Words Like Fire
Prophecy and Apocalypse in
Apollinaire, Marinetti and Pound

LEGENDA

LEGENDA is the Modern Humanities Research Association's book imprint for new research in the Humanities. Founded in 1995 by Malcolm Bowie and others within the University of Oxford, Legenda has always been a collaborative publishing enterprise, directly governed by scholars. The Modern Humanities Research Association (MHRA) joined this collaboration in 1998, became half-owner in 2004, in partnership with Maney Publishing and then Routledge, and has since 2016 been sole owner. Titles range from medieval texts to contemporary cinema and form a widely comparative view of the modern humanities, including works on Arabic, Catalan, English, French, German, Greek, Italian, Portuguese, Russian, Spanish, and Yiddish literature. Editorial boards and committees of more than 60 leading academic specialists work in collaboration with bodies such as the Society for French Studies, the British Comparative Literature Association and the Association of Hispanists of Great Britain & Ireland.

The MHRA encourages and promotes advanced study and research in the field of the modern humanities, especially modern European languages and literature, including English, and also cinema. It aims to break down the barriers between scholars working in different disciplines and to maintain the unity of humanistic scholarship. The Association fulfils this purpose through the publication of journals, bibliographies, monographs, critical editions, and the MHRA Style Guide, and by making grants in support of research. Membership is open to all who work in the Humanities, whether independent or in a University post, and the participation of younger colleagues entering the field is especially welcomed.

ALSO PUBLISHED BY THE ASSOCIATION

Critical Texts
Tudor and Stuart Translations • New Translations • European Translations
MHRA Library of Medieval Welsh Literature

MHRA Bibliographies
Publications of the Modern Humanities Research Association

The Annual Bibliography of English Language & Literature
Austrian Studies
Modern Language Review
Portuguese Studies
The Slavonic and East European Review
Working Papers in the Humanities
The Yearbook of English Studies

www.mhra.org.uk
www.legendabooks.com

STUDIES IN COMPARATIVE LITERATURE

Studies in Comparative Literature are produced in close collaboration with the British Comparative Literature Association, and range widely across comparative and theoretical topics in literary and translation studies, accommodating research at the interface between different artistic media and between the humanities and the sciences.

ALSO PUBLISHED IN THIS SERIES

Words Like Fire

Prophecy and Apocalypse in
Apollinaire, Marinetti and Pound

❖

JAMES P. LEVEQUE

l

LEGENDA

Studies in Comparative Literature 50
Modern Humanities Research Association
2021

Published by Legenda
an imprint of the Modern Humanities Research Association
Salisbury House, Station Road, Cambridge CB1 2LA

ISBN 978-1-78188-443-0 (HB)
ISBN 978-1-78188-444-7 (PB)

First published 2021

Copy-Editor: Richard Correll

CONTENTS

❖

ACKNOWLEDGEMENTS

❖

I want to give my profound appreciation to the team at Legenda for seeing this project to its final, printed-and-bound conclusion. Jacob Blakesley and Richard Correll both provided superb editing assistance that strengthened this work at almost every line. Graham Nelson patiently and diligently managed the whole process from the beginning, and he has my sincere gratitude.

This book would never have been written without the guidance of Peter Dayan who, in its earliest days, when it was a vague and unwieldy PhD thesis, helped me shape my rambling interests into a legitimate piece of scholarship.

I would also like to thank Giammario Impullitti, and Doctor Daniela De Marchi at the Comune of Portogruaro, for their help in securing permission for the cover image.

Lizzie Stewart's support and affection have been a gift that has helped me through some truly difficult times. And she has been a companion on many joyful adventures, the birth of our wonderful daughter Effie most of all.

This book is for my mom and dad, Jacques and Suzan Leveque. In the final stages of editing this work, Suzan passed away from ovarian cancer, and it's heartbreaking that only one of them will see it. They've given so much to me — emotionally, intellectually, and financially — that I hope a book about poetry and the future is even a small bit of a repayment they would never dream of asking for.

J.L., April 2022

LIST OF ABBREVIATIONS

❖

ŒP	Guillaume Apollinaire, *Œuvres Poétiques*
ŒPC, I–III	Guillaume Apollinaire, *Œuvre en proses complètes*, vols. I–III
MP	F. T. Marinetti, *Le Monoplan du pape*
CEP	Ezra Pound, *Collected Early Poems of Ezra Pound*
P	Ezra Pound, *Personæ: The Collected Shorter Poems*

What ciphers risen from prophetic script,
What marathons new-set between the stars!
  — Hart Crane, *Cape Hatteras*

... je voulais être tantôt pape,
mais pape militaire, tantôt comédien.
[... I wanted to be, on one hand, Pope,
but Pope Militant, on the other, a clown.]
  — Charles Baudelaire, *Mon Cœur Mis à Nu*

'Is my word not like fire?' says the Lord
'and like a hammer that breaks the rock into pieces?'
  —Jeremiah 23. 29

INTRODUCTION

❖

Prophecy, Apocalypse, and Modernity

Poets such as William Blake might rightly dominate discussions of prophecy and poetry of the post-Enlightenment world — a testament to the profound *belief* in the mutability of life that charged their prose and lyrics. Such strong faith often stuns the senses like the unexpected glimmer of a falling star across a night sky, both for its brightness and its brevity. With the technological, philosophical, and cultural developments that accompanied the arrival of the twentieth century, that glimmer was all the briefer and more intense; and poets caught in the great emergency of the age became associated with endlessly ephemeral avant-garde movements and trends and the most vocal advocates of the need to *modernize*. Poets and artists recognized a renewed sense of anxiety over the values and traditions potentially being threatened, and, as before, stepped into the breach with works that were often modelled on prophecy, envisioning a new world just over the horizon, the restoration of a lost paradise, or a divine judgement. The three poets of this study, Guillaume Apollinaire (1880–1918), F. T. Marinetti (1876–1944), and Ezra Pound (1885–1972) — all associated with the avant-garde in their unique and respective ways — deployed the themes and styles of prophecy as a mode of discourse that invited receptive audiences into newly structured universes as much as it alienated the 'unbeliever'. Audiences often felt that avant-gardism was nihilistic, treating no tradition or heritage as worth preserving, and tending even towards the self-effacement of the avant-garde work itself, being condemned to the churn of history. But the martial origins of the term, which denoted a small group that proceeded into enemy territory before the main force, also carries connotations of exploration, conquest, and invasion of new and potentially hostile spaces. In order to justify or bolster these acts of uncovering the new, avant-gardists, and poets in particular, were inclined to adopt a prophetic tone of unjustifiable optimism and faith in a future that corresponded to no contemporary evidence.

For some avant-gardists, modernity called the poet to prophesy what was 'to come'; for others — what William Marx describes as the arrière-garde: a phenomenon of avant-gardism that captures 'residual elements that remain behind' as the former charges ahead[1] — the poet was meant to champion traditional values that the modern world seemed to be in the process of obliterating. The latter current confronted the tension between history, as the various competing narratives of the past, and tradition, as a supposedly stable and transcendent meaning and value existing across histories. The former addressed the tension between the open possibilities of the future and an increasingly ordered, rationalized, and predictable daily life. These two tensions raised the question of the nature of the future: would it be a grand advent of a world so radically new that it was impossible to contemplate, the rebirth of tradition in modern form, or would it be T. S. Eliot's whimper? For the view of the future that each poet took was derived from their diagnoses of the consequences of society's embrace or refusal of the developments of modernity. At its most pessimistic, the poet conjectured the decline of a world that did not necessarily deserve redemption, freighting their poetry, like many of the biblical prophets, with moral judgement. More optimistic writings uncovered the potential revolution and liberation within and without the repetition of working life, the exponential variations of material reality, and technology's offerings for new sensory experiences. However, the dialectic of destruction and creation that the avant-garde tarried with situates judgment and reprieve within one another. Goading the world into the new age often began or ended with the poet outlining the spiritual malady of the modern world.

Cutting against the grain of modernity, or the anxieties that arose from modernity, many avant-garde poets reified a practice that was distinguished from the everyday lives of their contemporaries, but in the specifically paradoxical way of collapsing the distinction between the former and the latter. In that respect, this study accepts Doug Singsen's argument that Peter Bürger's much-criticized thesis that the driving force of the avant-garde was the desire to dissolve artistic autonomy into everyday life, can be valuable in certain specific cases and that 'engaging with mass culture precisely does break art out of its autonomous separation from everyday life'.[2] However, another way to understand the avant-garde as a reconfiguration of the autonomy of artistic and literary practice that makes it available to everyday life, and vice versa. Therefore, making the materials and practices of everyday life poetic offers the appearance of a collapsed autonomy only to heighten polemically the question of what artistic autonomy means in the modern world. This question has implications for perennial dichotomies such as new art versus tradition and popular versus 'high' art, which became all the more urgent at a time when crowds, nations, and classes asserted themselves in the realm of culture, economics, and politics. The values of modernity may very well have been located by avant-gardists in mass and popular culture, even though those values may not have been immediately evident, so the approach that the central poets of this study employed were not straightforwardly elitist. Rather, much of the work of prophecy is legitimizing public culture as evidence of an otherwise hidden history driven by forces that are more transcendent than the individual demands of everyday life.

In 1871, Walt Whitman (1819–1892) used prophetic rhetoric to assuage tensions around 'sacred industry' by identifying these changes in America with the achievements of classical and medieval Europe. Whitman engages in visionary speculation about American industry's many possibilities:

> As in a waking vision,
> E'en while I chant I see it rise, I scan and prophesy outside and in,
> Its manifold ensemble.[3]

That same year, Rimbaud (1854–1891) set forth his own description of the poet as a seer, in a famous letter to Paul Demeny (15 May 1871), as a cultural explorer and analyst whose sensual and emotional experience methodically cleaves towards more expansiveness and less rationality:

> Le Poète se fait voyant par un long, immense et raisonné *dérèglement* de *tous les sens*. Toutes les formes d'amour, de souffrance, de folie; il cherche lui-même, il épuise en lui tous les poisons, pour n'en garder que les quintessences. Ineffable torture où il a besoin de toute la foi, de toute la force surhumaine, où il devient entre tous le grand malade, le grand criminel, le grand maudit, — et le suprême Savant! — Car il arrive à l'*inconnu!*[4]

> [The poet makes a seer of himself through a long, immense and reasoned *derangement* of *all the senses*. All forms of love, suffering, madness; he searches, using up all the poisons within himself, to retain their quintessence. Ineffable torture where he needs all his faith, all his superhuman force, where he becomes the sickest, the most criminal, the most accursed amongst men, — and the supreme Scholar! — For he reaches to the *unknown!*]

The poet's vision uncovered a hidden reality or realities in Whitman's 'manifold ensemble' that could only be truly comprehended with a sight that makes eccentric connections, reveals occult causalities, recovers forgotten traditions, and re-constructs the world into a new nomos. However, the distinction of the poet is rendered in different ways by Whitman and Rimbaud. The former distinguishes himself by his identification not just with the people around him, but also with nature, faiths, and time, culminating in statements such as 'I am large, I contain multitudes'.[5] By refusing social individuation, the poet is defined by his pantheistic self-externalization: his own biography is identified with the world as a whole. On the other hand, Rimbaud's seer-poet is an outlaw figure — the last, least soluble element in a world of largely homogenous morality, undermining any stable perception of the world on which morality could be based. He leaves himself with no spirit other than his own. Both versions of the poet, well-established by the beginning of the twentieth century, will be evident in the works of Apollinaire, Marinetti, and Pound.

To address the problem of individuating the artist in the face of their evident dependency on a socially constructed world, aesthetic movements increasingly conceived themselves in terms similar to political parties, with all of the attendant activity of platforms, rivalries, and propaganda. This was the period of sectarian 'isms', where bohemian arts-of-living were politicized through ephemeral movements and polemical manifestoes. Avant-garde manifestoes frequently adopted the language of a 'we' to 'make a persuasive move from the "I believe" of the speaker toward the "you" of the listener or the reader, who should be sufficiently convinced to join in'.[6] The avant-garde was constantly engaged in attempts to assert the value of art and the wisdom of the artist in the broader spheres of politics, economics, or religion, while simultaneously attempting to retain art's integrity. Prophecy was not simply a rhetorical tool that the poet employed to retain that integrity, but also a means of speaking for a community that was itself not fully formed. This study is meant to elucidate how the use of prophetic rhetoric and imagery in the avant-garde of early twentieth-century European poetry is designed not so much to separate the poet from society, but to build around that prophetic/poetic activity the idea of a common sociality.

The effort to imagine such a society speaks to why I have chosen the Bible as the counterpoint to the writings of Apollinaire, Marinetti, and Pound. Along with classical myth, the Bible figures as the ur-text for canonical literature in the West; but unlike classical myth, the Bible holds a much larger claim to a popular readership and a role in everyday lives, throwing into confusion the premise of questions that automatically separate 'high' and 'low' art or assume artistic autonomy — a term with significant religious connotations, as I will explain below. Biblical literature was often in the background (and sometimes in the foreground) of these writers' aesthetics. Was this because they found aesthetic or ethical themes in the Bible that could be 'demonically' applied to orthodox religious traditions that they felt prevented a breakthrough into the truly modern? Was it because biblical myths of prophecy and apocalypse were too ingrained in Western society for these poets to simply discard? As Ernst Bloch says, 'nothing has been absorbed like the Bible, *despite its alien stock*'.[7] This 'alien stock' is, for Bloch, essentially the language of the Bible itself, with obscure phrases, such as 'Son of Man' and its apocalyptic undertones of defiance against the Bible's own language of divine sovereignty, read as 'uniquely native to all lands'.[8] Both foreign and familiar, this counter-movement of defiance indicates traces of belief and action that escape the closed and totalizing dogma of the church. These avant-gardists were certainly not blind to the irony of the continued relevance of religious thought in a period that often openly proclaimed its contempt of traditional or orthodox religious views and practice. Although not the same as favouring a diffuse 'spirituality' over religion, the openness to religion marked a scepticism of the secular, rationalist thought derived from the Enlightenment, which was increasingly seen — particularly since the rise of Romanticism — as precluding any experience of the transcendent or numinous through its alienating systems of classification and slavish insistence on logic and causality.[9] Artists and writers mined Greek, Roman, and biblical literature for prophetic themes, but also looked beyond into psychology and mysticism, 'primitive' art and society, or technology. Pagan religion and contemporary technology both behaved as a kind of refuge from the doctrines of orthodox or everyday religious practices. As Northrop Frye argues, the Bible provides 'mythical structures' that 'give shape to the metaphors and rhetoric of later types of structure', be those later structures social, historical, cultural, and so forth.[10] Moses, Elijah, Jeremiah, Daniel, or Jesus were too embedded into the structure of prophetic rhetoric for any poet who presented himself[11] as a modern prophet to simply discard these figures and still be identified *as prophetic*. Many of the new art-forms of the avant-garde were informed by a teleology, by the conviction, like that of the Bible, that the world is *going somewhere*, and both the avant-garde and the Bible are suffused with the conviction that, whether it can be seen or understood or not, history is heading in a direction, and providence has sent guides to point the way to the new Jerusalem.

Sociologies of Religion and Literature

This study begins by drawing on the peculiar similarities between those social organizations imputed to many avant-garde movements and those prophetic or eschatological congregations: liminal and antagonistic to convention, absolutist in their claims, totalizing in their demands. The parallels were recognized by avant-gardists themselves, who often referred, ironically, to such groups as conventicles and coenobia. Literary salons in the nineteenth and twentieth centuries upended the image of the lone *poète maudit* living against society, and the communities like the famous Abbaye de Créteil, rather than being a quiet monastery of writers, acted as waystation for writers and artists across France and beyond.[12] It was as if these avant-garde movements were mimicking the small, hermetic enclaves that appear in some of the Bible's first encounters with prophecy, and to engage with these groups was to have one's identity thoroughly changed. After Samuel anoints Saul as king of Israel, he tells Saul to meet a small prophetic band: 'as you come to the town, you will meet a band of prophets coming down from the shrine with harp, tambourine, flute, and lyre playing in front of them; they will be in a prophetic frenzy. Then the spirit of the Lord will possess you, and you will be in a prophetic frenzy along with them and *be turned into a different person*' (1 Samuel 10. 5–6; emphasis added). One's identity prior to prophetic activity — be it shepherd, merchant, or, as with Saul, anointed of Israel — is negated by the activity of the prophet who has become a proxy for the 'spirit of the Lord'. The public's response to Saul's 'prophetic frenzy' (v. 10) is to coin a proverb for someone who acts out of character: 'Is Saul also among the prophets?' (v. 12).

This example also provides a rare moment in the Bible when aesthetic activity — in this case music — is associated with prophetic ecstasy. Music and, as shown by the major prophets, poetry were implicated in states of rapture, elation, and euphoria, giving the participants 'another heart' (v. 9) and connecting them, both physically and mentally, to the 'spirit of the Lord'. Aesthetics, community, and prophecy were often bound up with one another, with each component providing the justification for the others. In terms of Apollinaire, Marinetti, and Pound, what this presents to the reader are works that may vacillate between the overtly avant-garde and the more classically Modernist, a vacillation described by Astradur Eysteinsson as a 'fluid difference' that 'takes the form of reciprocity and dialogue rather than opposition and contrast. A single text is very often both Modernist and avant-garde, even though the avant-garde elements may vary in their pronouncements.'[13] Nevertheless, I refer to these poets as avant-garde to lay stress on the minoritarian outlook that seems, at first glance at least, to conform to a similar tendency in their small sectarian 'isms'. Radical and often bewildering aesthetic practices can serve as the boundaries of a movement, and manifestoes can substitute collective ethos for individual identities. However, this framing implies that the sectarian nature of the avant-garde is its defining feature — a framework that, from the subjective standpoint of many individual avant-gardists, does not stand up. For example, Pablo Picasso (1881–1973), Jean Cocteau (1889–1963), and Marcel Duchamp (1887–1968) have been variously associated with Cubism, Dada, and Surrealism even though they had little interest in aligning themselves with any movement. The lifelong association of an avant-garde figure with a single movement, as is the case with Marinetti and Futurism, or André Breton (1896–1966) and Surrealism, is the exception rather than the rule. Nevertheless, the particular duration and intensity of the focus of Apollinaire, Marinetti, and Pound on any one movement is less of a concern for this study than the heuristic value of the diversity of such movements as an entrance into the unique effect of prophetic and apocalyptic language, and these poets' approaches to tradition and modernity, given that such approaches inform their poetic production and conception of what sort of utopian state they advocated. These 'isms' gained an identity and sense of purpose by being apart from society, being therefore able to speak 'prophetically' from an external viewpoint and broach the possibility of a 'clean break' with history.

Max Weber (1864–1920) argued that prophets belong to a certain *class* of leadership that he termed *charismatic*. This archetypal category attributes one's authority to certain ineffable and extraordinary attributes of personal magnetism rather than to one's credible alignment to tradition, or to their technical mastery of rational processes. Charisma, as he wrote, involves 'a certain quality of individual personality by virtue of which he is set apart from ordinary men and treated as endowed with supernatural, superhuman, or at least specifically exceptional powers or qualities'.[14] As opposed to professional religious practitioners such as priests, who stake their legitimacy on the authority of tradition as 'incumbents of an "occupation" [...] that is, men who have acquired expert knowledge and who serve for remuneration',[15] Weber distinguishes the prophet by a charismatic 'call' to service that cannot be accounted for through rational, much less economic, means. Whether these qualities originate from a secular or divine origin, they are believed by both the charismatic leader and his or her followers to be evidence of the former's transcendence of the profane and the everyday. Weber also identifies the prophet as the carrier of a doctrine, a specific ideal used as a yardstick to judge the behaviour of people and the events of history.[16] Moreover, this doctrinal yardstick is largely legitimized by the willingness of the prophet's followers to submit themselves to the demands of the doctrine at the expense of their own well-beings. In this way, Weber places the prophet in opposition to the orthodoxy of the hegemonic powers, typically represented by the priesthood or royal court. A fundamentally convulsive force, the doctrine can be based either on a recovery of a seemingly neglected tradition or an insistence on God's new creation. History is henceforth read through the tension between the rationalizing ideologies and practices of dominant religious and political institutions on the one hand, and the subversive or disruptive influence of the prophet's charisma and doctrine on the other.

The charismatic leader, however, is tragic for Weber in that the vitality of his or her authority is doomed by the routine (and routinizing) structures of law, economics, and politics. If a prophet is successful in challenging orthodoxy, his charismatic impulse is carried by his followers into subsequent institutions and increasingly standardized across subsequent generations. From the moment charismatic authority is established, its animating character is destined to diminish and fade away: 'Indeed, in its pure form charismatic authority may be said to exist only in the process of originating. It cannot remain stable, but becomes either traditionalized or rationalized, or a combination of both'.[17] The theme of a being that is, in its most ideal state, perpetually 'in the process of originating' will be one this study will return to, but at present it is fair to say that it captures distinctively avant-garde hopes and anxieties over that stability of identity, the vast multiplicity of urban life, the relationship between mind and body, and the possibilities of technological progress or, as Eysteinsson states, 'the avant-garde desire to unveil the contingency, the made-up-ness of grand meanings'.[18] The primary danger posed to charisma lies within the desire to extend it beyond its original bearer to new disciples or successive generations, which necessitates the establishment of rules and regulations for the identification of the original charismatic claim in these latter-day apostles, thereby extinguishing its most seductive aspect. The paradox of a charismatic tradition (Weber occasionally uses the term 'hereditary charisma')[19] is a common fate for charismatic authority.

Weber's analysis of religion fitted into a larger project of understanding how society operated within the constraints of economic organizations. Partly against what Weber felt were deterministic and rigid understandings of the economic conditioning of culture (largely inspired by economistic or 'vulgar' Marxism),[20] he hoped to demonstrate how social 'spheres', that is ways of life (Weber identified the economic, the political, the aesthetic, and the erotic as most important to the study of religion) that abnegated worldly values in favour of values particular to those ways of life,[21] could develop autonomously defined values and practices. More significant, however, is Weber's analysis, famously put forward in *The Protestant Ethic and the Spirit of Capitalism* (1905), of how the character of social spheres could shape each other, often in spite of their expressed intentions. Even as early as *The Protestant Ethic*, Weber began to apply, in some evocative but limited cases, the analysis of religious autonomy to art and literature, and why certain forms of art and literature arose in particular religious and social milieus. For example, after describing Puritanism's contempt for the theatre and fashion, Weber admits that the Puritan's division between a fallen, material and creaturely world on the one hand, and a transcendent, sacred world on the other developed an 'instinctive sense of the timelessly great in art' and 'that a unique genius like Rembrandt, however little his "conduct" would have found favor in the eyes of the Puritan God, was yet vitally influenced in the direction taken by his creative work by the sectarian milieu in which he lived.'[22]

Pierre Bourdieu's re-evaluation of Weber's theory of religion is perhaps most extensive in its application to art and literature, but it also included a number of critical questions: Why are some people responsive to the prophet's charisma (assuming such a thing even exists) when others are not? In what areas of social life do prophets appear more or less frequently? How does class stratification shape the prophet's message or doctrine? How does symbolic or material power affect the prophet's legitimacy? Bourdieu considers Weber's theory of charisma to be little more than 'une théorie psycho-sociologique' [a psycho-sociological theory] that has no foundation other than in 'un acte de "reconnaissance"' [an act of 'recognition'] which objectively does not significantly illuminate the potential variations in a prophet's audience, what their interests are in recognizing the prophet's charisma, what *forms* charisma might take for them, and how they might become a factor in influencing the prophet's doctrine.[23] Bourdieu felt that what prophets did was articulate changing conditions in the society that previously had been only implicitly felt, expanding the audience's ability of expression above and beyond, to use Weber's terminology, the routinized language of orthodoxy. This aspect of Bourdieu's analysis recalls the sense of the ineffable identified by Rimbaud and highlights a definitive link between prophecy and poetry. These changes, be they economic, political, historical, or cultural, altered for the religious community the nature of what 'salvation' actually constituted. The prophet legitimizes lay concerns by aligning with the audience's interests in a way that *seems natural* because the prophet 'porte au niveau du discours ou de la conduite exemplaire des représentations, des sentiments et des aspirations qui lui préexistaient mais à l'état implicite, semi-conscient ou inconscient' [brings to the level of discourse or exemplary conduct representations, feelings, and aspirations that pre-existed him but in an implicit, semiconscious or unconscious state].[24]

When confronted by a prophet, the orthodoxy has either to crush the subversion by re-asserting the validity of its doctrine or neutralize the prophetic insurgency through a tactical alteration that incorporates at least some of the prophet's concerns. Through the latter means, salvation can be effectively standardized and religious practice rationalized. Charisma undergoes, in Bourdieu's terms, 'la "banalisation" que le corps sacerdotal fait subir à la prophétie d'origine' [the 'banalization' that the sacerdotal body subjects to the original prophecy] and

> la recherche typiquement bureaucratique de l'*économie de charisme* qui porte à confier l'exercice de l'action sacerdotale, activité nécessairement banale et 'banalisée', parce que quotidienne et répétitive, de prédication et de cures des âmes, à des fonctionnaires du culte *interchangeables* et dotés d'une qualification professionnelle homogène.[25]

> [the typically bureaucratic search for the *economy of charisma*, which leads to trusting the exercise of sacerdotal action — necessarily banal and 'banalized' because habitual and repetitive — of preaching and treatment of souls to *interchangeable* cultic functionaries endowed with homogenous professional qualifications.]

However, prior to this rationalization, charisma establishes its legitimacy by offering something the orthodoxy cannot, producing a belief in the audience that salvation is available because it is heterogeneous to the values of the orthodoxy.

Bourdieu applied this framework to cultural fields in analysing literary production, and the material and intellectual acquisition of art and literature; but a key component of Bourdieu's sociology of art and literature, that artistic authenticity is demonstrated through its disinterest in material or monetary remuneration, was explicitly derived from Weber's theory of prophecy: 'comme la *prophétie* [...] qui, selon Weber, prouve son authenticité par le fait qu'elle ne procure aucune rémunération, la rupture hérétique avec les traditions artistiques en vigueur trouve son critère d'authenticité dans le désintéressement' [like prophecy [...] which, according to Weber, proves its authenticity by the fact that it receives no remuneration, the heretical rupture with current artistic traditions finds its criterion of authenticity in disinterestedness]. This disinterest represents an 'économie charismatique fondée sur cette sorte de miracle social qu'est l'acte pur de toute détermination autre que l'intention proprement esthétique' [charismatic economy founded on this kind of social miracle that is the act free from any determination other than the properly aesthetic intention].[26] The paradoxical phrase 'économie charismatique' suggests that the logic of investment and production is at work, but not at the material level — at least not in the most immediate sense — which must be transposed or converted into symbolic or spiritual rewards in order to maintain legitimacy.

What Bourdieu called the 'production of belief' operated in both religious and artistic fields, and through similar processes of socialization, which could include class, family and community traditions, race and gender, or language, certain producers (priests or prophets in religion, artists or critics in the artistic field) and consumers (laity or audience) were more naturally inclined to identify with each other. Bourdieu writes that the nature of religious 'goods and services' depends upon

> l'harmonie qui s'observe entre les produits religieux offerts par le champ et les demandes des laïcs en même temps que de l'homologie entre les positions des producteurs dans la structure du champ et les positions dans la structure des rapports de classe des consommateurs de leurs produits.[27]

> [the harmony observed between the religious products offered by the field and the demands of the laity at the same time as the homology between the positions of producers in the structure of the field and the positions in the structure of class relationships of the consumers of their products.]

What constitutes 'salvation', the essential religious 'product', is a result of a seemingly natural and unspoken 'harmony' between religious practitioners and laity. Class position finds an analogue, or 'homology', in the universe of religious choices, which nevertheless are not reducible to class position as these choices are refracted through the ways in which an individual might perceive them at a given moment in their own history and the history of the religious field. The sociology of artistic production, on the other hand, accounts for 'la signification et de la fonction que les pratiques et les œuvres comme prises de position doivent à la *position* de ceux qui les produisent dans le champ des rapports sociaux de production et de circulation' [the significance and function that the practices and works, as position-takings, owe to the *position* of those who produce them in the field of social relationships of production and circulation].[28] Artistic production and consumption, much like the mutual work of clergy and laity, requires a deeply intuitive familiarization with the stakes (what Bourdieu refers to as 'prises de position') of artistic products and practices instilled over a long period of time. This familiarity becomes an individual's *habitus* through educational institutions, family upbringing, and social milieu, naturalizing artistic appropriation:

> Il s'ensuit que les connaisseurs les plus avertis sont les défenseurs naturels de l'idéologie charismatique, [...] qui oppose l'expérience authentique de l'œuvre d'art comme 'affection' du cœur ou illumination immédiate de l'intuïtion aux démarches laborieuses et aux froids commentaires de l'intelligence, en passant sous silence les conditions sociales et culturelles d'une telle expérience[29]

> [It follows that the most savvy connoisseurs are the natural defenders of charismatic ideology, [...] which opposes authentic experience of the work of art as 'affection' of the heart or immediate, intuitive illumination, to laborious procedures and cold, intellectual commentaries, while passing under silence the social and cultural conditions of such an experience]

Artistic appreciation is not, from the point of view of charismatic ideology, a transferable skill to be learned, but a pre-disposition embodied in habits and tastes, therefore making them seem to be a 'gift'; any attempt to grasp a work through a detached and analytical exegesis betrays the rote and mechanical learning of the parvenu, whose authenticity is subject to doubt for that very fact. Rather than a passive attribute of the prophet — as with Weber — Bourdieu conceives the charismatic ideology as an unacknowledged and unacknowledgeable pact, grounded by similarities in *habitus* between artists and art consumers.

Bourdieu was then able to show that religion and art are both founded upon the ability to produce in the audience the belief that the values and perspective asserted by the religious or artistic product represent salvation, or grace, or social distinction, or 'good taste'. The prophet or artist never really produces this belief *sui generis*, but his or her articulation of changing social conditions as experienced from the perspective of members of similar social positions can appear as a secret affinity between speaker and audience. Moreover, the articulation of how one's social position leads to this unspoken understanding can threaten the 'charismatic illusion'. In this way, art and literature were subject to the same cycle of prophetic attack and orthodox defence described by Weber: established institutions (political, educational, religious, etc.) maintain a monopoly on what constitutes 'legitimate' art, while more marginal challengers attack those institutions by embracing 'the new', arguing that the institutions are sclerotic and out-dated. Or, in agitating for a return to tradition or 'the basics', re-emphasizing the 'letter of the text' or the canon, prophetic attacks argue that the institutions have become cynical and corrupt. What a prophet tries to do, vis-à-vis the social world, is

> à déplacer ainsi la frontière du pensé et de l'impensé, du possible et de l'impossible, du pensable et de l'impensable, [...] permet au prophète d'exercer une action mobilisatrice sur une fraction suffisamment puissante des laïcs en symbolisant par son discours et sa conduite extraordinaires ce que les systèmes symboliques ordinaires sont structuralement incapables d'exprimer[30]

> [to displace the frontier of the thought and the unthought, the possible and the impossible, the thinkable and the unthinkable, [...] allow the prophet to exercise a mobilizing action over a sufficiently powerful fraction of the laity by symbolizing, through his extraordinary discourse and conduct, what the ordinary symbolic systems are structurally incapable of expressing]

Similarly, what the avant-garde artist tries to do is (re)set the terms of a debate between 'les tenants de l'"art pur"' [the keepers of 'pure art'] and the 'tenants de l'"art bourgeois" ou "commercial" [...] pren[ant] inévitablement la forme de conflits de *definition*, au sens propre du terme: chacun vise à imposer les *limites* du champ les plus favorables à ses intérêts' [keepers of 'bourgeois' or 'commercial art' [...] inevitably taking on the form of conflicts over *definition*, in the proper sense of the term: each aims to impose the *limits* of the field that is most favourable to their interests].[31] From this particular perspective, the relationship between religion and art is founded in the way they achieve legitimacy and challenge orthodoxy, by continually struggling over the definition and stakes of spiritual or aesthetic 'grace'.

Too Many Prophets, and Never Enough

The sociology of religion and literature, as I have sketched it out above, provides a foundation for the imaginaries of the avant-gardists for this study — an implicit relationship between prophet and the audience that artists could accept, refuse, ironize, or innovate. For example, Apollinaire may have been recalling Numbers 11. 29, where Moses wishes that 'all the Lord's people were prophets' — a utopian desire for all Israelite people to maintain an intimacy with God similar to that of Moses himself — when he wrote in 'Sur les Prophéties' [On Prophecies] (1914) that 'Tout le monde est prophète' [Everyone is a prophet] (*ŒP*, 186). But Apollinaire's statement is likely also a provocation — surely not *everybody* can be a prophet, for a prophet's legitimacy is derived from his or her tension with the broader society. But the truth might, at one time, have been closer to Apollinaire's quip than he knew. In the ancient Near East, prophets were not uncommon, and ancient texts from Egypt to Mesopotamia abound in stories, anecdotes, and legal documents that make reference to various prophets, seers, oracles, diviners, and mediums and their supernaturally speculative activities. The book of Deuteronomy, with its prescriptions on how to know if a prophet is true or false (18. 15–22), addresses the problem of Israel's confrontation with a wide variety of individuals claiming to speak for the divine. Later biblical evidence confirms the prolific vocation of prophecy: Elijah enters into a contest with 450 prophets of Baal and 400 prophets of Asherah who are in the employ of Queen Jezebel (1 Kings 18. 19); Jezebel's husband, Ahab, consults about 400 prophets in the decision to go to war (1 Kings 22. 6); when King Josiah's royal court need to authenticate a sacred text (widely thought by scholars to be the historic book of Deuteronomy), they seek out a prophetess named Huldah (II Kings 22. 11); Jeremiah 28 recounts a prophetic dispute between the eponymous prophet who preaches submission to Babylon and a rival prophet, Hananiah, who favours resistance to the empire. Prophets held roles as royal seers, public representatives, healers, miracles-workers, and diviners of the word of God. In this light, the prophet often assumes the role of speaking within and on behalf of various religious and political institutions, and fractions of society, rather than establishing an absolute independence.

And yet, the Bible repeatedly locates *the one* prophet who stands beyond the rest. Frye states:

> The great majority of prophets, the Old Testament itself makes clear, were well-broken-in functionaries either of the court or of the temple. So it is all the more interesting that the Old Testament should highlight so strongly a number of prophets who spoke out against royal policies and exposed themselves to persecution as a result. [...] the prophet with the authentic message is the man with the unpopular message.[32]

Truth results in scorn and condemnation of the prophet because he or she lifts the veil on those aspects of human existence that our painfully human qualities — ambition, greed, ignorance, cowardice, spite — prevent us from acknowledging. The denial of truth, in this sense, however, is not simply one of face-saving, but, much more fundamentally, one of preserving the foundations upon which our worldviews rest. Of the 400 prophets whom Ahab consults, all predict victory for the king except one, Micaiah ben Imlah, whom Ahab dislikes because 'he never prophesies anything favorable about me, but only disaster' (1 Kings 22. 8). When Ahab's messenger reaches Micaiah, he states that 'the words of the prophets with one accord are favorable to the king; let your word be like the word of one of them' (22. 13), to which Micaiah replies, 'whatever the Lord says to me, that I will speak' (22. 14). Micaiah's recalcitrance, which results in his imprisonment (22. 27), is not merely an insult to Ahab's ego, but strikes at the core of the relationship between king and cosmos. Ahab is not part of the order of the universe, but evidence of the disorder that God will correct.

The postures of the poets of this study, who confront modernity in such a way to highlight the persistence of their devotion despite a dismissive public, can be effective ways to garner a particular sort of anti-legitimacy. Much of the analysis of the relationship between the avant-garde and the public will be in the spirit of Frye's observation that certain forms of literature demonstrate

> not merely an intense vision of the present, but an unusual ability to see a conditional future, the consequence of tendencies in the present. This in turn may give the sense of a *distinctive kind of knowledge hidden from most of society* [...] indicat[ing] the quality of the poet's authority.[33]

In some cases, the Bible's presentation of a single prophet on one side of a conflict and hundreds on the other side is an exaggeration meant to highlight the seemingly insurmountable challenges confronting God's prophets. Again, there are biblical precedents to which we can turn. In the prophetic contest on Mount Carmel, Elijah is said to confront 400 prophets of Baal, a hyperbole meant to emphasize the extent to which Israel had fallen to religious syncretism. Moreover, Elijah's isolation calls into question his chances of success when he laments, 'I, even I only, am left a prophet of the Lord' (1 Kings 18. 22). This lament serves to underscore the strength of his faith, which ultimately is shown as compensation for the apparent weakness of his social position. The sociologist Peter L. Berger conceptualized a 'plausibility structure', that is, an exercise in world-building that is fundamental to religion and is the product of continuous *social activity* that maintains the objective and subjective validity of the world that a particular religion proposes.[34] But what is a plausibility structure proposed by a single individual? It is this question that Elijah, and the poets examined in this study, confront. 'Since every religious world', states Berger, 'is "based" on a plausibility structure that is itself the product of human activity, every religious world is inherently precarious in its reality.'[35] A liminal social position would, in theory, express itself as an inability to render a plausibility structure as Berger describes it, leading to the prophet's reflection on, and necessity for, a social 'base' of activity. What this study attempts to demonstrate is not even that the anomic experience of modernity provides fertile soil for the building a social base in which a plausibility structure might be reified, as it may not always do so, but that the poetry of these avant-gardists resolves or circumvents that problem by dissolving artistic autonomy in order to reclaim it at the level of an imagined future that is often allegorized through the figure of the poet.

Weber's definition of the prophet as a carrier of *charisma*, conceived in the fount of European Modernist culture, registered the acute sense of alienation that was a central theme of the culture.[36] Robert Wilson's summery of charismatic authority is sensitive to Weber's intuition that charisma is the dialectal negative of alienation:

> For Weber, charismatic authority is distinct from traditional authority. [...] the former has no system of abstract rules but involves new demands which frequently break with tradition. The charismatic figure is thus the prophet who brings a new divine word to challenge the traditional structures of society.[37]

Bible scholars, however, have taken issue with Weber's influential thesis as overly subjective, and have sought to place greater attention on the possibilities for prophecy inherent in particular audiences. These theories developed a framework of prophecy as mediation between the divine and a receptive public. For example, Thomas Overholt proposed:

> Prophets speak for some deity, which necessarily implies that they speak to a particular group of persons. Indeed, we may define *religious intermediation* as a process of communication between the human and the divine spheres in which messages in both directions are 'channelled' through one or more individuals who are recognized by others in the society as qualified to perform this function.[38]

Such a framework groups prophets with the other supernatural mediators, such as shamans, mediums, magicians, sorcerers, and diviners, but the Bible makes a distinction between the latter and the prophet *qua* prophet. Deuteronomy 18. 9–14 makes the unequivocal statement that God's word will be received through prophets and never through any other sort of intermediary. The distinction seems to be based on the verbal-literary methods of the properly biblical prophet as opposed to the practical-technical craft of proscribed forms of divination. Of greater concern, however, is the initiative taken by biblical prophets, suggestive of their ultimate service to God: 'diviners wait to be consulted and rely on mechanical means such as lots to arrive at their message, while prophets come forward at Yahweh's direction and have their message directly from the deity.'[39] The 'true' prophet speaks extemporaneously, inspired and compelled by a 'higher' power. The implication of the intermediary waiting to be consulted, likely charging for such a service, suggests that he or she works at the behest of a client, whereas the true prophet only works for God. And unlike other intermediaries, their prophetic craft is not simply a series of technical skills, which could theoretically be learned by anyone, but a gift of the divine. The suggestion that prophecy is a transferrable technique implies that the choice of prophet ultimately lies outside the will of God. This is not to suggest that the transfer of prophetic inspiration does not occur in biblical literature: the tradition of Elijah passing his commission to Elisha is the most notable, but it fully relies on God's plan (I Kings 19. 16; II Kings 2. 9–15): Elisha is not shown to *learn* anything, in any practical sense, so much as simply *receive* Elijah's spirit and faith.

Overholt adds that biblical 'prophets were religious intermediaries who functioned at the national level'.[40] Apollinaire, Marinetti, and Pound also conform in their respective ways to another important attribute of biblical prophets in their relationship to a figure that speaks to the public on behalf of some conception of the national character. The European avant-garde, filled as it was with expatriates and refugees, inevitably had conflicted views of the nation, but inevitably folded nationalism and patriotism within the boundaries of aesthetics as *the* transcendent force in the world, often presenting themselves as national poets recasting their respective national histories in terms of the beautiful, dramatic, tragic, comedic, or heroic. As intermediaries between God and Israel, biblical prophets must be representative of both, but not fully identifiable with either. The communication that they do receive, however, generally retains some identification with a foundational, but often obscured or forgotten aspect of the nation. This complex and fraught relationship to the nation — of speaking both to and from the nation — has implications for the questions of *who* is allowed to speak and *why*, and in this respect raises questions of religious or aesthetic labour and production.

Beginning at the End

Apocalypse, derived from the Greek term *apokalypsis*, revelation, denotes a genre of visionary literature, and as such, inevitably draws a comparison to prophecy. As will be described, apocalyptic literature is often viewed as an extreme form, or 'doubling down', on prophecy in the face of disconfirmation and in that sense bears some continuity with prophecy. However, whereas biblical prophecy largely tends to the day-to-day trials of people and nation, apocalyptic literature sends its visionaries to wild, cosmic scenes. John J. Collins defines apocalypse as

> a genre of revelatory literature with a narrative framework, in which a revelation is mediated by an otherworldly being to a human recipient, disclosing a transcendent reality which is both temporal, insofar as it envisages eschatological salvation, and spatial insofar as it involves another, supernatural world.[41]

Rather than the pretence of a prophet speaking extemporaneously to an audience, apocalyptic literature is, by comparison, presented in a manner that highlights its thorough — even overwrought — composition. Visions and messages are related, recorded, and kept secret until the proper time. Furthermore, by communicating the revelation through multiple mediators (usually angels), the divine becomes more distant even as it becomes more infinitely cosmic. Finally, with apocalyptic literature, reality is increasingly presented as illusory, and the end of this world is merely the end of a dream or nightmare from which the elect will awake. In these cases, eschatologies offer a new beginning so radically different than the current situation that they cannot do anything less than encompass the totality of life and history. Indeed, the premise of apocalyptic literature is that history's meaning is obscure, and only revealed in the form of its conclusion. Or, more theologically, God's 'hidden' relationship to the world is only made known when the current phase of that relationship comes to an end. In biblical literature — though not exclusively in biblical literature — the new phase of this relationship, which will be the final phase, is communal and ideal — such as the prophecy in Revelation that states that God is 'among the mortals' (21. 3) — rather than hierarchical and material.

The obverse side of apocalyptic literature, as an expression of beliefs concerning humanity's place in the cosmos, is the practices and behaviours of communities that produce and read such literature. Apocalypse is a form of social organization in which members share in apocalyptic beliefs and prepare themselves for the imminent End Times. Paul D. Hanson defines apocalyptic social organization as the crisis of anomic experience *within* the broader social order:

> the crisis which sociologists find at the root of every apocalyptic movement is a minority phenomenon. This crisis is the collapse of a well-ordered worldview which defines values and orders the universe for a group of people, thrusting them into the unchartered waters of chaos and anomie. While the majority continues on the course defined by past norms, the apocalyptic minority calls attention to signs indicating that the course leads to perdition and offers in its place a new vision of life's values.[42]

Since this social organization is predicated on the belief that no hope for salvation can be found within the major institutions and ideologies of this world, studies of apocalypticism have frequently focused on the marginalized or self-marginalized status of individuals and groups with apocalyptic beliefs. Social organization and behaviour are apocalyptic when those actions are aligned with the imagined world 'to come'. David G. Bromley's description of apocalypticism emphasizes this aspect of social organization by marginal groups:

> Particularly as apocalyptic groups create their own space organized as part of the new order that they construct to authorize ongoing social relations within the group, they inevitably leave themselves in a position of spatial liminality. The community they create is specifically constructed, both to be part of an order that does not yet exist and to be distanced from the existing social order.[43]

While the apocalyptic group may be objectively liminal, it is subjectively consistent with an ordered society and universe *to come*. Apocalyptic communities feel themselves on the cusp of a total transformation of humanity's relationship to the cosmos, and the social structures such communities establish in response metonymically conform to that future relationship, being images of the new dispensation. The apocalyptic group is therefore driven by an exclusive knowledge of the new order; and that liminality can be experienced as a sense of being chosen from the common population. In this respect, the dominant social order no longer offers a refuge from anomie but becomes the source of feelings of estrangement and exile, against which the apocalyptic community struggles to defend itself. For example, Roland Boer, in an analysis of Bloch's eschatology, also characterizes the disillusionment with bourgeois religion relevant to the avant-gardists in this study:

> What we get instead is a purely individualistic focus on existence. What counts for the individual is the encounter with the Word, an encounter in which we find contact from one existence to another. And the essence of that encounter, the address from God to the individual person, has no content, it is not about anything. In the end, for Bloch, such a position is barely Christian, or rather, by abandoning any eschatological and political change, it preserves 'highly unchristian conditions in the world.'[44]

Scholars such as Bromley and Hanson regard the relationship between prophecy and apocalypse not as one of absolute distinction, but as two opposing ends of a continuum. Bromley understands apocalyptic social organization as a radical form of what he calls the 'prophetic method' of legitimizing one's understanding of the events and ideas of the external world. Adopting Weber's framework of prophet's contrarianism versus the priest's conservation of the establishment worldview, Bromley describes the 'prophetic method' that

> deconstructs and delegitimates the ultimate understandings established by the priestly method to authorize organizations and relationships in the existing social order and to connect human and transcendent purpose. Apocalypticism simply extends this process. Its assertions — that the organizing logic of the dominant social order is so antithetical to transcendent purpose that unilateral intervention is mandated [...] — mount a challenge to the established social order that is direct, total, and on highest authority.[45]

By identifying the social relations of apocalyptic organization with 'transcendent purpose', that is, the will of the divine, that social organization grants itself an unassailable sense of legitimacy. But apocalyptic de-legitimations are essentially no different from the historically narrower de-legitimations performed by the prophet. Hanson clarifies the distinction within the varying forms of eschatology employed by prophetic and apocalyptic literature. He defines the difference between prophetic eschatology and apocalyptic eschatology as the relative ability to envision salvation occurring within the political and social structures of the existing order: while the prophetic office feels that salvation can be found within the contemporary order, the apocalyptic visionary has no such confidence. When the historical situation has become dire enough,

> The prophets no longer have the events of a nation's history into which they can translate the terms of Yahweh's cosmic will. Hence the successors of the prophets, the visionaries, continue to have visions, but they increasingly abdicate the other dimension of the prophetic office, the translation into historical events. At that point we enter the period of the transition from prophetic to apocalyptic eschatology.[46]

The context of this study, in the years leading up to, and during World War I, is an apt timeframe for tracking this transition from the prophetic to the apocalyptic, but it should be stressed that such a transition is not always chronological. As will be argued in this study, one of the major drivers of apocalyptic thought is a loss of faith in prophecy as an applicable model of comprehending historical events when those events seem to outstrip *any measure* of understanding, which implies that apocalyptic thought typically follows after prophetic rhetoric. The reality is rarely so unidirectional. We will discover that the prophetic and apocalyptic are often expressed in close proximity, but with a more tactical and less chronological frame of reference, owing as much to personal predilection as to the wider zeitgeist that the poets found themselves in, which is nevertheless evidence of the close conceptual relationship between the two modes of writing.

Ideologists, Propagandists, Poets

The arts innovated at the beginning of the twentieth century in innumerable ways, in the practices employed, the materials and technologies used, and theories designed to elucidate them. Poets, however, with a notable frequency, assumed the role of ideologists and publicists of new artistic movements. Even when it can be argued that literature had not made advances comparable to painting, sculpture, photography, and film, the poets of this study also acted as critics, editors, and polemicists for a range of forms well beyond their own literary practice. They became the messengers of aesthetic doctrines that were justified by nothing more than the charismatic will of the poet. From Marinetti's prolific Futurist manifestoes, to Tristan Tzara's (1896–1963) parody of the form among the Dadaists, to André Breton's extensive and dogged Surrealist efforts, poets felt called to announce and propagate the aims, methods, and values of these movements in a way that was often designed to baffle and offend audiences. Indeed, rationality and comprehensibility were sometimes viewed as craven sops to the middle classes, which limited audiences to like-minded artists and poets more inclined to respond with approval to unusual, heterodox, absurd, and offensive art and literature. These predisposed audiences would likely form the core of avant-garde sects, but the race to continually innovate and modernize made such audiences highly unstable — the avant-garde of one year becoming the arrière-garde of the next. In this way, the declaration of the avant-garde mission involved aggressiveness and non-conformity in artistic form as well as content. They were as vociferous in their attacks on genteel bourgeois morality as they were enthusiastic in their radical incorporation of the newest developments, seeking to represent simultaneous perspectives, unheard-of speeds, or fledgling technologies.

Apollinaire, Marinetti, and Pound stand out for the fact that each of them, in their own specific ways, took up a position of leadership in a variety of avant-gardist movements, and situated these movements vis-à-vis religion. The European avant-garde was alternatively constructed by these poets as a challenge to, continuation of, or transformation through religion or religious thought. These poets were certainly ambivalent about the Jewish and Christian literature from which they drew prophetic and apocalyptic themes, being fully cognizant of the irony of engaging with millennia-old practices while advocating for the modernization of art and culture. Secondly, their personal experience of dislocation from a national home — Apollinaire's birth in Italy to a Polish mother and unknown father, Marinetti's Egyptian childhood and Parisian success, Pound's expatriation from America — gave each a sense of separateness that is a characteristic of the prophet. However, none of these poets accepted a completely rejectionist position when it came to the nation, and much of the content of their poetry is concerned with the problem of developing or identifying a national tradition. Furthermore, World War I compelled them to confront the tenets that energized their work and thought, such as the dialectic of destruction and creation, the place of tradition, and the value of national culture. By limiting this study to the few years preceding the war and its immediate aftermath, I mark a number of crucial events for these poets and for the avant-garde: Apollinaire's death at the end of 1918, Marinetti's alignment of Futurism with fascism after the war, and Pound's permanent departure from London and its literary culture in 1920. The most extreme agents of avant-garde art expressed themselves in terms of warfare and battle, but when confronted with the reality of modern war, of the apocalyptic possibility of total destruction, Apollinaire, Marinetti, and Pound were forced to incorporate this new reality into their prophetic tone and outlook.

Apocalyptic attitudes and prophetic poses were used by Apollinaire, Marinetti, and Pound to establish poetry as the authoritative voice on the meaning of the war and the potential for the post-war future. The political agitation in Europe in the months leading to World War I was preceded by the aggression of the avant-gardes' manifestoes, where rival movements were slandered and new styles were promoted, and by avant-garde shows and cabarets often designed to offend bourgeois sensibilities. Avant-gardism, adopting a name that elicits the image of a warrior-class in the realm of art and culture, in some ways predated the European conflict in representing 'the idea of spirit at war'.[47] Modris Eksteins explains that for avant-gardists, 'whether considered as the foundation of culture or as steppingstone to a higher plateau of creativity and spirit, war was an essential part'.[48] War and art together were offered up as an alternative way to advance human civilization rather than the tedium and sclerosis associated with parliamentary politics. But when confronted by the actual event itself, the millenarian attitudes often, if not always, gave way to a sense of generalized horror, and rather than a rebirth, the war became the best evidence of the inevitable decline of Western civilization.

Even in this period prior to World War I, combat and warfare fascinated and intrigued European writers and artists, and they began to laud it for its aesthetic possibilities. One of the earlier pieces that I will examine is Marinetti's 1912 *Le Monoplan du pape: roman en vers libre*. In the final few months of 1911, Marinetti went to Libya to report on the Italo-Turkish War (1911–12) for the French newspaper *L'Intransigeant* and was stunned by the sensory experience of modern warfare. *Monoplan*, as well as the collection of his dispatches during the war, *La Bataille de Tripoli* (1912), expresses awe at the ways in which war marshals cultural and material resources, achieving the status of an aesthetic benchmark in Futurism. Like Marinetti, Apollinaire had direct experience of war, enlisting in the French army in 1914 and serving until 1916, when he was famously wounded in the head. The majority of his collection *Calligrammes: poèmes de la paix et de la guerre* (1918) was written during his time in the war. While somewhat more ambivalent than Marinetti, the collection often approaches modern warfare with a feeling of wonder, excitement, and enthusiasm.

The title of the English translation of Geert Buelens's study of the poetic output of World War I, *Everything to Nothing* (2015), already suggests where this enthusiasm would lead by the end of the war. It was the nadir of European civilization. Several poems in *Calligrammes* express the sorrow, disorientation, and regret of soldiers in the war, and while Apollinaire maintained his French nationalism to the end of his life, many of his later works, such as the posthumously published verse-play *Couleur du Temps* (1949), ruminate on the tragedy of warfare and the desire for peace. Pound never experienced the war first-hand, being exempt from conscription in Britain, and never enthusiastically supported it. *Hugh Selwyn Mauberley* (1920), was published almost a year and a half after the war ended, but several sections of the sequence address the disappointment at the war's cause and cost. It condemns, in no uncertain terms, the deception and propaganda of the British war effort.

The choice, exacerbated by the political and cultural lines drawn by World War I, between a cosmopolitan, experimental, and international aesthetic on the one hand, and the advocacy of specific national cultures on the other, perhaps proved to be more than these writers could negotiate. Whether through transformation or cessation, the war brought this particular period of the avant-garde to an end. In his early career, for example, Marinetti, being fluent in French and highly responsive to the literary world of Paris, wrote and published most of his poetry and manifestoes in French before translating them into Italian. Most notably, the first Futurist manifesto was published in 1909, not in an Italian publication, but in the French *Le Figaro*. But in 1912, after spending time at the Italian front in Libya, Marinetti's increasing nationalism and belief in Italy's imminent resurgence on the imperial stage prompted him to address himself to Italian audiences more directly than before. *Monoplan*, therefore, is the last major work of his to be initially published in French. While World War I did not end his Futurist activities, the so-called 'heroic' phase of Futurism ended after two of the movement's guiding lights, the painter Umberto Boccioni (1882–1916) and the architect Antonio Sant'Elia (1888–1916), were both killed in the war and Futurism became explicitly aligned with fascist politics.[49] Apollinaire's early poetry that was collected in *Alcools* (1913), much of it written during his travels in Germany and Eastern Europe while engaged as a tutor in 1901 and 1902, demonstrates a highly cosmopolitan outlook. This cosmopolitanism never receded completely in his work, but Apollinaire's personal affection for France and the increased pressures of the war led towards overtly pro-French writings, culminating in *L'Esprit nouveau et les poètes* (1918), which explicitly champions France, precisely for its sense of universalism, as the most important cultural producer. After his discharge, however, he wrote some of his most powerful poetry, much of which expresses a deep ambivalence and mourning over the war. Pound did not serve in the war, and his immediate reactions to it are largely critiques of the 'home-front' attitudes, rather than the delirious synaesthesia or despondency of poets at the front. He had moved to London in 1908, so had a different relationship to the pressures of nationalism from Marinetti and Apollinaire. Partly behind his engagement with the avant-garde was the intent to re-invigorate art and culture, and the *Cantos* can be read as Pound's lifelong attempt to rise to that impossible challenge. Many parts of *Hugh Selwyn Mauberley* explicitly expressed Pound's disappointment with London's literary milieu, and, as this study will examine, such aesthetic 'failure' is perceived as a result of the propaganda and cynicism he encountered during the war.

Apollinaire's expansive relationship to the avant-garde will be the starting point for this study. Although he was absolutely dedicated to the idea of being modern, he was often ambivalent about avant-gardism's sectarian formations, and never fully identified with any one movement, acting as a champion and theorist of several. He is the most well-known promoter of Cubism in the visual arts, and his own poetry's occasional disruption of logical continuity and context has earned it the description of Cubist (although the appellation is debatable).[50] He briefly theorized the aesthetic of Orphism, the practice of painting from non-visual elements, along with the painter Robert Delaunay (1885–1941), and he coined the term Surrealism in the programme to the ballet *Parade* (1917) by Picasso, Cocteau, and Erik Satie (1866–1925). His brief association with Futurism led him to write *L'Antitradition futuriste* in 1913, which contains a list of artistic comrades, Futurist and otherwise, as well as condemnations attacking everything from professors and critics to Shakespeare and Tolstoy. And though he easily acquainted himself with Futurist artists and writers (in no small part due to being able to speak Italian), including reading Marinetti's *Monoplan du pape*, which provided some background to his own poem 'Zone', Apollinaire ultimately disagreed with Futurism's strident attacks on tradition. *L'Esprit nouveau et les poètes*, his most important theoretical statement on the relationship between poetry, tradition, and modernity, intentionally avoids association with any specific movement. Although an excellent Modernist example of Weber's charismatic leader, inasmuch as his aesthetics seemed to be as much a product of his own lifestyle as any intellectual reflection, he was never particularly doctrinaire, nor did he ever suggest that there was no room for artistic tradition, but rather defended artistic tradition as concertedly as he advocated expressions of the new.

Marinetti and Futurism were dedicated to an enthusiasm for technology and sought to modernize nearly every aspect of life, from day-to-day activities such as cuisine and fashion, to national political engagement. From an early age, Marinetti was a rising star in the Parisian literary scene, finding success and camaraderie with a number of poets who were writing in the wake of Symbolism, which certainly had an effect on Marinetti's work. Marinetti himself might have agreed with this assessment, as he sometimes referred to the Symbolists as his former 'maîtres'. But after the publication of the first Futurist manifesto in 1909, and his self-presentation as the prophet of Futurism, Marinetti dedicated himself to the popularization of the movement for the remainder of his life. He travelled extensively promoting Futurism, giving well-publicized talks in Paris, London, South America, and Russia, and had a notable influence on avant-garde artists wherever he went. Futurism drew from a paradoxical array of anarchist and nationalist trends, championing bohemian individualism at the same time as promoting irredentist causes advocating for the recovery by force of cities now part of north-eastern Italy, which were controlled by Austria at that time. After World War I, Futurism became aligned with Mussolini's fascist movement, and while Marinetti's dual commitment to politics and art was often strained, he remained a supporter of fascism throughout his life, even if his active involvement in the party waned somewhat.

Pound, while ultimately abandoning the avant-garde movements of London by the end of World War I, spent several years theorizing Imagism and Vorticism. As a somewhat later avant-garde development, the term being coined in 1912, Imagism had the advantage of hindsight, and was hence more reflective about the tropes and trends that defined avant-gardism in Europe. The Imagists' 'statements of purpose' — F. S. Flint's 'Imagisme' (1913) insisted that they did not write manifestoes[51] — sometimes denied being a 'movement' and claimed that they had no aesthetic doctrine, but only a loose collection of principles. Disagreements about leadership, whether by a sole theorist or through democratic means, compelled Pound to depart Imagism, as his sense of individualism clashed with a movement that might otherwise *collectively* decide upon an aesthetic direction. Pound later joined with the writer and painter Wyndham Lewis (1882–1957) and the sculptor Henri Gaudier-Brzeska (1891–1915) to form Vorticism. They collaborated with a number of other artists in the release of the journal *Blast*, which only lasted for two issues between 1914 and 1915. After Gaudier-Brzeska's death in the war, just before the release of the second issue of *Blast*, the Vorticist group collapsed and while Pound continually worked with avant-garde writers and artists afterwards, his leadership of such groups had come to an end.

Apollinaire, Marinetti, and Pound were familiar with each other's works, just as they were with contemporary artistic developments across Europe in general. Each was also aware of the ways in which the others presented themselves as charismatic individuals who could speak authoritatively of the relationship between modernity and tradition, the past and the future, art and society. Apollinaire developed a personal friendship with a number of Futurist painters showing their work in Paris. He and Marinetti met on a few occasions, and, as described above, Apollinaire found some interest in Futurism. Both Apollinaire and Marinetti were visitors to the quasi-utopian Abbaye de Créteil — an enclave for writers and artists just outside Paris. Pound was somewhat more distant, in location as well as temperament, to the avant-garde movements on the continent. While he never met Apollinaire, he acquired a copy of Apollinaire's *Alcools*, and in September 1913 he wrote a series of articles on French poetry in which he cited Apollinaire as a major French poet.[52] When Pound collaborated with Lewis in the publication of *Blast*, they employed lists of praises and condemnations very similar to Apollinaire's in *L'Antitradition futuriste*, which Apollinaire seems to have been happily aware of.[53] Pound was also aware of Marinetti's activities, especially his public lectures on Futurism in London between 1910 and 1912. Moreover, parts of *Blast* were dedicated to criticisms of Futurism, even as it clearly borrowed from the tone and style of the Futurist manifestoes.

The choice of the Bible as the main comparative point for these avant-gardists is also rooted in how the biblical literature provides a series of mythical analogues for death and resurrection, from the individual Jesus, to the nation of Israel, to humanity in Revelation. Apollinaire's religious attitudes are infused with themes of martyrdom and sacrifice, and a longing for an ever-receding utopia that the poet cannot but continually reach for. One of his final poems, 'La Jolie Rousse' (1918), written after Apollinaire had served in the war and reflecting a melancholic attitude toward the avant-garde's aggressiveness, still regards the modern poet as a kind of soldier battling his way into a new age. Apocalyptic thought often involved the tendency towards collective establishments of a way of life that was understood to be only actualized in the future.[54] This is one tendency that Apollinaire sought in his associations with the avant-garde, and while it is certainly questionable whether he ever found such a community in the here-and-now, I examine a number of poems from *Alcools* and *Calligrammes* to show how both the artistic avant-garde and soldiers of World War I were intimations of that community. Apollinaire's religious imagery, then, draws from the figure of the biblical prophet even as the poet seeks to explore the modern world and, in doing so, predicating much of his poetry on a failure to achieve the truly modern. And while Apollinaire does not frequently use the term 'apocalypse', the concept is alluded to in a variety of themes and images that also derive from biblical literature: the end of the world; rebirth and the return of the dead; new eras and a new humanity.

Le Monoplan du pape: roman en vers libre, the primary work by Marinetti that this study will examine, has received little critical attention,[55] and yet brings together the aesthetic trends of his early, pre-Futurist poetry with the social, political and religious pronouncements of Futurism. From his first collection in 1902, *La Conquête des étoiles*, until the publication of the first Futurist manifesto in 1909, Marinetti was a prolific poet and playwright, and yet this was Marinetti's only major work of poetry between the launching of Futurism and the end of World War I.[56] In this respect, *Monoplan* is significant in its placement between the early theorizations of Futurism and Marinetti's eventual turn towards fascist politics after World War I. *Monoplan* adopts the voice of a pilot, and that of his aeroplane, flying across the Italian peninsula on a mission to incite the country to war against Austria. Halfway through the story, the pilot kidnaps the Pope and, at the end, drops him into the Adriatic Sea in a move that can be read as an attempt by Marinetti to express Futurism as an oppositional force to Christianity, and Catholicism in particular. Furthermore, this pilot clearly presents himself as the prophet of Futurism, which, in some of Marinetti's manifestos, is treated as a religion as well as an aesthetic. In his 1914 Italian translation of *Monoplan*, Marinetti signalled the work's prophetic pretensions by changing the subtitle to 'Romanzo Profetico', prophetic novel, and his 'prediction' of war against Austria looked significantly more accurate in hindsight (Italy declared war on Austria on 23 May 1915). Furthermore, Marinetti's time as a journalist in the Italo-Turkish War, when *Monoplan* was composed, gave him an insight into the nature of modern war that most of his contemporaries in the avant-garde had not yet imagined. War is presented as a total change in the sense of the self and the world, and it is in this context that, like Apollinaire, Marinetti engages in the imagery of destruction and rebirth. The sense of apocalypse makes itself felt in the attention to destruction as a potentially creative force.

The selection of Pound's work is drawn primarily from the period prior to his initiation of the *Cantos* — a period in Pound's thinking where the challenge to a modern aesthetic was conceived as a spiritual challenge. Like Apollinaire and Marinetti, Pound's work at this time is animated by the sense of crisis and progress, and the question of what it means to be modern. However, Pound's work reflects a deeper concern for literary tradition, and its potential loss in this modern era, than either Apollinaire's and certainly Marinetti's. Pound's use of personae, for example, is drawn from historical and mythical figures, adopting their voices and outlooks to bring out a theme or idea that Pound considers endangered. While Pound rarely references the biblical prophets directly, there is a strongly prophetic element in his work, defined by Louis L. Martz's in his study of the subject's relation to Modernist English literature: that the prophet can be seen as one who speaks for another.[57] So the prophetic voice, in this work, involves the *pretence* of obscuring the poet's own historical self. Pound did not share Apollinaire's or Marinetti's embrace of war as a sublime aesthetic experience, but he did share their belief that modern war — and World War I in particular — was part of an absolute and fundamental change in the world. This change could provide, assuming the poet is perceptive enough to see it, and dogged enough to profess it, a revelation, if not of a new era then at least of a new formation of a transcendent truth.

The works examined in this study represent an exercise in poets attempting to be prophetically authoritative and apocalyptically modern. They spoke for themselves, but also spoke *on behalf of* an ideal that modernity was either just bringing into view or was threatening to destroy. The apocalyptic impulse also tries to reveal a new, potentially utopian sense in the world — a totality that can speak to the history these poets are living in but is discontinuous from it. Both of these modes of discourse are caught, however, within the tension between the individual view of the poet and the society they are trying to find or construct. The emergence, or re-emergence, of the poet as a charismatic individual — acting not simply as an artist, but as a prognosticator and mediator between society and something more super-mundane — calls for a more systematic understanding of the place of prophecy within the poetry of this period. Moreover, the central place of the Bible in this study is meant to demonstrate the place of myth in the challenge that the avant-garde posed towards artistic autonomy. Frye argues that the Bible maintains a peculiar place in history because it is myth that has retained strong aspects of *logos*, or propositional, dialectical language, unlike classical myths that have largely drifted into a status of pure literature.[58] As literature, but never just literature, the Bible is a model for reinvigorating *logos* within Modernist myths. The reconfiguration of artistic autonomy that the beginning of the twentieth century demanded required the foundation of a social knowledge that myth is adept at providing, but also needed to break out of the expression of pure art in order to demand, urge, and insist on this radically new era. Apollinaire, Marinetti, and Pound, in their own unique ways, nominated their poetry as the place in which the values of the new era, and new society, could be explored.

Notes to the Introduction

1. William Marx, 'The 20th Century: Century of the Arrière-Gardes?', in *Europa! Europa? The Avant-Garde, Modernism and the Fate of the Continent*, ed. by Sascha Bru et al. (Berlin: Walter de Gruyter, 2009), p. 63.
2. Doug Singsen, 'The Historical Avant-Garde from 1830 to 1939: l'art pour l'art, blague and Gesamtkunstwerk', *Modernism/Modernity*, 5.2 (2020) <https://doi.org/10.26597/mod.0154> [accessed 6 December 2020].
3. Walt Whitman, *Leaves of Grass* (New York: The Modern Library, 2001), p. 249.
4. Arthur Rimbaud, *Œuvres complètes*, ed. by Antoine Adam (Paris: Gallimard, 1972), p. 251.
5. Whitman, *Leaves*, p. 133.
6. Mary Ann Caws, 'The Poetics of the Manifesto: Nowness and Newness', in *Manifesto: A Century of Isms*, ed. by Mary Ann Caws (Lincoln: University of Nebraska Press, 2001), pp. xix–xxxii (p. xx).
7. Ernst Bloch, *Atheism in Christianity: The Religion of the Exodus and the Kingdom*, trans. by J. T. Swann (London: Verso Books, 2009), p. 10; emphasis added.
8. Ibid.
9. At the end of his study on the confrontation between spiritual thought and scientific practice in the nineteenth and twentieth centuries, J. W. Burrow provides a concise overview of the relationship between the European avant-garde and the rejection of rationalist thought that connects many of the movements discussed in this study to major intellectual figures like Nietzsche and Bergson. An important theme that Burrow addresses, which this study will return to in a different context, is the confrontation of the avant-garde with language as the carrier of logic, and its attempt to de-couple that relationship (*The Crisis of Reason: European Thought, 1848–1914* (New Haven, CT: Yale University Press, 2000), pp. 234–53).
10. Northrop Frye, *The Great Code: The Bible and Literature* (London: Routledge & Kegan Paul, 1982), p. 35.
11. The prophetic pose, particularly among these poets, frequently took on a deeply chauvinistic tone, where the masculine poet or prophet is juxtaposed to a feminized, bourgeois culture. This affect will be examined in detail below, but it does suggest the value of further examining prophetic discourse in the work of female authors.
12. Marianne W. Martin, 'Futurism, Unanimism, and Apollinaire', *Art Journal*, 28.3 (Spring 1969), 258–68 (p. 259).
13. Astradur Eysteinsson, '"What's the Difference?" Revisiting the Concepts of Modernism and the Avant-Garde', in *Europa! Europa? The Avant-Garde, Modernism and the Fate of the Continent*, ed. by Sascha Bru et al. (Berlin: Walter de Gruyter, 2009), pp. 21–35 (p. 33).
14. Max Weber, *The Theory of Social & Economic Organization*, ed. by Talcott Parsons, trans. by A. M. Henderson and Talcott Parsons (New York: The Free Press, 1947), p. 358.
15. Max Weber, *From Max Weber: Essays in Sociology* (London: Routledge & Kegan Paul, 1977), p. 245; see also Max Weber, *The Sociology of Religion*, trans. by Ephraim Fischoff (Boston, MA: Beacon Press, 1991), p. 46.
16. Weber, *Sociology of Religion*, p. 47.
17. Weber, *Theory of Social & Economic*, p. 364.
18. Eysteinsson, '"What's the Difference?"', p. 22.

19. Ibid., p. 372.

20. The following statement by Weber is a paradigmatic example of his approach to historical materialism: 'We intend, rather, to establish whether and to what extent religious influences *have in fact* been *partially* responsible for the qualitative shaping and the quantitative expansion of that "[capitalist] spirit" across the world, and what concrete aspects of capitalist culture originate from them. [...] the only possible way to proceed is to first investigate whether and in what points particular *elective affinities* between *certain* forms of religious belief and the ethic of the calling can be identified. At the same time, the manner and general *direction* in which, as a result of such elective affinities, the religious movement influenced the development of material culture will be clarified as far as possible' (Max Weber, *The Protestant Ethic and the 'Spirit' of Capitalism and Other Writings*, ed. by Peter Baehr and Gordon C. Wells (London: Penguin Books, 2002), p. 36). The qualifications and caveats Weber employs in the above passage, and throughout much of *The Protestant Ethic*, have signalled Weber's diminished status as the anti-Marxist sociologist *par excellence*. Rather, Weber is often seen by sociology and critical theory as approaching the same problems as Marx from a different angle.

21. See in particular 'Religious Rejections of the World and Their Directions' in Weber, *From Max Weber*, pp. 323–59.

22. Weber, *Protestant Ethic*, pp. 114–15.

23. Pierre Bourdieu, 'Une interprétation de la théorie de la religion selon Max Weber', *European Journal of Sociology*, 12.1 (May 1971), 3–21 (p. 15).

24. Ibid.

25. Ibid., p. 20.

26. Pierre Bourdieu, *Les Règles de l'art: genèse et structure du champ littéraire* (Paris: Seuil, 1992), p. 300.

27. Pierre Bourdieu, 'Genèse et structure du champ religieux', *Revue française de sociologie*, 12.3 (June–September 1971), 295–334 (p. 319).

28. Pierre Bourdieu, 'Le Marché des biens symboliques', *L'Année Sociologique*, 22 (1971), 49–126 (p. 106).

29. Pierre Bourdieu, 'Éléments d'une théorie sociologique de la perception artistique', *Revue internationale des sciences sociales*, 22.4 (1968), 640–64 (pp. 659–60).

30. Bourdieu, 'Genèse et structure', p. 331.

31. Bourdieu, *Les Règles de l'art*, p. 310.

32. Frye, *The Great Code*, p. 126.

33. Northrop Frye, *Words with Power: Being a Second Study of the Bible and Literature* (New York: Harcourt Brace Jovanovich, 1990), p. 53; emphasis added.

34. Peter L. Berger, *The Sacred Canopy: Elements of a Sociological Theory of Religion* (New York: Anchor Books, 1967), p. 45.

35. Ibid., p. 50.

36. Weber has taken endless grief for his reliance on 'ideal types' often without the acknowledgement that such types were meant as heuristic models: 'the ideal type was a fiction, like, for example, the assumption of perfect rationality — on the analogy of the frictionless engine — from which hypothetical consequences could be deduced which could then be compared with actual outcomes' (Burrow, *Crisis of Reason*, p. 63).

37. Robert Wilson, *Prophecy and Society in Ancient Israel* (Philadelphia, PA: Fortress Press, 1973), p. 57.

38. Thomas Overholt, *Channels of Prophecy: The Social Dynamics of Prophetic Activity* (Minneapolis, MN: Fortress Press, 1989), p. 17.

39. Thomas Overholt, 'Prophet, Prophecy', in *Eerdmans Dictionary of the Bible*, ed. by David Noel Freedman, Allen C. Myers, Astrid B. Beck (Grand Rapids, MI: William B. Eerdmans Publishing Company, 2000), p. 1087.

40. Ibid., p. 1086.

41. John J. Collins, 'Introduction: Towards the Morphology of a Genre', *Semeia*, 14 (1979), 1–20 (p. 9).

42. Paul D. Hanson, *The Dawn of Apocalyptic: The Historical and Sociological Roots of Jewish Apocalyptic Eschatology* (Philadelphia, PA: Fortress Press, 1979), p. 2.

43. David G. Bromley, 'Constructing Apocalypticism: Social and Cultural Elements of Radical Organization', in *Millennium, Messiahs, and Mayhem: Contemporary Apocalyptic Movements*, ed. by Thomas Robbins and Susan J. Palmer (Routledge: New York, 1997), pp. 31–46 (p. 39).

44. Roland Boer, 'The Privatization of Eschatology and Myth: Ernst Bloch vs. Rudolph Bultmann', in *The Privatization of Hope: Ernst Bloch and the Future of Utopia*, ed. by Peter Thompson and Slavoj Žižek (Durham, NC: Duke University Press, 2013), pp. 106–20 (p. 114).

45. Ibid., p. 37.

46. Paul D. Hanson, *The Dawn of Apocalyptic*, p. 16.

47. Modris Eksteins, *Rites of Spring: The Great War and the Birth of the Modern Age* (London: Black Swan, 1990), p. 19.

48. Ibid., p. 135.

49. Cinzia Sartini Blum, *The Other Modernism: F. T. Marinetti's Futurist Fiction of Power* (Berkeley: University of California Press, 1996), p. 126.

50. See L. C. Breunig's introduction to the concept of 'cubist poetry', where the question of whether or not cubist poetry even existed was raised, and sometimes rejected, by these same poets (L. C. Breunig, ed., *The Cubist Poets in Paris: An Anthology* (Lincoln: University of Nebraska Press, 1995), p. 1.

51. F. S. Flint, 'Imagisme', in *The Norton Anthology of English Literature*, ed. by Jahan Ramazani and Jon Stallworthy, 6 vols (New York: W. W. Norton & Company, 2012), vol. F, p. 2065.

52. Willard Bohn, *Apollinaire and the International Avant-Garde* (Albany: State University of New York Press, 1997), p. 28.

53. Ibid., p. 22.

54. See Bromley, 'Constructing Apocalypticism', p. 42.

55. A notable exception is Maria Pia De Paulis-Dalembert's study on Marinetti's translation and re-writing of his own works from French to Italian ('F. T. Marinetti: la réécriture de l'imaginaire symboliste et futuriste entre le français et l'italien', *Chroniques italiennes web*, 12 (December 2007), 1–30), but *Monoplan* only constitutes a small portion of this article. While Cescutti has perhaps the most extensive study of Marinetti's early French works she explicitly excludes *Monoplan* from her study because of the work's overtly political and anticlerical dimensions (Tatiana Cescutti, *Les Origines mythiques du futurisme: Marinetti, poète symboliste (1902–1908)* (Paris: Presses de l'Université Paris–Sorbonne, 2008), p. 16). Blum's *The Other Modernism*, while the most extensive English-language study of Marinetti's works, makes no reference to *Monoplan*.

56. Marinetti's *Zang Tumb Tumb* (1914) demonstrates some poetic properties, but it seems that he was far more interested in exploring the visual possibilities of typography, or the sound quality of onomatopoeia, both of which constitute the majority of the work.

57. Louis L. Martz, *Many Gods and Many Voices: The Role of the Prophet in English and American Modernism* (Columbia: University of Missouri Press, 1998), p. 7.

58. Frye, *Words with Power*, pp. 33–34.

PART I

❖

Prophecy

CHAPTER 1

❖

Making False Gods

Apollinaire's religious outlook vacillated between devotion and rejection — though a pious Catholic school pupil who claimed atheism in his teenage years, he nevertheless often returned to the nostalgic and animating energy of his early faith. 'Zone''s pivot from a generous attitude towards the symbols and rituals of the poet's Catholic upbringing, to a bitter loneliness amongst 'fétiches' [fetishes] — all being civilization's failed attempts to recapture that sense of oneness with the divine — encapsulates this inability to maintain that earlier religious sensibility. The poem is constantly surprised by the impulses of faith in the modern life of early twentieth-century Europe, even as those impulses are partial, temporary, and superficial. While always keeping one eye on the future, the poet nevertheless often presents himself as a prophet for whom the recovery of tradition is the most avant-garde act possible. He speaks to and for tradition within the modern world because he is 'naturally' in tune with it, inclined not so much to what tradition *says* but what it *means*, perhaps in the sense that Walter Benjamin posits 'language as such' as a pre-linguistic communicability when he states that 'mental being communicates itself *in* language and not *through* language'.[1] Such communicable 'contents of the mind', which again Benjamin distinguishes from 'communication in words',[2] receives its first elaboration in speech or text as a kind of revelation, and it's possible to say that the poet's vocation is to recreate that revelatory sense of first elaboration. Similarly, Frye postulates three phases of language: metaphorical, metonymic, and descriptive. He states that in metaphorical or 'poetic' phase, 'the central conception which unifies human thought and imagination is the conception of a plurality of gods, or embodiments of the identity of personality and nature',[3] and that

> it is the primary function of literature, more particularly of poetry, to keep re-creating the first or metaphorical phase of language during the domination of the later phases, to keep presenting it to us as a mode of language that we must never be allowed to underestimate, much less lose sight of.[4]

Apollinaire's most frequently invoked judgement of tradition was the 'solide bon sens' [solid good sense] and 'esprit critique assuré' [assured critical spirit] (*ŒPC*, II, 943) that it imparts to the reader, but in this case, taken from 'L'Esprit nouveau et les poétes', Apollinaire refers not so much to tradition, but to the 'classiques', the wealth of masterpieces that modernity must advance from, but whose ability to re-create language and reality in identity with itself presents a challenge to the prophetically inclined poet. This poet, as I will show, will seek out and meet a substrate of cultural tradition that pulls him towards the construction of an autonomous existence; whereas the poet, as an inevitably social being, is not meant to *prevail* in this challenge, but simply to unite the two sides of order and adventure by offering himself as the terrain of struggle.

The prophet, positioned at 'la frontière du pensé et de l'impensé, du possible et de l'impossible, du pensable et de l'impensable' [the border of the thought and unthought, of the possible and impossible, of the thinkable and unthinkable],[5] must begin with familiar religious and cultural materials that provide the basis for the 'thought' and the 'thinkable', but also must simultaneously be able to intimate in them something not yet 'thinkable'. Although the religious or spiritual message of the Bible was too often yoked to its historical and social context for any sort of orthodox use in Apollinaire's poetry, it did provide a wealth of fantastic and mythical imagery that Apollinaire gladly severed from its textual source in order to play on the divisions between sincerity and irony, authenticity and artificiality. Biblical heroes such as Samson and David were 'chers à Guillaume Apollinaire en raison de leurs prouesses amoureuses' [dear to Guillaume Apollinaire for their erotic prowess] and 'les prophètes l'intéressent pour leur aspect merveilleux; ce sont des *enchanteurs* qui dominent le temps et l'espace et reculent les limites de l'existence humaine' [the prophets interest him for their marvellous aspect; these are *enchanters* who dominate time and space and draw back the limits of human existence].[6] Prophets explore new opportunities for experience and new modes of representation and perception. Couffignal's argument that there is 'aucun souci du message spirituel que délivreraient les prophètes' [no concern for the spiritual message that the prophets deliver][7] — which, given that he very rarely quotes these parts of scripture, seems to be the case — suggests that Apollinaire's approach to biblical prophetic literature is critically focused on the *figure* of the prophet and the rhetorical functions of prophetic speech. These aspects of prophetic literature were a way to understand his own vocation as a poet in modern society and to provide rhetorical force to the values he expressed in his poetry.

With his repeated references to biblical figures and themes, it's clear that Apollinaire conceded the Bible's literary and aesthetic value, even as he militated against the supposed value of its historical veracity. His approach to the biblical text is more invested in the 'magical' properties of its poeticized language, and the possibilities of those properties for the modern era. That is, following Frye's extrapolation of metaphorical language from the magic and religion that unifies thought, speech, and nature, poetry is now

> detached from faith, power, or truth, as we ordinarily understand these words, even when it expresses them. And yet the release of metaphorical language from magic into poetry is an immense emancipation of that language. [...] Poetry does not really lose its magical power thereby, but merely transfers it from an action on nature to an action on the reader or hearer.[8]

A similar point might be made about history, where the scientific, evidentiary study that grew out of the Enlightenment extracted it from the transformative properties of cultural tradition, leaving the latter liberated to speak more directly to experience. Modernist poets like Apollinaire reacted to the extraction of history from myth, folklore, and religious tradition with a defence of the imagination on the grounds that it engaged the elements of emotion and desire within history. An article entitled 'Des Faux' that Apollinaire wrote in 1903 illuminates this distinction between the aesthetic and historical. In it, Apollinaire addresses the scandal of the Tiara of Saitafarnes. This crown, acquired by the Louvre in 1896, and supposedly belonging to an ancient Scythian king, was discovered to be a forgery. Using the Bible as his example, Apollinaire argued that art and literature's value is hardly dependent upon its historical authenticity: 'Les Évangiles sont postérieurs aux personnages auxquels on les attribue et n'expose-t-on pas dans quelque sanctuaire une image de la Vierge peinte par saint Luc?' [The Gospels are posterior to the figures that we attribute to them, and have we not exposed in some sanctuary an image of the Virgin painted by Saint Luke?].[9] In the wake of historical methods of biblical criticism that arose in the nineteenth century, the faithful and non-faithful alike increasingly accepted that the historical attributions of religious literature and artefacts were often fictional. Apollinaire, as many others did, looked at the aesthetics of biblical literature as its legitimating factor, especially insofar as those aspects enhanced or mediated the theological, philosophical, or ritualistic aspects of the Bible. Regardless of the question of authorship, these 'fakes', 'forgeries', and 'imitations' were attempting, often successfully, to recapture and renew the initial creative impulse derived from the events of Jesus's life, death, and resurrection. Apollinaire extended this point to a rejection of nostalgia: 'La tiare de Saïtaphernès donnera au public, j'espère, un grand mépris pour le passé' [The tiara of Saitaferne will give the public, I hope, a great contempt for the past]. Note that Apollinaire refers to the past, and not to tradition. 'Le mépris est un sentiment libérateur. Il exalte une belle âme et l'incite aux grandes entreprises' [Contempt is a liberating sentiment. It exalts a beautiful soul and incites it to great enterprises]. The pejorative notion of the 'fake' betrays an attachment to the past, to an ever-receding original object rather than the animating spirit behind that object. A contemptuous attitude towards the past, however, shocks certain 'belle[s] âme[s]' back into the present, recognizing the contemporaneity already extant in a great work. In this way, the tiara is 'beau *comme l'antique*' [beautiful *like the ancient*],[10] inciting the viewer to look beyond everything in a work of art that identifies it as belonging to a particular historical context, and to locate a quality of beauty that places the most modern works of art side by side to the most antique. The fact that the public, as well as the Louvre, was deceived for a time by the tiara shows that in spite of its historical provenance, in spite of its status as a 'forgery', it demonstrated a genuine quality of beauty not essentially different from that of other modern works of art. Quoting an unnamed, and probably fictional, forger, 'un vieillard fort bizarre, vivant en ermite' [a very bizarre old man, living as a hermit], Apollinaire summarized this mischievous view of beauty in explicitly supernatural terms: 'J'ai fabriqué un dieu, un faux dieu, un vrai joli faux dieu' [I have made a god, a false god, quite a lovely false god].[11] Placing the words 'vrai' and 'faux' in such close proximity, Apollinaire projects contradictory ideas onto a single artistic object. This 'god', perhaps explicitly meant to be seen as an idol (and who better than a prophet to judge idols?), is false because it exists in defiance of a particular sense of reality understood as historical, specifically made against history. Yet, it exhibits genuine beauty ('vrai joli'), no less real for its formal inauthenticity. Moreover, Apollinaire inverts the relationship between creator and created: the god, in this instance, is the object of creation, and the artist is, as Apollinaire will insist through much of his poetry, the creator of realities. Forgery, fabrication, and fiction — these words express the ambivalent nature of the imagination, and the next section will argue that such efforts at manufacture are extended, in Apollinaire's work, to the life of the poet as well, inviting an audience to mingle in the poetic allegory of the childhood and maturity of the modern poet.

The Devoted Son

Apollinaire often grounded his poetry in the conflict between a pious youth and a secular maturity, an allegorical rendering, through the life of the poet, of modernity's confrontation with itself. Apollinaire received a Catholic education, gaining significant exposure to Catholic and biblical literature as well as a working understanding of Latin, Greek, and Hebrew, and his later writings demonstrate a familiarity with a broad range of saints and biblical characters. The piety described in 'Zone' manifested itself sporadically and spontaneously throughout Apollinaire's life, despite an early-life distancing from Catholicism. The poem itself places 'those elements of his poetry which are concerned with spiritual matters, in a widely based non-Christian tradition which is closer to heresy than to atheism'.[12] As often as he fixated on the biblical prophets or the figure of the Virgin, his wide-ranging reading habits brought him into contact with such bodies of work as ancient Middle- and Near-Eastern mythology and Kabbalah,[13] developing his capacity for 'an out-of-the-ordinary sensibility and a particular capacity for whole-hearted devotion to an ideal'.[14] He declared himself an atheist by the time he arrived at lycée in Nice, and he began to favour more 'profane' and classical literatures; Couffignal speculates that in a poem of this period, 'Lecture', the reference to a 'grimoire rongé des vers' [grimoire gnawed by worms] was the Bible.[15] This was also the period in which some of the irreverently blasphemous stories of *L'Hérésiarque et Cie* were written.[16]

From a reading of 'Zone', one might be forgiven for assuming that Apollinaire still maintained his religious devotion into adulthood, as it opens with clear and seemingly sympathetic references to Catholic symbols and practice. However, the focus on the young poet's evening prayer is less a recommitment to Catholic faith than a meditation on his eventual loss of faith — the ecstatic visions of the first half of the poem heightening that loss in the second half. Apollinaire became naturally sceptical of religious authority but the spiritual symbols, practices, and emotions of his youth made a deep impression, the search for which he never entirely abandoned:

> Voilà la jeune rue et tu n'es encore qu'un petit enfant
> Ta mère ne t'habille que de bleu et de blanc[17]

> Tu es très pieux et avec le plus ancien de tes camarades René Dalize
> Vous n'aimez rien tant que les pompes de l'Eglise (*ŒP*, 40)

> > [Here is a young street and you are only a small child
> > Your mother dresses you in blue and white
> > You're very pious and with your oldest comrade René Dalize
> > You love nothing so much as the pomp of the Church]

The church's 'pompes' might justly be read as vanity, gaudiness, or needless pretension, and signal the way it imposes itself on the youth. The youth can be criticized for his naïveté, but the image, rather, contrasts the young poet's more transient fascinations to the 'heart' of Christianity: the hope of the resurrection as a myth that is nevertheless relevant to modernity itself. The following lines take on a more serious tone, describing the young poet sneaking into a chapel at night to pray. The stanza shifts at this point to the vision of Christ, and from a contemplation of youth to a consideration of eternity:

> Tandis qu'éternelle et adorable profondeur améthyste
> Tourne à jamais la flamboyante gloire du Christ
> [...]
> C'est la torche aux cheveux roux que n'éteint pas le vent
> [...]
> C'est l'arbre toujours touffu de toutes les prières
> C'est la double potence de l'honneur et de l'éternité (*ŒP*, 40)

> > [While deep amethyst eternal and adorable
> > The flaming glory of Christ turns forever
> > [...]
> > It's the red-haired torch that the wind doesn't extinguish
> > [...]
> > It's the tree always stuffed with every prayer
> > It's the double potency of honour and eternity]

The contrast is striking: from the youthful and fleeting 'pompes de l'Eglise', whose spirit has since been found in the modern city, to the eternally burning flame (as with the sacrificial sun of the final line). And along with the words 'éternelle' and 'éternité' appearing in close proximity, the torch, unable to be extinguished by the wind, provides a comparative measure of stability. The image occurs again in *Calligrammes*'s prophetically themed poem 'Les Collines' as the 'Torche que rien ne peut éteindre' [Torch that nothing can extinguish] (*ŒP*, 175) and in *Alcools*'s 'Le Brasier', which identifies the condition of the flame with Apollinaire's ever-changing soul: 'Qu'au brasier les flammes renaissent | Mon âme au soleil se dévêt' [How the flames rekindle in the brazier | My soul undresses in the sun] (*ŒP*, 108). In contrast to a poem like 'Cortège', which celebrates the poet's shifting identity, the religious sentiments from his youth provide an unlikely anchor within the peripatetic search of the modern poet. This paradox, symbolized in the image of the eternal flame is a constant metaphor for Apollinaire's self-consuming desires that nevertheless renew his soul, and for the youth that he's always searching for but can never entirely leave behind.

Biblical literature infrequently addresses the prophet's youth, but on the occasions in which it does, youthful events themselves foreshadow the character of the individual, and in so doing, write prophecy into his or her very biography. For example, the story of a young Jesus debating with the scholars in the temple, related in Luke 2. 41–52, demonstrates his precocious intellect and anticipates his career as a future rabbi. A similarly auspicious childhood was already part of Apollinaire's biography, having an unknown father, which gave him freedom to spin fantastic stories about his paternity, and a mother who was active in his religious upbringing. Several lines in this section of 'Zone' suggest the stories of the prophet Samuel as a possible source. Writing in the second person, the poet recalls, 'Ta mère ne t'habille que de bleu et de blanc' [Your mother clothes you only in blue and white] (ŒP, 40), prompting Couffignal to observe that 'Ce monde porte les couleurs de l'enfance; ce monde *est* celui de l'enfance' [This world wears the colours of childhood; this world *is* that of childhood].[18] In a mention of the prophet's mother, 1 Samuel 2. 18–19 states: 'Samuel was ministering before the Lord, a boy wearing a linen ephod. His mother used to make for him a little robe and take it to him each year [...]'. Hannah, Samuel's mother, takes charge of the young boy's religious fidelity by making for him the proper clothing for a future member of the priesthood, just as the poet's mother dresses him in blue and white, the colours of the Virgin.[19] Hannah, a barren woman who is made pregnant through divine intervention (1 Samuel 1. 19–20), serves as a precedent for the Virgin Mary and such modelling of significant figures is a crucial way for biblical prophecy to assert a continuity of legitimacy. Joshua's and Elijah's parting of the Jordan river (Joshua 3. 14–17; II Kings 2. 8) clearly models Moses leading Israel across the Red Sea, an image that Apollinaire also famously borrows in 'La Chanson du Mal-Aimé'. Like Apollinaire's mother, Angélique, Hannah takes a leading role in the story while Samuel's father, Elkanah, is significantly more passive (for example, Hannah has seventeen verses of speech whereas Elkanah has only two) — an absence that likely resonated with the Apollinaire. Another small detail suggests the possible influence of the book of Samuel, where Apollinaire writes: 'Il est neuf heures le gaz est baissé tout bleu vous sortez du dortoir en cachette' [It is nine o'clock the gas is dimmed to blue you sneak out of your dormitory] (ŒP, 40). This line invokes several other parallels with Samuel, including the period of time over the course of an evening ('Samuel lay there until morning'; 1 Samuel 3. 15), Samuel's sleep ('Samuel was lying down in the temple of the Lord'; 1 Samuel 3. 3), and the description of the low flame of the lamp ('the lamp of God had not yet gone out'; 1 Samuel 3. 3). And finally, the narrative remarks on Samuel's young age ('Now the boy Samuel'; 1 Samuel 3. 1), grounding Samuel's narrative in the formative experiences of his youth.

The attention to the youth of the poet/prophet has two results: highlighting their receptiveness and withdrawing them from the timeline of the surrounding society. In terms of the former, the city is composed of both 'real' and imagined signals — advertisements and books, bells and sirens regulating the city's rhythm and shaping the public's ideas. But the poet, hearing the 'singing' of posters and catalogues, is receptive to a message beyond the 'plain meaning' of these signals. Aesthetic and cultural possibilities ('la poésie est partout diffuse [...]; la littérature est descendue dans la rue, abondante, riche, foisonnante' [poetry has diffused all over [...]; literature has descended into the street, abundant, rich, flourishing])[20] divorce these artefacts of everyday life from their general functions, conveying messages, rather, to and about the poet's shame and enthusiasm; and the workers he encounters, who might regard such objects as merely quotidian, are relegated to the background of the poet's experience — a condition that the second half of the poem addresses with some reservation — even as these objects are rescued as totems of art and literature. In particular, the 'clairon' of the sun seems directed specifically at the poet, whose sensitivity absorbs surroundings as if he were again a youth seeking communion with God. His heightened receptivity, in both the present-day street and in the chapel of his memory, is comparable to Samuel's 'Speak, for your servant is listening', and as much or more the product of the poet's *desire* to conceive modern life against the routines of daily life. In order to do so, he recalls youth's innocence — perhaps even naïveté — but also the spiritual sensitivity necessary for the young prophet.

Being 'called' as a youth also places the poet or prophet within a timescale above and beyond the workdays and weekends of 'Les directeurs les ouvriers et les belles sténo-dactylographes' [The directors and workers and beautiful shorthand typists] (*Œ P*, 39). He is, as S. I. Lockerbie states, 'un poète échappant à l'ordre du temps habituel' [a poet escaping the order of habitual time].[21] The Bible performs a restructuring of history around God's salvation, which compels prophets to experience time on a scale that is not simply longer, but one that develops through the actions of the divine. When God calls Jeremiah, He states, 'Before I formed you in the womb I knew you, and before you were born I consecrated you' (Jeremiah 1. 5). This indication of Jeremiah's destiny suggests that, even in utero, his life is tuned to the fluctuations of God's salvation history, rather than the daily lives of his contemporaries. So if, as Lockerbie argues, Apollinaire has escaped from the daily order of time, what has he escaped into? It seems to be an unfolding of an aesthetic that is intimately tied to the poet's formative, spiritual experiences, recognized, like Jeremiah, as a divine calling. The attention to the calling in the prophet's or poet's youth marks him as a figure of both the past and the future in an alternative history. Moreover, the poeticized call externalizes his inner experience as the very aesthetic that he 'objectively' encounters: the poet is himself evidence of that alternative history.

Suggestive of multiple interpretations, the final image of 'Zone', 'Soleil cou coupé' [Sun cut throat] (*Œ P*, 44), can be read as the poet bidding farewell to the past, which is for him now dead and lost.[22] But the violence of the image indicates that there is no seamless transition from youth to maturity in Apollinaire's work. The transition is wrenching, dangerous, and always constitutes a loss as well as a gain. The distinction between youth and maturity, past and future is rarely sharper than the opening of 'Les Collines' and its image of two aeroplanes, 'L'un était rouge et l'autre noir' [One being was red and the other black] (*Œ P*, 171), which transitions into the image of the spiritual or cosmological conflict between Lucifer and the archangel, and the inevitable contradiction between youth and future.[23] In stanzas 2 and 3, Apollinaire writes:

> L'un était toute ma jeunesse
> Et l'autre c'était l'avenir
> Ils se combattaient avec rage
> Ainsi fit contre Lucifer
> L'Archange aux ailes radieuses
>
> Ainsi le calcul au problème
> Ainsi la nuit contre le jour (*ŒP*, 171)
>
> [One was all my youth
> And the other was the future
> They battle each other with rage
> As the archangel with radiant wings
> Did against Lucifer
>
> As the calculation does against the problem
> As the night does against the day]

The last two lines define a relationship of thesis and antithesis, completing, and therefore negating, each other. The problem is made redundant by the calculation that solves it, turning a question into an answer; night succeeds but cannot coexist with day, although each implies the other. Youth is itself the preparation for its own end. In interpreting the famous image of the sun that concludes 'Zone', Couffignal explicitly compares it the end of youth: 'Adieu au soleil claironnant, tout neuf; salut à un astre mort, guillotiné, soleil des morts, soleil infernal. Adieu à l'enfance, à sa pureté, à son dieu Jésus-Christ' [Farewell to the proclaiming sun, completely new; greetings to a dead star, guillotined, sun of the dead, infernal sun. Farewell to childhood, in its purity, to his god Jesus Christ].[24] This metaphor is carried through in 'Les Collines' where Apollinaire writes several times of the death of youth in terms that are not always enthusiastic about the future:

> Jeunesse adieu jasmin du temps
> J'ai respiré ton frais parfum
> [...]
> Adieu jeunesse blanc Noël
> Quand la vie n'était qu'une étoile
> Dont je contemplais le reflet
> Dans la mer Méditerranée (*ŒP*, 174)
>
> [Goodbye youth jasmine of time
> I have breathed your fresh perfume
> [...]
> Goodbye youth white Noel
> When life was only a star
> Whose reflection I contemplated
> In the Mediterranean sea]

The reflection of the star in the sea, as the image of youth itself, is a symbol of a distant idealization[25] — it is indeed only a reflection — within the ever-shifting sea. In a similar, but even more erotic, manner, the symbol of the dying and sea was taken up by Marinetti in his own work, such as the end of *La Conquête des étoiles*, where the sky has been defeated by the ocean — a metaphor in Marinetti for materialism or chaos. The narrator of *Conquête* encounters a dying star by the ocean and kisses it by way of saying goodbye: 'Longtemps, je savourai ce funèbre baiser | pour en mourir, pour en mourir!' [For a long time, I savoured this funereal kiss | so I could die from it, so I could die from it!].[26] The poet in 'Los Collines' is under no real obligation in this state to dedicate himself to faith or the world, and hence experiences life as a fragrance or free contemplation. However, the obverse side of youth's end is a more immediate experience of life, which entails both positive and negative qualities:

> Il vient un temps pour la souffrance
> Il vient un temps pour la bonté
> Jeunesse adieu voici le temps
> Où l'on connaîtra l'avenir
> Sans mourir de sa connaissance (ŒP, 174)

> [There comes a time for suffering
> There comes a time for kindness
> Youth goodbye this is the time
> When one will know the future
> Without dying from knowing]

The future is neither strictly positive nor negative, carrying both 'souffrance' and 'bonté', and this dual aspect, the future being neither better nor worse than youth, is not moral. What does distinguish youth and maturity is the prophetic fortitude of knowing and facing the future. When the poet states that this is the time where one can know the future 'Sans mourir de sa connaissance' [Without dying of his knowledge], there is a subtle allusion to the survival of the prophet when confronted by God. In Exodus 33. 20, God states that anyone who sees His face will die, presumably from the power of the full presence of the Lord. Moses has the strength to speak with God 'face to face, as one speaks to a friend' (Exodus 33. 11), although later in the passage, God insists that Moses should not look at His face (vv. 20–23). Regardless of the potential contradiction, the meaning for Apollinaire is clear. If God is read as a figure for the totality of humanity's aspirations, that is, the future,[27] then Apollinaire confronts the notion that we cannot know that utopian state, except in death. The prophet, however, is an exception to this rule, being the very individual who must see, experience, and proclaim the future in this life.

Youth ends not when the prophet reaches a certain age, but when the commission of God is forced onto him, when the burden of the vocation of poet/prophet imposes itself, opening up an entirely new understanding of the self, the world, and time. The prophetic call is structured around this pivot from youth to maturity. 'La fin de la jeunesse', states Lockerbie, 'doit avoir une valeur plus qu'anecdotique. Elle figure plutôt le moment capital où une nouvelle dimension s'ouvre' [The end of youth must have a value more than anecdotal. Rather, it figures the capital moment where a new dimension opens itself up].[28] Jeremiah's call is a useful example in this sense. Jeremiah protests God's commission by pleading immaturity:

> Then I said, 'Ah! Lord God! Truly I do not know how to speak, for I am only a boy.' But the Lord said to me, 'Do not say, "I am only a boy"; for you shall go to all to whom I send you and you shall speak whatever I command you.' (Jeremiah 1. 6–7)

While it is tempting to speculate on Jeremiah's protest about being too young in terms of his possible age at the time of his call, such speculation misses the point of the protest, which is a show of humility or inexperience.[29] God counters the phrase 'I am only a boy' to the act of prophesying, arguing that prophecy is not prevented by being a boy, but is instead the means by which the prophet will reach maturity.[30] Apollinaire writes his youth into the past and writes the future into existence, surviving the violence of that transition. Weber also eschews the naïve definition of age as 'a date registered on a birth certificate', arguing that

> what is decisive is the trained relentlessness in viewing the realities of life, and the ability to face such realities and to measure up to them inwardly. [...] [I]t is immensely moving when a *mature* man — no matter whether old or young in years — [...] acts by following an ethic of responsibility and somewhere reaches the point where he says: 'Here I stand; I can do no other.'[31]

The august tone of this statement, however, presents maturity as essentially a form of fatalism, and neglects the subversive basis of charisma: the ability to clearly see the 'realities of life' and decline to accept them. The paradox of charisma is that its pure or ideal form is the essence of newness and discontinuity, but when it confronts the world it becomes developed and rationalized as a practical response to the world. If the charismatic moment in Apollinaire is viewed as the free, spontaneous apprehension of poetry, analogously associated with the youthful and prophetic communion with God, then the tension arises when that moment imposes itself as a regularized ethic that must be followed in the world.

The tension between tradition and modernity that opens 'Zone' is resolved, though never completely, through the poet as a mediating force between a world that is both 'ancient' and new, crystallized in the paradoxical image of the Eiffel Tower as a 'shepherdess'. The tower is called 'Bergère' and the bridges of the Seine are 'le troupeau des ponts [qui] bêle ce matin' [the flock of bridges [that] bleat this morning] (ŒP, 39) — quaintly pastoral figures that appear as unusually atavistic. Ezekiel 34 has a long discourse on shepherds who both betray and rescue their flock: initially, the shepherds are rulers who fail to properly tend to the flock (i.e., Israel); but by the end of the passage, God assumes the role of shepherd, stating, 'I myself will be the shepherd of my sheep' (Ezekiel 34. 15). The metaphor is then applied to King David: God will 'set up over them one shepherd, my servant David, and he shall feed them: he shall feed them and be their shepherd' (34. 23). On the other hand, the shepherd can occur in a military context: Jeremiah 6. 3 describes invading armies as 'Shepherds and their flocks', and similarly Apollinaire's 'Saillant' (1915) describes an artillery shell as a 'Berger suivi de son troupeau mordoré' [Shepherd followed by his bronzed flock] (ŒP, 227). There are indications in 'Zone' of people needing guidance in the modern world, and the Eiffel Tower acts as a symbol of stability, but also a more democratic sense of prophecy unified by the urban and pastoral imagery. Amos 6. 14–15, a potent parallel to 'Zone', likewise establishes the analogy between prophet and shepherd: 'Then Amos answered Amaziah, "I am no prophet, nor a prophet's son; but I am a herdsman, [...] and the Lord took me from following the flock, and the Lord said to me, 'Go, prophesy to my people Israel.'"'.

Amos appears to undercut his position as a prophet by appealing to his status as a *mere* herdsman. But the act is ironic insofar as both prophecy and shepherding are vocations of leadership if we think of tending a flock as analogous to tending to God's people, which God appears to do in his command to Amos. What Apollinaire might take from these associations of prophecy and shepherding is that the poet is not only a guide but is also *being guided* by something more transcendent and mysterious.

Guidance suggests that the guide has a dedication to the future as well as a feel for the past, a sense of where he is going as well as where he is coming from, and that he is fulfilling a need that is lacking in the broader society. But the poet's deeply conflicted relationship to religious thought and practice in 'Zone', also presenting themes of misdirection, wandering, and migration, raises the question of whether or not the past and future are universal experiences, or individual journeys. Therefore, no guidance is ever quite adequate, even when directed towards a wider population, and so demonstrates the tension between the sense of individual and common experience:

> Si tu vivais dans l'ancien temps tu entrerais dans un monastère
> Vous avez honte quand vous vous surprenez à dire une prière
> Tu te moques de toi et comme le feu de l'Enfer ton rire pétille
> Les étincelles de ton rire dorent le fond de ta vie (*ŒP*, 41)

> [If you were living in former times you would have entered a monastery
> You are ashamed when you surprise yourself saying a prayer
> You mock yourself and like the fire of Hell your laughter sparkles
> The sparks of your laughter gild the background of your life]

These lines express a series of incompatible aspects of the poet's personality — nostalgia and unsentimentality, faith and rationality, insincerity and earnestness. The shifts in the second-person, from the plural, formal 'vous' to the singular, informal 'tu', complicates the integrity of the speaker: is he acting as a stand-in for a broader humanity? Does he see himself, as in 'Cortège', as a composite figure? The *common* — as both frequent and as communal — practice of prayer incites a conflicted reaction in the poet: the habitual act of prayer associates him with a most un-modern, religious public. Likewise, the monastery is an image of withdrawal from society but is itself a communal form of life. The analogy works, however, at cross purposes: the poet is fundamentally modern and shares the apparent secularism of contemporary society, yet still feels longings and inclinations towards certain aspects of his Christian upbringing; on the other hand, religious practice is profoundly social *and* outmoded, mitigating the avant-gardist pretensions of the poet. Yet, Apollinaire makes the most of this contradiction, as it enlivens and defines the poet in relation to the society. He finds a transcendent energy in religion that nonetheless does not sit well with modern secularism and bourgeois morality, and which causes friction with society: he is both guide and peripatetic wanderer.

Images of ascent in the Bible — mountains and hills, ladders or stairs, angels' flights — are related to what Frye terms 'the intensifying of consciousness'[32] that comprehends God's creation in new ways. He states that, 'Creation is rather an intensely vivid image of the objective world as a spread-out picture of intelligibility awaiting discovery and interpretation';[33] and where better to consider creation than from the top of a mountain or hill, where many of the biblical prophets typically meet God? 'Zone', as a poem that figures the urban space as a new creation, likewise reflects Modernism's broader re-considerations of the relationship between time and space, which reaches its zenith, sometimes in more-or-less literal ways, in Futurist writing. The impulse to be modern is re-figured as another historical iteration of religious myth, represented in one era by the ascent of Christ into heaven, and recurring again in the twentieth century, abetted by the mechanical possibilities of flight. The title of the poem signifies a horizontal space that must be navigated, and indeed the poet spends much time recounting his travels across Europe. But the opening stanzas' imagery establishes the spatial element as more vertical, which will be further re-iterated by the extensive sections on the flight and ascent of the modern Christ. The obvious image is again the Eiffel Tower extending into the sky, straining to escape the 'antiquité grecque et romaine' (ŒP, 39). The following lines then state that Christianity is entirely modern:

> La religion seule est restée toute neuve la religion
> Est restée simple comme les hangars de Port-Aviation
>
> Seul en Europe tu n'es pas antique ô Christianisme
> L'Européen le plus moderne c'est vous Pape Pie X (ŒP, 39)
>
> [The only religion has remained entirely new religion
> Has remained simple like airport hangars
>
> Only in Europe you are not ancient O Christianity
> The most modern European is you Pope Pious X]

Apollinaire considers — which is certainly not the same as advocacy — the emergence of Christianity from Greece and Rome as a model for the struggle of modernity to realize itself in the twentieth century. This conflation of the contemporary and ancient implies that the former must, somehow, develop from the latter, mitigating the definitiveness of the break between the past and future, and anticipates Apollinaire's oft-cited correlation of tradition and invention. 'Zone' presents the struggle for the modern as a literal upward movement equally embodied both by the ascent or resurrection of Christ, the flight of aeroplanes, or the vertical construction of the Eiffel Tower. Indeed, even the description of the pope as 'le plus moderne' is likely a tacit riposte to Marinetti's Le Monoplan du pape, which concludes with the downward movement of the pope falling into the sea. It's a measure of the prophetic historiography of the poem that events and developments of the 'here-and-now' are connected, by the poet, to the celestial sphere. After recounting his own youthful religious practice, the poet envisions the aeroplanes as another reiteration of the ascension of Christ to heaven:

> C'est le Christ qui monte au ciel mieux que les aviateurs
> Il détient le record du monde pour la hauteur (ŒP, 40)
>
> [It's Christ who rises to the sky better than any aviator
> He holds the world record for the highest]

Like the pope, Christ himself becomes the paradoxical symbol of modernity:

> Pupille Christ de l'œil
> Vingtième pupille des siècles il sait y faire
> Et changé en oiseau ce siècle comme Jésus monte dans l'air (*ŒP*, 40)

> [Christ pupil of the eye
> Twentieth pupil of the centuries he knows his stuff
> And this century transformed into a bird like Jesus rising into the air]

The phrase 'il sait y faire' demonstrates an assuredness on the part of Christ that is paralleled in the figure of the prophet, mimicking Christ's ascent in the following lines. Apollinaire writes: 'Icare Enoch Elie Apollonius de Thyane | Flottent autour du premier aéroplane' [Icarus Enoch Elijah Apollonius of Tyana | Floating around the first aeroplane] (*ŒP*, 40). Alongside figures of Greek myth and legend the poet envisions the biblical prophets Elijah and Enoch. The choice of these prophets is not coincidental, as these two figures of Hebrew literature share a particular trait: 'les deux prophètes ont tous deux été *enlevés* par Dieu sans avoir connu la mort' [the two prophets have both been *lifted up* by God without having known death]:[34] Elijah is taken to heaven in a fiery chariot (II Kings 2. 11), and Enoch is lifted up by God before death (Sirach 44. 16). In the context of 'Zone', in which flight and ascent are images of distinctly modern acts, the prophet is a figure of both the past and the future, embodying the kind of idealized purity of poetic temporality described by Robert Champigny. After the death of God and, I would add, subsequently severed from the salvation-history of the Bible, Champigny states that 'le temp représente la dignité de l'homme par rapport aux choses' [time represents the dignity of man by a relationship to things].[35] This profane state of affairs presents a problem for Modernist art. However, any attempt at 'purifying' language of its necessary reliance on the utility of 'things'[36] requires that 'le véritable pureté poétique doit être trouvée, non pas en deçà du temps prosaïque, mais au-delà. Il ne s'agit pas tant d'ignorer la chronologie que de la surmonter' [true poetic purity must be found, not within prosaic time, but beyond it. It's not so much a matter of ignoring chronology as of overcoming it].[37] The effort to 'overcome' chronology is certainly embodied by the choice of Elijah and Enoch, as neither Elijah nor Enoch experienced death in the popular conception of the figures, and yet both still reached heaven. Elijah, as well, is thought, as early as the prophet Malachi (4. 5), to return as a sign of the eschaton. So, rather than 'ignoring' the state of the world, Apollinaire draws energy from the shear impossibility of the demands that religion makes upon the world. The power of these images — of resurrection, of flight — is derived by comparison to the poet's grounding in conditions of the present, and so the second movement in 'Zone' is downwards into the more visceral, sordid, and deadly world.

The following section of 'Zone' examines the fine line between the experimental wanderings of the modern poet and the experience of being astray. Is the modern poet a shepherd or another part of the flock? After the visionary experience of Christ, aeroplanes, prophets, and birds, induced by a memory of religious devotion, the poet finds himself 'dans Paris tout seul parmi la foule' [in Paris all alone among the crowd] (*ŒP*, 41). This returns the poet to a more social level, existing, objectively, as one more indistinguishable piece of the world itself, a traumatic fracture and repair between the internal orientation of the poet and the world. This double-movement in 'Zone', from the inspired ascent at the beginning of the poem to the descent into the depths of Paris or Europe, can be read as Apollinaire's farewell to the religious energy of his youth, and acceptance of the necessity to engage with the world. But this engagement is by turns humiliating, corrupting, and shameful, a repeated 'processus que décrit le poète, le *"déclin"*, la dégradation' [process that describes the poet, '*decline*', degradation];[38] that is, it is the opposite of the purifying and invigorating feelings of the first half of 'Zone'. The themes of sin and death are more prominent in this half of the poem, where Apollinaire begins by stating: 'Aujourd'hui tu marches dans Paris les femmes sont ensanglantées | C'était et je voudrais ne pas m'en souvenir c'était au déclin de la beauté' [Today you are walking in Paris the women are bloody | It was and I don't want to remember that it was the decline of beauty] (*ŒP*, 41) The intimation of death ('les femmes sont ensanglantées'), connected to feelings of guilt and sin, expands and darkens into an infernal space. The Catholic images that he revered as a youth engulf him:

> Entourée de flammes ferventes Notre-Dame m'a regardé à Chartres
> Le sang de votre Sacré-Cœur m'a inondé à Montmartre
> Je suis malade d'ouïr les paroles bienheureuses
> L'amour dont je souffre est une maladie honteuse (*ŒP*, 41)

> [Surrounded by flames Our Lady watched me at Chartres
> The blood of your Sacred Heart flooded me at Montmartre
> I am sick of hearing words of wellbeing
> The love of which I suffer is a shameful malady]

If the love experienced by the poet as a child — from his mother, from the Virgin, from Christ — was at that time a source of life, then the same love is now a source of shame. After the initial ascension of the first half of 'Zone', the poet experiences, as Couffignal explains, 'une série de parcours qui, souvent commencés dans la lumière et le bonheur, s'achèvent dans les ténèbres et le malheur, conduisant le promeneur au fond d'une impasse barrée, dans un étranglement qui l'emprisonne; butant sans cesse contre une cloison, il recommence indéfiniment son errance à travers ces circuits labyrinthiques' [a series of journeys which, often commenced in light and happiness, concludes in shadows and evil, leading the wanderer to the foot of a barricade, in a web that traps him; stumbling without end against a wall, he indefinitely resumes his wandering across labyrinthine circuits].[39] Between the ecstatic flight and pathetic fall, the wanderings around Europe and the perennial return to Paris, the poet finds himself caught between duelling and irreconcilable tendencies that are similarly expressed in 'La Chanson du mal-aimé' (1909):

> Je suivis ce mauvais garçon
> Qui sifflotait mains dans les poches
> Nous semblions entre les maisons
> Onde ouverte de la mer Rouge
> Lui les Hébreux moi Pharaon

Que tombent ces vagues de briques
Si tu ne fus pas bien aimée
Je suis le souverain d'Egypte (Œ*P*, 46)

[I followed this malevolent boy
Who whistled hands in pockets
We seemed among the houses
Open wave of the Red Sea
He the Hebrews myself Pharaoh

How these waves of bricks fall
If you were not well-loved
I am the sovereign of Egypt]

Apollinaire employs the biblical myth of the exodus to understand the image of following 'ce mauvais garçon', which, as in 'Zone', objectifies Apollinaire's youth so that he may critically examine it. The walls on either side are imagined as the divided Red Sea that provided the Hebrews with a passage to safety. The 'bien aimée' is pursued by the poet in the guise of 'le souverain d'Egypte', which suggests how affection might easily slip into a mode of domineering possessiveness, driven not by rationality, but by pharaoh's heart hardened by God. Describing this scene, Susan Harrow makes an observation that is also applicable to the ambivalence that characterizes 'Zone': 'Those pressures are summed up powerfully [...] where the distinctions between urban violence and human vulnerability, biblical persecution and personal guilt, myth and the everyday collapse together in a searing expression of anxiety and desire'.[40] Therefore, the poet, like the prophet, is buffeted from either side by desire and responsibility, the high-flown aesthetic or religious ideal and the fallen nature of the world. In this sense, the poet-as-prophet is both guide and in need of guidance in the way that the Bible can simultaneously present both God and prophet as shepherd.

Maintaining the dialectical character of much of his thought, the poet's liminality in life is only heightened by his grounding in the social sphere, modelling biblical prophecy's formation as an anti-elite discourse. For instance, Robert Wilson describes Elisha's 'sons of the prophets' as 'peripheral individuals who had [...] been forced out of the political and religious establishments.'[41] And Norman Gottwald argues that prophets with radical messages 'could find a hearing in the community [...] as their fellow Israelites also became critical of the institutions whose powerful effects upon their lives could not be escaped.'[42] Aspirations towards an ideal are reflections of the disappointments and sins of the poet's life. The movement of descent into the shameful aspects of humanity, in spite of his desire for the light and the air, is an act of conviction and credibility — to experience sin is to know what it means to transcend it. An obvious comparison to the poet's punishment — 'Comme un criminel on te met en état d'arrestation' [Like a criminal they place me under arrest] (Œ*P*, 42) — is Jeremiah's arrest and imprisonment (Jeremiah 37. 11–38. 6). Another comparison is to Jesus' association with tax collectors, prostitutes, and sinners (e.g. Matthew 9. 10; 21. 32), placing him among the most socially marginal. Similarly, the poet finds himself among emigrants: 'Tu regardes les yeux pleins de larmes ces pauvres émigrants | Ils croient en Dieu ils prient les femmes allaitent des enfants' [Eyes full of tears you look at these poor emigrants | They believe in God they pray women breastfeed children] (*ŒP*, 43). The second line above echoes the poet's previous memory of prayer, processing feelings of dislocation by turning to religion. However, while the emigrants are hoping to return 'après avoir fait fortune' [after having made their fortune], the poet's goal is presumably much less tangible. This placement among the migrants and criminals aligns the poet's outwardly lived experience with theirs, perhaps in the quest for a partial credibility among the public, as well as the anti-institutional elements of avant-garde thought. Like the prophet Elisha's prophetic conventicle, identifying with the desire of the poor and the outcast, as related in the miracle stories of II Kings (2. 19–22; 4. 1–6. 7), makes a virtue of necessity. The poet-as-prophet asserts an experience that both garners the credibility to speak to and on behalf of the liminal individuals and groups, while simultaneously redirecting the assumptions the public might have about such experiences. The poet's brief visualization of his erstwhile religious belief extends those moments of youthful inspiration to the modern social world, envisioning the possibility of a restoration or return to that earlier state of being, or the simplicity and dedication of something like the monastic community. Francis Carmody has argued that 'The role of the poet is defined by his need or longing for purity and renewal',[43] and Bourdieu states that artistic and cultural revolutions can take the form of a return 'to the purity of origins'. The legitimacy of the poet lies in the charged ambivalence of the forward-looking prophet of modernity, and simultaneously, the self-representation of the person who is driven back to that 'purity of origins'. Similarly, the avant-garde as a whole stakes it ground on a new origin, and all of the possibilities that implies, freedom from the constraints (which, for Apollinaire, was not necessarily a lack of respect) of literary tradition an opportunity for experimentation.

The Call

Samuel's call, while neither as fraught with mystery as that of Moses before the burning bush, nor as glamorously supernatural as Isaiah's or Elisha's, stresses the experience of *hearing* and *listening* for the prophet. The young Samuel initially hears the voice of God in the night, in the sanctuary where he sleeps, and assumes that the priest Eli is calling him. Eli cannot hear the voice himself and, after being woken several times by the attentive Samuel, concludes that God is communicating with the boy and tells him to return to the sanctuary and wait for the call: 'Now the Lord came and stood there, calling as before, "Samuel! Samuel!" And Samuel said, "Speak, for your servant is listening."' (I Samuel 3. 10). Is Samuel gifted with unique kinds of perception, or is he simply more vigilant than the priest Eli (who, earlier in the story, is indicted by the narrator as a corrupt officiant of the Lord)? The text supports both readings: the voice seems to be silent to Eli; Samuel's act of listening is shown both in his actions and verbal response. Poets are frequently, and perhaps necessarily, presented as especially sensitive to their environment, but there is a distinction in degree if not in the kind of observance the prophet manifests. If a poet can occasionally get away with drawing out relationships between the exterior aspects of the world, the prophet penetrates, improbably, to an 'inner' meaning of the physical world or history itself. When Apollinaire initially sets out on his reverie in 'Zone', prompted by the view of a street, the sounds that he perceives prime him to receive the call that the people around him, trapped in the routines and rhythms of daily life, cannot. He writes:

> Neuve et propre du soleil elle était le clairon
> [...]
> Le matin par trois fois la sirène y gémit
> Une cloche rageuse y aboie vers midi
> Les inscriptions des enseignes et des murailles
> Les plaques les avis à la façon des perroquets criaillent (*ŒP*, 39)

> [New and clean it was the sun's clarion
> [...]
> The siren whines three times each morning
> A raging bell barks around noon
> The inscriptions of signs and murals
> Plaques and notices cry like parakeets]

Only the bell and siren in these lines make an actual sound, and so the 'clairon' of the sun and the bird-like twittering of the signs suggest an aural experience beyond what the poet is hearing in everyday life, and so only audible to him. He is connecting to something between the basic human sense of hearing and a more profound revelation of the world around him. But does this mean that such a revelation is ultimately available only to him? Or, could it be, as he states in 'Sur les prophéties', that 'tout le monde est prophéte' [everyone is a prophet]? Despite its seeming singularity, the call is a synecdoche of a possible *social* transformation.

The call is a crucial moment in most prophetic narratives, and Apollinaire's appeals, both implicit and explicit, to the myth of the prophet describe the position of tension between the demands of the everyday world and the ideal to which he is called. What makes this tension so difficult to mediate is that the call is not simply the moment in which the prophet's vocation is revealed, but that their service is required, and set against day-to-day life. The Christian imagery of 'Zone' and other works frame the call in terms of resurrection, repentance, and salvation, positing the division of life and death as the stakes for both the poet and his potential audience in adhering to the call. Life, after the call, becomes so acutely felt that existence prior to the call is a sort of death. This stark understanding of the poet's position in relation to art and society devalues the latter, but only insofar as the experience of society concentrates the sense of artistic autonomy that is apparently untenable in modern life. Weber acknowledged an intimate relationship between artistic production and religion, but concluded that the relation had been strained in his own era, where 'the conscious discovery of uniquely esthetic values [...] causes the disappearance of those elements in art which are conducive to community formation and conducive to the compatibility of art with the religious will to salvation'.[44] To employ Bourdieu's more strategic terminology, the prophetic *prise de position* can be read as an ironic play on the inability of art to maintain its autonomy in the modern world, yet it takes seriously the concern for community formation that art and religion might offer.

'Les Collines' is considered one of Apollinaire's 'manifestes poétiques' and its prophetic outlook, both in terms of its future-oriented themes and its position as one of the first poems in *Calligrammes*, has been aptly described by Scott Bates:

> Le poème prophétique par excellence de *Calligrammes* exigea un lieu privilégié d'où il pourrait dominer — comme une colline — les beaux territoires situés au-delà. Le poète s'octroya ainsi une autorité de prophète et de législateur du Parnasse dès le commencement du livre et donna en même temps plus d'importance et d'unité à *La Victoire* et à *La Jolie Rousse*, les deux autres manifestes poétiques de l'esprit nouveau qui suffisaient en eux-mêmes pour accorder au livre sa conclusion prophétique.[45]

> [The prophetic poem par excellence of *Calligrammes* claimed a privileged place from where it could dominate — like a hill — the beautiful territories located beyond. The poet thus granted himself an authority of the prophet and legislator of Parnassus from the commencement of the book, and at the same time gave more importance and unity to 'La Victoire' and 'La Jolie Rousse', the other two poetic manifestoes of the new spirit which sufficed in themselves to bestow on the book its prophetic conclusion.]

In stanza 5, at a moment when Apollinaire proclaims himself as spokesperson for a new vision of the world, he places himself between his past and the future:

> Où donc est tombée ma jeunesse
> Tu vois que flambe l'avenir
> Sache que je parle aujourd'hui
> Pour annoncer au monde entier
> Qu'enfin est né l'art de prédire (*ŒP*, 171)

> [So where has my youth fallen
> You see that the future burns
> Know that I speak today
> To announce to the entire world
> How that art of prediction is finally born]

The first and second lines echo the division of youth and future in 'Zone' but the image of the flame in the second line, and the interrogative phrasing of the first, emphasizes the confidence in the future. Overall, the lines transition from a personal, doubtful tone, to an objective 'Tu', to a commanding ('Sache que') 'Je' in the third line. The vision of the flaming future recalibrates the orientation and identity of the speaker as a prophetic advocate. The poet creates a mythic version of the self through the agonizing transition from youth to maturity or from past to future. The image suggests a prophetic call wrenching the subject into a new awareness, which compels certain attitudes and actions on the part of the subject.

The poem's title alludes to the common prophetic motif in the Bible as Moses, Elijah, and Jesus all received theophanies on the tops of a hill or mountain, to command a wider view of time and space than the average individual. Immediately after announcing 'l'art de prédire' in 'Les Collines', Apollinaire claims:

Certains hommes sont des collines
Qui s'élèvent d'entre les hommes
Et voient au loin tout l'avenir
Mieux que s'il était le présent
Plus net que s'il était passé (Œ*P*, 172)

[Certain men are hills
That rise up from among others
And see the entire future from a distance
Better than if it was the present
Neater than if it was past]

The eponymous hills refer to those notable individuals who see the future, and of whom Apollinaire explicitly notes in stanza 12: 'Voici s'élever des prophètes | Comme au loin des collines bleues' [Here prophets arise | Like blue hills in the distance] (Œ*P*, 172). In one respect, these lines imply that the poet is innately different from the public. Moses' encounter is distinctive in this regard, as he is the only Israelite who can directly communicate with God and survive — both an exception and a model for others, saying to the Israelites: 'The Lord your God will raise up for you *a prophet like me from among you, from your fellow Israelites*. You must listen to him. For this is what you asked of the Lord your God at Horeb on the day of the assembly when you said, "Let us not hear the voice of the Lord our God nor see this great fire anymore, or we will die." The Lord said to me: "What they say is good. I will raise up for them *a prophet like you from among their fellow Israelites* [...]"'' (Deuteronomy 18. 15–17; emphasis added). The repetition of 'raise up' (קוּם, *qûm*) in this passage from Deuteronomy parallels the use of 'élever' in the lines from 'Les Collines' above as a possible allusion for these lines.[46] Apollinaire's statement that only 'certains hommes' are 'collines' distinguishes, at first glance, this poem from the more democratic view of 'Sur les prophéties', where 'Tout le monde est prophète' (Œ*P*, 186). However, reflecting on the comparison of 'Les Collines' to Deuteronomy, the latter makes clear that the prophet's identity will remain with their 'fellow Israelites' as a more nationalistic position. Conversely, the poet in 'Les Collines' occupies a position above national and cultural ephemeral borders, being drawn 'd'entre les hommes' though perhaps resembling 'des collines bleues' — that is, the poet is an aspirational figure for others in the manner of the shepherd. When Apollinaire writes 'Tout le monde est prophète', there is a hopeful echo of the prophet Joel's prediction that 'your sons and daughters shall prophesy, your old men shall dream dreams, and your young men shall see visions' (2. 28). The contradiction between the public and the poet is even less pronounced when in Apollinaire's subsequent statement in 'Sur les prophéties':

Mais il y a si longtemps qu'on fait croire aux gens
Qu'ils n'ont aucun avenir qu'ils sont ignorants à jamais
Et idiots de naissance (Œ*P*, 186)

[But for such a long time people have been made to believe
That they have no future that they are always dumb
And idiots from birth]

The attitude of 'We Chosen Few', common among the avant-garde, is cast in less strictly elitist terms. Everybody has the potential to prophesy, but it takes the 'certains hommes' who must shake the people out of their pessimism towards themselves and the future. The prophet's call is then read as a possibility that exists against a kind of 'realism', a moment that perhaps can be collectively experienced in embracing the changes and transformations of modern life.

The advocacy of the future and 'l'art de prédire' suggests that the poem is, overall, an experience of the prophetic call or commission. As opposed to professional religious functionaries such as priests, who stake their legitimacy on the authority of tradition as 'incumbents of an "occupation" [...] that is, men who have acquired expert knowledge and who serve for remuneration',[47] Weber distinguishes the prophet by a charismatic call to adhere to and express a firm belief or ideal. For example, Apollinaire echoes the prophetic call of Isaiah in stanza 30 of 'Les Collines':

> L'on ne me donna qu'une flamme
> Dont je fus brûlé jusqu'aux lèvres
> Et je ne pus dire merci
> Torche que rien ne peut éteindre (ŒP, 175)

> [They gave me only a flame
> That burned me up to the lips
> And I could not say Thank You
> Torch that nothing could extinguish]

The poet is burnt up to his lips, called with an action similar to Isaiah in the temple. The silence of the poet, however, is a reversal on Isaiah who, when given his call by the angel of God, immediately assumes the role of God's intermediary and asks to preach:

> Then one of the seraphs flew to me, holding a live coal that had been taken from the altar with a pair of tongs. The seraph touched my mouth with it and said: 'Now that this has touched your lips, your guilt has departed and your sin is blotted out.' Then I heard the voice of the Lord saying, 'Whom shall I send, and who shall go for us?' And I said, 'Here I am; send me!' (Isaiah 6. 6–8)

Isaiah's call narrative presents several parallels and differences with Apollinaire that elucidate the latter's understanding of the structure of prophecy in relation to modern poetry. Apollinaire has a conception of the prophet as a liminal figure, who nevertheless occupies crucial points of convergence, and even adulteration, of conceptual boundaries. Likewise, Isaiah's call narrative occurs within a space of convergence, the temple, which was thought to be the site of meeting between heaven and earth, transforming 'the prophet from being a witness to being a participant in the heavenly council'.[48]

Images of flames and burning are frequent themes for Apollinaire, recalling how 'le Passé, le Dieu de (sa) jeunesse, et d'autres symboles d'une vie antérieure, furent jetés dans le feu' [the Past, the God of (his) youth, and other symbols of an anterior life, were thrown into the fire].[49] For instance, in the poem of *Alcools*, 'Le Brasier' (1908), Apollinaire writes:

J'ai jeté dans le noble feu
Que je transporte et que j'adore
De vives mains et même feu
Ce Passé ces têtes de morts
[...]
Où sont ces têtes que j'avais
Où est le Dieu de ma jeunesse (Œ*P*, 108)

[I have thrown into the noble fire
What I carry and what I adore
Of living hands and even fire
This Past these heads of the dead
[...]
Where are these heads that I had
Where is the God of my youth]

That poets and prophets can only exist for the briefest moment in time is evoked at the end of 'Les Collines', where Apollinaire states that 'Tout n'est qu'une flamme rapide' [Everything is only a rapid flame] (Œ*P*, 177). The moment, that is, that a poet truly resonates with the spirit of modern life is, in the great span of history, relatively small. That moment feels like a burst of flame that consumes, as when Apollinaire writes in 'Les Fiançailles' (1908): 'Un Icare tente de s'élever jusqu'à chacun de mes yeux | Et porteur de soleils je brûle au centre de deux nébuleuses' [An Icarus tries to rise up to each of my eyes | And carrier of suns I burn between two nebulae] (Œ*P*, 130). In 'Zone' Icarus appears alongside the flying Christ, as well as the prophets Elijah and Enoch. The brief and ecstatic flight of Icarus is external to the poet in the first verse, but then Apollinaire imagines himself burning at the centre of the two nebulae/eyes in the following line. The poet is caught between two spheres, and while these spheres are not strictly identifiable, they may loosely correlate with the great dichotomies the poet attempts to transcend: the ideal and material, art and society, the sacred and the profane. This relationship between flight and fire is also anticipated by Isaiah's call narrative: the live coal is flown to the prophet by seraphs, themselves creatures of fire.[50] The prophet's location is therefore somewhere between heaven and earth. And the unstable state of fire suggests that its brief life is inherently tied to its explosiveness; a prophet must 'burn' brighter and faster to introduce new ideas into the world.

This explosive flash of inspiration recalls the tragic element of charisma in Weber, in its role in the de-banalization of institutional structures and daily life. The vitality of the charismatic individual's authority is ultimately doomed by the routine structures of law, economics, or politics. A danger is posed to charisma when the desire to extend it beyond its original bearer to new disciples or successive generations necessitates the establishment of rules and regulations for the identification of the original charismatic claim in these latter-day apostles. The irony in Apollinaire is that the poet's charisma or creativity is actualized, at least partially, in the materials and routines of everyday life — the very sphere that threatens the charismatic experience. Attempting to work against this trend of routinization, Apollinaire's poet-as-prophet both represents the brief and instantaneous aspect of inspiration as well as the aspect of inspiration as a continual referent for the poet. On the one hand, Apollinaire highlights the disruptive prospects of modern literature, stating in *L'Esprit nouveau et les poètes* that 'La surprise est le grand ressort nouveau' [Surprise is the great new spring],[51] pushing outside of the realm of the expected or the routine. The attempt is meant to always push beyond an experience that is 'n'est qu'une flamme rapide', willing a 'Torche que rien ne peut éteindre'. The latter is the inverse of the all-too-material process of charisma — the eternal fire of the burning bush that 'was blazing, yet was not consumed' encountered by Moses.

Weber recognizes in charisma a force that 'repudiates any sort of involvement in the everyday routine world',[52] and Apollinaire pronounces dead much of everyday life. In the conclusion of 'Les Collines', Apollinaire leaves behind much of the cosmological, mythical, and psychological imagery to 'reset' the poem and present himself as a poet 'à ma table' [at my table], and consequently, the remainder of the poem is perhaps the most grounded in the material world. Nevertheless, the list of everyday objects in this part of the poem — hats, hair, fruit, gloves — repeatedly foreshadow death. Stanza 37 begins with disparate, banal, as well as somewhat morbid, imagery:

> Un chapeau haut de forme est sur
> Une table chargée de fruits
> Les gants sont morts près d'une pomme
> Une dame se tord le cou
> Auprès d'un monsieur qui s'avale (*ŒP*, 176)

> [A top-hat set upon
> A table filled with fruit
> The dead gloves are near an apple
> A lady twists her neck
> Next to a gentleman who swallows himself]

The gloves are dead, the lady's neck has been wrung, and the gentleman has swallowed himself, the latter suggesting a surreal kind of suicide. Yet, images of death are often paired with images of explosiveness and creativity, as shown in stanza 38, where a representation of killing immediately reverses itself to demonstrate the technical brilliance of the poet:

> Le bal tournoie au fond du temps
> J'ai tué le beau chef d'orchestre
> Et je pèle pour mes amis
> L'orange dont la saveur est
> Un merveilleux feu d'artifice (*ŒP*, 176)

> [The dance spins at the end of time
> I have killed the handsome conductor
> And for my friends I peel
> The orange whose flavour is
> A marvel of fireworks]

The reference to 'mes amis', echoing poems like 'Les Fiançailles' or 'Cortège', indicates a shift in perspective, where an act of death, from one viewpoint, might easily be an act of creation from those allied with the poet. Again, in stanza 39, Apollinaire begins with an image of death: 'Tous sont morts le maître d'hôtel' [Everyone is dead the hotel manager] (ŒP, 176) But then then he finishes the stanza off with images of the bubbling activity of the poet's mind:

> Leur verse un champagne irréel
>
> Qui mousse comme un escargot
> Ou comme un cerveau de poète
> Tandis que chantait une rose (ŒP, 176)
>
> [Pours them an unreal champagne
>
> Which foams like a snail
> Or like a poet's brain
> While a rose sang]

The singing rose is itself and 'an affirmation over death'.[53] By stanzas 40 and 41, Apollinaire writes parallel images of death and rebirth:

> L'esclave tient une épée nue
> Semblable aux sources et aux fleuves
> Et chaque fois qu'elle s'abaisse
> Un univers est éventré
> Dont il sort des mondes nouveaux
>
> Le chauffeur se tient au volant
> Et chaque fois que sur la route
> Il corne en passant le tournant
> Il paraît à perte de vue
> Un univers encore vierge (ŒP, 176–77)
>
> [The slave takes a naked sword
> Similar to fountains and rivers
> And each time it's lowered
> A universe is gutted
> From which new worlds arise
>
> The chauffeur holds onto the wheel
> And each time on the road
> He sounds the horn while making a turn
> From just out of view there appears
> Another virgin universe]

The slave and chauffeur, both subject to the demands of work and routine, are paralleled by their action of grasping the sword and steering wheel, respectively. The curved motion of the blade mimics the curve of the automobile around the corner, and in both cases the motion, indicating a turning or change of direction, releases 'nouveaux mondes'.

The dialectic between autonomy and engagement in Apollinaire, and the avant-garde more generally, is expressed as reappropriation of the everyday so that autonomy can be established again on another level. Peter Read locates one of the central conflicts in Apollinaire's poetry as that 'between high idealism, the

Symbolist quest for perfection in which the poet is prophet and magician, and a more modern desire to find poetry in the inspiration of every moment, every situation.'[54] The materials of the everyday world in Apollinaire are evidence of the everyday, but also provide the passage out of the everyday and into a less alienated world. In this respect, Apollinaire anticipates the utopian techniques of the Surrealists or intellectuals such as Walter Benjamin. These techniques are not the same as earlier Symbolist efforts to sequester art into an impermeable void, but rather, states Susan Harrow, 'the sheer proliferation of palpable things — via their signifiers — imparts the desirability of "thickening" and reclaiming the real against the levelling effects of a mechanized, streamlined world. [...] The subjective engagement with accessible, alterable objects generates acts of transformation — real and imaginary — as the everyday is reworked.'[55] This outlook, which seeks to look beyond the economic rationality of the profane world, stimulates a form of charisma that is not necessarily oriented towards a Beyond that looks away from this world:

> Charisma [...] may involve *a subjective or internal reorientation* born out of suffering, conflicts, or enthusiasm. It may then result in a radical alteration of the central systems of attitudes and directions of action with a completely new orientation of all attitudes toward the different problems and structures of the 'world'.[56]

This struggle with death, which is to say the struggle with two mutually exclusive modes of existence separated by an threshold of the will, is fundamental to poetry and prophecy. By attempting to detect new cultural possibilities out of the fragments of modern culture, the poet in 'Les Collines' necessarily risks himself through engagement with the necrotic character of everyday life prior to its transformation by the poet. Ultimately, the prophets straddle the line between life, death, and rebirth — always facing what must be destroyed in order to speak of what is new. After receiving his call, Isaiah is instructed to predict destruction on Israel, however within the destruction of the land lies a kernel of redemption:

> [']Even if a tenth part remain in [the land], it will be burned again,
> like a terebinth or an oak whose stump remains standing when it is felled.'
> The holy seed is its stump. (Isaiah 6. 13)

Despite the prophecy of doom Isaiah offers up, God leaves 'the holy seed' from which a new civilization might grow. Calling for something genuinely new in the world risks death, perhaps including the death of the very poet or prophet making that call, but that death opens the world to the possibility of resurrection, also including for the subject. In 'Le Brasier', Apollinaire writes:

> Voici le paquebot et ma vie renouvelée
> Ses flammes sont immenses
> Il n'y a plus rien de commun entre moi
> Et ceux qui craignent les brûlures (ŒP, 109)

> [This is the boat and my renewed life
> Its flames are immense
> There is nothing in common left between me
> And those whom the burns frighten]

The boat and the fire are images of transition, but the other side of the transition cannot necessarily be articulated and understood. The poet evades the doubt of that transition by allegorizing the renewal of the world through in the renewal of his own life.

★ ★ ★ ★ ★

Whereas Isaiah finds inspiration from a deity whose message he resolves to proclaim, the secular context of Apollinaire proves a bigger challenge in terms of describing the 'discoveries' of artistic inspiration. The poet announces 'l'art de prédire', but he falls into silence, or at least a silence with respect to what *ought* to be said, ('je ne pus *dire* merci') after the prophetic inspiration of the 'Torche que rien ne peut éteindre'. Stanza 31 then begins:

> Où donc es-tu ô mon ami
> Qui rentrais si bien en toi-même
> Qu'un abîme seul est resté
> Où je me suis jeté moi-même
> Jusqu'aux profondeurs incolores (Œ*P*, 175)

> [So where are you my dear
> Who withdrew so much into yourself
> That only an abyss remained
> Where I threw myself
> Into colourless depths]

Lockerbie reads this moment as

> ce point tourné vers le monde intérieur, le rôle de l'imagination ne peut plus être de contribuer à la 'magnifique exubérance de (la) vie': il faut en attendre un profit plus subtil. C'est plutôt vers la compréhension de l'homme secret qu'elle sembler aller.[57]

> [this point turned towards the interior world, the role of the imagination can no longer be to contribute to the 'magnificent exuberance of (the) life': it must achieve a more subtle profit. It is, rather, towards the comprehension of the secret man that it seems to go.]

Just as the poet is struck by the inspiration of the torch, the self-contemplation and even solipsism of this private experience resembles a form of mysticism. As in 'Zone', where the inspirational high of the vision in the first half leads to an experience of shame and death in the second half, the 'poetic afflatus'[58] in 'Les Collines' is authentically powerful, yet lacks distinction, colour, and feeling. The experience might represent a *tabula rasa* of the unused imagination, or the sterile emptiness of the poetic ego. In either case (or both), the prophetic aspect of the poet has reached the heart of the aesthetic experience and finds it incommunicable.

The unutterable nature of the prophetic experience or prophetic message is a central theme of Isaiah's call-narrative. When Isaiah is confronted with the vision of God on his throne and seraphs before him, his first response is one of regret: 'And I said: "Woe is me! I am lost, for I am a man of unclean lips; and I live among a people of unclean lips; yet my eyes have seen the King, the Lord of hosts!"' (Isaiah

6. 5). Isaiah's focus on the 'unclean lips' implies that his *ability* to speak is based on the conceit of purity or impurity, that is the alignment of the individual with the divine character. The word that the NRSV translates as 'lost' (דמה, *dāmâ*)[59] relates to silence or cessation of speech, leading some translations to render the phrase as Isaiah declaring himself as unclean, and therefore refusing to speak in the name of the Lord. Of course, once he has been cleansed by the angel touching his lips with the coal, the prophet's immediate response is to declare himself ready and able to speak, but then the question turns on the precise content the prophecy. God's words, via Isaiah are thus:

> ["]Keep listening, but do not comprehend;
> keep looking, but do not understand.'
> Make the mind of this people dull, and stop their ears, and shut their eyes,
> so that they may not look with their eyes, and listen with their ears,
> and comprehend with their minds, and turn and be healed." (Isaiah 6. 9–10)

Almost half of Isaiah's prophecy concerns God's refusal to allow for the public's comprehension of the prophecy. Moreover, it suggests that the prophecy itself will become the element of confusion among the people, preventing them from repenting because to hear the prophecy is to misunderstand it, 'until the Lord sends everyone far away, | and vast is the emptiness in the midst of the land' (Isaiah 6. 12). Isaiah ends where Apollinaire does, with a prophecy that turns in on itself, unable to be articulated because the content of the prophecy is bound to the idea of incomprehensibility. The silent or ineloquent prophet is not unique to Isaiah, and occurs in the call of Moses, who claims: 'O my Lord, I have never been eloquent, neither in the past nor even now that you have spoken to your servant; but I am slow of speech and slow of tongue' (Exodus 4. 10). The meaning of prophecy is not precluded by this silence, but is displaced back onto the subject of the prophet's transformation in the call. Herbert Marks states, in somewhat psychoanalytic language, that

> Obscuration corresponds rather to the moment of blockage that marks the mind's defeat before the unattainability of the object. It symbolizes not the transcendent order but the prophet's relation to the transcendent order, a relation that includes his mute intuition of his own infinitude.[60]

Therefore, both poet and prophet vacillate between the ability and inability to speak, and the prophetic doctrine and its incomprehensibility. In these particular moments, Marks sees the prophet's realization of being both a subject and object of the call, both an identification with the infinite and called upon to produce the infinite in the prophecy, ultimately conveying 'nothing more than the fact of conveyance itself'.[61]

Calligrammes makes use of the image of the mouth or the voice as one that has the ability to proclaim with the authority of a Moses without specifying exactly what is to be conveyed. 'Chef de Section' (1917) imagines the mouth with a deep sense of power, having both 'des ardeurs de géhenne' [fires of Gehenna], referring to the Greek term for Hell (see Matthew 10. 28), and even suggests the biblical association with Isaiah's call: 'Les anges de ma bouche trôneront dans ton cœur' [The angels of my mouth will be enthroned in your heart] (*Œ P*, 307). Apollinaire heightens the martial imagery by referring to 'Les soldats de ma bouche' [The soldiers of my mouth] (*Œ P*, 307), similar to Isaiah 49. 2, which states '[The Lord] made my mouth like a sharp sword' or the description of the resurrected Christ in Revelation 1. 16: 'from his mouth came a sharp, two-edged sword'. In this way, the modern poet presents possibility, as in stanza 10 of 'Les Collines':

> Voici le temps de la magie
> Il s'en revient attendez-vous
> A des milliards de prodiges
> Qui n'ont fait naître aucune fable
> Nul les ayant imaginés (*Œ P*, 172)

> [This is the time of magic
> It is returning you may wait
> On billions of prodigies
> That have given birth to no fables
> None having imagined them]

The poet here resembles the prophet Habakkuk when the latter receives not a vision, but the *promise* of the vision: 'For there is still a vision for the appointed time; it speaks of the end, and does not lie. | If it seems to tarry, wait for it: it will surely come, it will not delay.' (Habakkuk 2. 3) The poet does not foretell what 'le temps de la magie' will bring, but simply promises its eventuality.

Apollinaire presents the poet's role in society as an effort to continually orient people towards a sense of the future without defining it in way that might close it off as the only possibility. The poet-as-prophet embodies annunciation of the future with a self-consciously public voice in his poetry, replete with second-person imperatives, such as in 'Chant de l'Honneur' (dated 17 December 1915), a dialogue between the poet, France, and the war:

> Prends mes vers ô ma France Avenir Multitude
> Chantez ce que je chante un chant pur le prélude
> Des chants sacrés que la beauté de notre temps
> Saura vous inspirer plus purs plus éclatants
> Que ceux que je m'efforce à moduler ce soir (*Œ P*, 306)

> [Take my verse O my France Future Multitude
> Sing what I sing a pure song the prelude
> Of sacred songs the beauty of our time
> Will inspire you more pure more explosive
> Than those I force myself to modulate tonight]

What the multitude should sing is both the song of the poet himself and the 'prélude' to even more pure and beautiful 'chants sacrés'. These songs are sung by the wider milieu of France, to which the poet is prophet, but deferred to an unknown future. The final line, however, brings the focus back to the poet himself, struggling ('je m'efforce'), in the midst of the war, to sing songs less pure and brilliant than those of the future — a struggle necessary for that purer music. In 'Les Collines', adopting a more commanding tone, Apollinaire writes:

> Habituez-vous comme moi
> A ces prodiges que j'annonce
> A la bonté qui va régner
> A la souffrance que j'endure
> Et vous connaîtrez l'avenir (Œ*P*, 176)

> [Adjust yourself like me
> To these prodigies that I announce
> To the goodness which will reign
> To the suffering that I endure
> And you will know the future]

The poet has aligned himself with the future and demands the same of the reader. Again, he places himself in the position of 'souffrance' or martyrdom that meets the burdens of the unknown future. Like similar themes in 'Zone', sin, guilt, death, and suffering derive not exclusively from the terror of plunging headlong into the future, but also from the way such a plunge compels a reflection on the mistakes and disappointments of the past. In this sense, the future 'la bonté' and present 'la souffrance', and vice versa, are two perspectives on the same process of poetic experience.

This specific prophecy of progress or modernity is itself not tied to any static utopian state, but to progress itself as a push for constant change and challenge reminiscent of the rhetoric of Futurism. As an art critic, promoter of a new generation of painters, and theorist of aesthetics, Apollinaire promoted himself as among the vanguard of artistic thought, and cultivated the self-image of an outsider on the margins of culture. This self-image is not simply vanity, but figures the poetic self as a door from which the future might arrive or an instrument by which the future is built. In stanza 24 of 'Les Collines', he writes:

> Un serpent erre c'est moi-même
> Qui suis la flûte dont je joue
> Et le fouet qui châtie les autres (Œ*P*, 174)

> [A serpent wanders it's myself
> That is the flute that I play
> And the whip that chastens others]

In an allusion to Orpheus, utilizing the power of song, the poet transforms into the flute that he himself plays, tempting the audience in the manner of a pan or pied-piper. In the very next line, the serpent then becomes the image of the chastising whip. All three images are an aspect of the poet's own self, tempting and enticing the public like the serpent in the Garden of Eden. This enticement, however, results in a discipline that drives society forward or, to use Pound's term (discussed further below), a 'sledging' or chastising of society. In the end, because this serpent is still 'moi-même', the elision of subject and object turns back on itself and remains, once again, 'nothing more than the fact of conveyance itself'.

The irony then is that for Apollinaire to present himself as an innovator, radical, or vanguard, he must establish himself within the basis of tradition that, in theory, is a barrier to the future. The poet who wishes to speak prophetically of the 'new age', as Apollinaire expresses it, is never meant to imply an utter disregard for the traditions that formed the basis of literary institution from which the poet speaks. With the authority of a respected figure or tradition, the poet can enlist the trust of the public he seeks to speak to at the cost of losing his own identity within that tradition. When Apollinaire states in 'Les Collines' that 'Certains hommes sont des collines' (ŒP, 172), he is placing himself within a tradition of 'promethean' poets who extend themselves beyond the limits of culture for the benefit of the wider public, nation, or audience.[62] This manoeuvre recalls Baudelaire's 'Les Phares': great artists as lighthouses alone on the rocky coast, serving as guides for the present and future, but the image is two-fold: the lighthouse or beacon suggests a beam of light illuminating the distance, but it also implies one that can *be seen* from a distance — immovable and immobile. The 'phares' or 'collines', because of their visibility, provide a basis upon which a tradition can be constellated and innovated.

Though the mouth might then be silent or stunned in poems such as 'Les Collines', when expressing the anticipation of the future, it is equally capable of presenting itself in other poems as the advocate of tradition and order. In 'La Jolie Rousse' (1918), the mouth, as the image of God, is placed on the side of the past or tradition:

> Vous dont la bouche est faite à l'image de celle de Dieu
> Bouche qui est l'ordre même
> Soyez indulgents quand vous nous comparez
> A ceux qui furent la perfection de l'ordre
> Nous qui quêtons partout l'aventure (ŒP, 313)

> [You whose mouth is made in the image of God
> Mouth that is order itself
> Be indulgent when you compare us
> To those who were the perfection of order
> We who quest everywhere for adventure]

With an echo of Adam's creation in the image of God, the mouth represents order and considers the poet according to 'la perfection de l'ordre'. If, recalling the conflict between youth and maturity in 'Zone' and 'Les Collines', the annunciation of the future is at the price of the death of the young poet, then the mouth of order acts as constant judgment over the poet, who is necessarily always dwelling in a state of deviation or sin relative to that order. In contrast to the quasi-divine, creative voice present in so much of his poetry, the mouth made in the image of God resides on the side of tradition and of order in the 'longue querelle de la tradition et de l'invention | De l'Ordre et de l'Aventure' (ŒP, 313), but this is not to suggest that order and tradition are constraining or arbitrarily punitive. Rather, the truly prophetic voice creates tradition in its wake, as its resonance, suggesting a view of the broad sweep of history. The poet, aspiring to the 'heights' of 'ceux qui furent la perfection de l'ordre', can locate the traditional within the modern and vice versa through the unique vantage point of poetry. The image of the 'collines' also implies a critical assessment of the past's value rather than an unthinking nostalgia or sentimentality. In *L'Esprit nouveau et les poètes*, Apollinaire insists that the new spirit strives to avant tout hériter des classiques un solide bon sens, un esprit critique assuré, des vues d'ensemble sur l'univers et dans l'âme humaine, et le sens du devoir qui dépouille les sentiments et en limite ou plutôt en contient les manifestations.[63]

[inherit from the classics, before everything else, a solid good sense, an assured critical spirit, collected outlooks on the universe and into the human soul, and the sense of duty which bares sentiments and limits them, or rather, contains their manifestations.]

Danger or risk — a wandering into the unknown — is then the fate of the poet, who must always toil at 'la frontière du pensé et de l'impensé, du possible et de l'impossible, du pensable et de l'impensable'. Whether or not the poet chooses to start with tradition and look forward, or vice versa, he always aims at a point unknown even to himself, brought up within a tradition, but then always balancing himself against that tradition:

> Pitié pour nous qui combattons toujours aux frontières
> De l'illimité et de l'avenir
> Pitié pour nos erreurs pitié pour nos péchés (*ŒP*, 344)

[Pity us who always battle at the borders
Of infinity and the future
Pity our errors pity our sins]

The language of wandering and sin implies the inevitability of missteps for such artists and prophets labouring on the outskirts of culture.[64] Therefore, tradition in the later Apollinaire takes on the same function of religion in 'Zone', as both the cradle of the poet's identity and the obstruction he must transcend: 'Les apparitions divines torturent le pécheur, mais ne lui ouvrent pas le chemin du Paradis' [The divine apparitions torture the sinner, but don't open the way to Paradise to him].[65] This dichotomy is described by Scott Bates as the fundamental characteristic of Apollinaire's 'new spirit':

L'esprit nouveau se divise ainsi en deux: d'un côté, l'esprit classique français qui apporte l'ordre, la moralité, le devoir, l'honneur, le patriotisme; de l'autre, l'esprit romantique apportant l'aventure, les visions d'avenir, l'audace, la liberté, l'exploration, l'invention et la prophétie. Entre ces deux tendances un moteur puissant: la volonté.[66]

[The new spirit divides itself in two: on one side, the classical French spirit which carries order, morality, duty, honour, patriotism; on the other, the romantic spirit carrying adventure, visions of the future, audacity, liberty, exploration, invention and prophecy. Between these two tendencies is a powerful motor: the will.]

The will,[67] the fulcrum on which Order and Adventure pivot, is the driving force of poetic and human progress, and both ideal and material creations derive from it:

> On scrutera sa volonté
> Et quelle force naîtra d'elle
> Sans machine et sans instrument (*ŒP*, 173)

[We will study his will
And what force will be born from it
Without machine and without instrument]

Through the individual will or charisma of the poet, the routinization of tradition can be overcome. 'The bearers of charisma', states Weber,

> the oracles of prophets, or the edicts of charismatic warlords alone could integrate 'new' laws into the circle of what was upheld as tradition. Just as revelation and the sword were the two extraordinary powers, so were they the two typical innovators. In typical fashion, however, both succumbed to routinization as soon as their work was done.[68]

For Apollinaire, the classical tradition was itself once established by charismatic, prophetic, or artistic genius, which could serve as a check on the less restrained impulses of the prophetic vision of the modern poet — but these very impulses ultimately pressed the poet forward into the modern world and beyond. The next two chapters, assessing the approaches of Marinetti and Pound, respectively, to prophecy and the biblical tradition, which show how that tradition is mediated in ways that aggressively confront it as a form of (perhaps even model for) propaganda, or sublimate it into a deeper, more rarefied form of human activity.

Notes to Chapter 1

1. Walter Benjamin, 'On Language as Such and On the Language of Man', in *Walter Benjamin: Selected Writings, Volume 1: 1913–1926*, ed. by Marcus Bullock and Michael W. Jennings, trans. by Edmund Jephcott (Cambridge, MA: Harvard University Press, 1997), pp. 62–74 (p. 63).
2. Ibid., p. 62.
3. Frye, *The Great Code*, p. 9.
4. Ibid., p. 23; Frye's further discussion of demotic speech remind us that these 'phases' of language should not be regarded entirely chronologically, and that all three remain in a synchronic tension and conversation. The extent to which such phases are chronological is dependent on how 'culturally inherited knowledge' (p. 22) corresponds to an objective or, perhaps more specifically, *objectified* and *objectifiable* world.
5. Bourdieu, 'Genèse et structure', p. 331.
6. Robert Couffignal, *L'Inspiration Biblique dans l'œuvre de Guillaume Apollinaire* (Paris: Lettres Modernes, 1966), pp. 96–97.
7. Ibid., p. 101.
8. Frye, *The Great Code*, p. 25.
9. Guillaume Apollinaire, *Œuvres en prose complètes*, ed. by Michel Décaudin, 3 vols (Paris: Gallimard, 1991), II, 76.
10. Ibid., II, 74; emphasis added.
11. Ibid., II, 77.
12. Peter F. Read, *Society and Religion in the Poetry of Guillaume Apollinaire* (unpublished doctoral dissertation: University of Hull, 1981), p. 68.
13. Couffignal, *L'Inspiration Biblique*, p. 24.
14. Margaret Davies, *Apollinaire* (Edinburgh: Oliver & Boyd, 1964), p. 13.
15. Couffignal, *L'Inspiration Biblique*, p. 23.
16. Marcel Adéma, *Apollinaire: le mal-aimé* (Paris: Libraire Plon, 1952), p. 15.
17. The poem 'Prière', first published in *Le Guetteur mélancolique* (1952), contains a nearly identical line that reinforces the association with the Virgin: 'Ma mère ne m'habillait que de bleu et de blanc | O Sainte Vierge | M'aimez-vous encore' [My mother dressed me only in blue and white | O Holy Virgin | Do you still love me] (*ŒP*, 580).

18. Robert Couffignal, *'Zone' d'Apollinaire: structure et confrontations* (Paris: Minard, 1970), p. 8.

19. Guillaume Apollinaire, *Alcools*, ed. by Garnet Rees (London: Athlone Press, 1975), p. 124.

20. Couffignal, *'Zone' d'Apollinaire*, p. 8.

21. S. I. Lockerbie, 'Le Rôle de l'imagination dans *Calligrammes*, deuxième partie: les poèmes du monde intérieur', in *Guillaume Apollinaire 6*, ed. by Michel Décaudin (Paris: Lettres Modernes, 1967), pp. 85–105 (p. 91).

22. Couffignal, *'Zone' d'Apollinaire'*, p. 18.

23. See Guillaume Apollinaire, *Calligrammes: Poems of Peace and War (1913–1916)*, ed. by Anne Hyde Greet and S. I. Lockerbie (Berkeley: University of California Press, 2004), p. 359.

24. Couffignal, *'Zone' d'Apollinaire*, p. 18.

25. See also 'Tristesse d'une étoile', written after his injury in the war. The star is again presented as a symbol of Apollinaire's ideals but, in this poem, is presented as the wound in his head.

26. F. T. Marinetti, *La Conquête des étoiles: poème épique* (Paris: E. Sansot & Cie, 1902), p. 128.

27. This formulation owes something to Ernst Bloch's humanist reading of biblical literature, reconfiguring God not as the face of absolute transcendence, but as the central figure of utopian thinking, first truly exhibited in the exodus, not only as an escape from Egypt, but from the 'lord-of-the-manor' model of Yahweh: 'Exodus from every previous conception of Yahweh was now possible, with the *Futurum* as the true mode-of-being of that which is thought of as God' (Bloch, *Atheism in Christianity*, p. 79).

28. Lockerbie, 'Le Rôle de l'Imagination', p. 91.

29. Robert P. Carroll, *Jeremiah: A Commentary* (London: SCM Press, 1986), pp. 98–99.

30. Ibid.

31. Weber, *From Max Weber*, pp. 126–27.

32. Frye, *Words with Power*, p. 151.

33. Ibid., p. 156.

34. Couffignal, *L'Inspiration Biblique*, p. 97.

35. Robert Champigny, 'Le Temps chez Apollinaire', *PMLA*, 67.2 (1952), 3–14 (p. 3).

36. Here, Champigny references Symbolism as the origin of such linguistic purification. Although modernist prose — Woolf, Proust, Joyce — highlighted the inadequacy of 'l'arrangement vulgaire' (p. 3) of time (past, present, future), poetry could go further in challenging chronological time. Although he doesn't use the term, Somigli's reading of Mallarmé's and Symbolism's aspiration towards a non-functional language, which will be examined further in this study, also suggests a form of purity. Luca Somigli, *Legitimizing the Artist: Manifesto Writing and European Modernism, 1885–1915* (Toronto: University of Toronto Press, 2003), p. 132.

37. Champigny, p. 4.

38. Couffignal, *'Zone' d'Apollinaire*, p. 15.

39. Ibid., p. 5.

40. Susan Harrow, *The Material, the Real, and the Fractured Self: Subjectivity and Representation from Rimbaud to Réda* (Toronto: University of Toronto Press, 2004), p. 63.

41. Wilson, *Prophecy and Society*, p. 202.

42. Norman K. Gottwald, *The Hebrew Bible in Its Social World and in Ours* (Atlanta, GA: Scholars Press, 1993), p. 116.

43. Francis J. Carmody, *The Evolution of Apollinaire's Poetics, 1901–1904* (Berkeley: University of California Press, 1963), pp. 83–84.

44. Weber, *Sociology of Religion*, p. 243.

45. Scott Bates, 'Les Collines, dernier testament d'Apollinaire', in *Guillaume Apollinaire 1*, ed. by Michel Décaudin (Paris: Lettres Modernes, 1962), pp. 23–39 (p. 38).

46. Ironically, Apollinaire's 'élever' is semantically closer to the Hebrew verb (קום, *qûm*), which means to 'get up', than to the French translations widely available at Apollinaire's time, Ostervald (1724) and Segond (1910), which both use the more excitable 'susciter'.

47. Weber, *Theory of Social & Economic Organization*, p. 245; see also Weber, *Sociology of Religion*, p. 46.

48. Otto Kaiser, *Isaiah 1–12: A Commentary*, trans. by John Bowden, 2nd edn (London: SCM Press, 1983), p. 122.

49. Lockerbie, 'Le Rôle de l'Imagination', p. 92.
50. The plural noun for these angelic beings, שרפים, *s*ʳā*pîm*, is derived from the verb שרף, *śārāp*, 'to burn'. Couffignal speculates from the following line in 'Fusée' (1915) that Apollinaire may have been aware of this etymology: 'Qu'agitent les chérubins fous d'amour' (*ŒP*, 261). He writes that 'Les chérubins sont identiques aux séraphins, dont le nom signifiant: les *brûlants* est traduit par "*fous d'amour*"' (Couffignal, *L'Inspiration Biblique*, p. 105).
51. *ŒPC*, II, 949.
52. Weber, *Theory of Social & Economic Organization*, p. 362.
53. The foam of the poet's brain is also linked by Greet and Lockerbie to Apollinaire's head-wound (Greet and Lockerbie, eds, *Calligrammes*, p. 370).
54. Read, *Society and Religion*, p. 131.
55. Harrow, *The Material, the Real*, p. 72.
56. Weber, *Theory of Social & Economic Organization*, p. 363; emphasis added.
57. Lockerbie, 'Le Rôle de l'Imagination', p. 97.
58. Weber, *Sociology of Religion*, p. 119.
59. Several cognates provide illustrative associations: for example, דממה, *dᵉmāmâ* (1 Kings 19. 12), the 'still, small voice' encountered by Elijah, or the noun דמי, *dᵉmî*, the silence or rest condemned in Isaiah (62. 6).
60. Herbert Marks, 'On Prophetic Stammering', in *The Book and the Text: The Bible and Literary Theory*, ed. by Regina Schwartz (Oxford: Blackwell, 1990), pp. 60–80 (p. 63).
61. Ibid. p. 62.
62. Greet and Lockerbie, eds, *Calligrammes*, p. 358.
63. *ŒPC*, II, 943.
64. Apollinaire claimed in *L'Esprit nouveau et les poètes* that the new poetry 'est plein de dangers, plein d'embûches.' (Ibid., p. 947).
65. Couffignal, *'Zone' d'Apollinaire*, p. 13.
66. Bates, 'Les Collines', p. 27.
67. This term can safely include its Nietzschean connotations, given the philosopher's well-documented influence on Apollinaire. See, Read, *Society and Religion*, pp. 77–78.
68. Weber, *From Max Weber*, p. 297.

CHAPTER 2

❖

Accelerating Visions

Marinetti, perhaps more than any avant-gardist before André Breton and the Surrealists, was dedicated to the avant-garde as a full-scale social movement encompassing the full range of public life, from art to politics. It was, in part, this desire to spearhead an Italian cultural revolution that led him to eventually support Mussolini and the fascists as a mass political movement. Although it's not the intention of this study to examine Marinetti within a fascist context, the ways in which his early works and later Italian fascism rejected politics *qua* parliamentary struggle, suffrage, and political representation is a strong indication of Futurism's post-war tendency. Other than the manifestoes, *Monoplan du pape: roman politique en vers libre* is also perhaps the most explicitly political of Marinetti's creative works insofar as it advocates war against Austria, is ruthlessly critical of parliamentary democracy and the Catholic Church, and contains moments of anti-feminism and antisemitism. The early years of Futurism were intoxicated with the possibility of uniting humanity with emerging technologies and machinery in a cultural, mental, and spiritual revolution in which politics, as generally understood, would cease. To this end, Marinetti understood his craft as a form of prophecy that announced the following aspects of Futurism: technology and speed as an experience of the sublime; aggressiveness, often towards women or femininity; Italian nationalism; love of war. Additionally, *Monoplan*'s anti-Catholicism tracks with the broader Modernist rejection of bourgeois morals and social conventions; and the church, as the traditional guarantor of such conventions, became an obvious target. These Futurist themes, extensively enumerated in dozens, perhaps hundreds, of manifestoes, were effectively designed to be unpopular and antagonistic and, as Luca Somigli concludes, 'it is only by not accepting the exhortations of [the manifesto] that the reader becomes the enemy'.[1] Marinetti can find no shortage of enemies in any case, but this chapter will demonstrate how *Monoplan* defines the Futurist not simply against classes or institutions that categorize and measure value (whether material or spiritual), but against the imposition of judgment that such institutions represent. However, the challenge posed by Marinetti is, ultimately, against the sense of confinement within the self and its internal experience, expressed most saliently in his antipathy towards Catholicism and Romanticism.

 Monoplan is neither as distinctly poetic as Marinetti's earlier, pre-Futurist or Symbolist works such as *La Conqête des étoiles* (1902), *Destruction* (1904), or *La Ville*

Charnelle (1908), nor as visually and acoustically inventive as *Zang Tumb Tumb* (1914). However, *Monoplan* holds a unique place in Marinetti's *oeuvre*. It was one of the last major works he wrote originally in French, which had been his normal practice before World War I — writing and publishing in French, and translating the piece into Italian, sometimes many years later.[2] The Pilot[3] who narrates the work kidnaps the Pope, engages in parliamentary debate, and leads a successful attack on the Austrian navy — all interspersed with a series of bizarre visions reminiscent of those found in the biblical books of Isaiah, Ezekiel, Daniel, or Revelation. Written in a tone of near-religious ecstasy and enthusiasm, this work is often comical and at times quite sensitive, but is also at turns autocratic in its cultural and political outlook, as well as containing passages that are misogynistic, homophobic and antisemitic.

Monoplan was inspired by Marinetti's experience as a correspondent for the French newspaper *L'Intransigeant* during the Italo-Turkish war; he was stationed in Tripoli, where the book was written and completed in November 1911. However, it was Marinetti's second attempt at an epic war-poem; his first, *La Conquête des étoiles*, which gives an extensive account of the ocean attacking the sky, contains a similar style of prophetic vision and voice. *Monoplan* was published in French in January 1912 and an Italian translation followed in 1914, where the subtitle was changed from 'Roman politique' [Political novel] in the French version to 'Romanzo profetico' [Prophetic novel] for the Italian. More than any other movement, Futurism revelled in the narrow space between binaries such as this: is Futurism an artistic style or social movement? Should the Futurist engage primarily in expression or action? But why, asks Marinetti, should we assume that they are separate? Is it not, as Bourdieu writes, that 'L'*action* charismatique du prophète s'exerce fondamentalement par la vertu de la *parole* prophétique, extraordinaire et discontinue' [The charismatic *action* of the prophet is fundamentally exercised by virtue of the prophetic *word*, extraordinary and discontinuous]?[4] The prophet's collapse of word and action, like Marinetti's (implied) collapse of prophecy and politics, are indeed elements in the broader Futurist project of destroying the division between art and life.

The Artist, Numerous and Swarming

By 1909, with the publication of the *Manifeste et fondation du futurisme* on the front page of *Le Figaro*, Marinetti declared his intention to act not only as an artist, but as a propagandist of the new movement of Italian painters and poets. Fittingly, his most powerful artistic legacy was Futurism's dissemination. The numerous manifestoes[5] that he and his fellow Futurists published blended poetry and polemic, visual art and politics, typographical experiments and quasi-mathematical theories. The Futurist *soirées* of the pre-war years consisted of early performance art, music, and theatrical readings of the manifestoes. But if the intent of the manifesto form was to enumerate specific principles for new literature, painting, music, theatre, film, dance, cooking, and any other aspect of art and life that the Futurists set their sights on, these techniques and principles were often more aspirational than practical.

Perhaps as the modern prophetic mode *par excellence*, the manifesto was an instance of proclaiming *what could be* against any reasonable expectations — the 'extraordinaire et discontinue' [extraordinary and discontinuous] prophetic action. Manifestoes do not simply convey a series of concepts, but also attempt to embody the reality in which those concepts could be meaningful. If the manifesto writer fails to adhere to his or her own dogma, that only re-establishes the necessity of their claims. For example, in 1931, Marinetti published the *Manifesto dell'aeropoesia* that retroactively identifies *Monoplan* as the first instance of *aeropoesia* and provides an extensive list of twenty-two prescribed techniques for this style of airborne verse. But *Monoplan*'s correlation with this list is spotty at best: extensively employing points #3 ('evoke clouds, fog, and other atmospheric phenomena') and #8 ('evoke independence'), occasionally employing point #10 ('employ terms borrowed from art and especially music'), and almost never employing points #6 ('avoid terrestrial images') and #12 ('avoid being bombastic'). Point #12 in particular seems so contrary to the general character of Futurism that it's difficult to take the list seriously at all. But this is not unusual in Marinetti's manifestoes. The same year he published *Monoplan*, Marinetti also published the 'Manifeste technique de la littérature futuriste' which famously calls for the suppression of the analogical terms 'like' or 'as', the abolition of adjectives and adverbs, and the exclusive use of the verbal infinitive — none of which *Monoplan* actually does.[6] The manifesto form and style is strongly rooted in the Decadent and Symbolist influences, a combination of prescription and excess, that Marinetti was attempting to transcend in Futurism, so Marjorie Perloff's statement that 'The 1909 manifesto reflects Marinetti's program for the future rather than his own poetic practice'[7] can be potentially extended to all his manifestoes on poetry. The principles and themes of any given manifesto declared an allegiance to the future, and a radical break with the present as lived by the writer himself. It was a momentary denial of the writer's self from a future standpoint — Marinetti's own attempt to put Rimbaud's *Je est un autre* into practice.

Moreover, by breaking the continuity between a present and future self, the manifesto is one strategy by which to disrupt the values that reproduce the artistic 'establishment' insofar as they assume the continuity of the artist's self just as they assume the unity of content and form. The manifestoes parallel biblical prophecy's un-thinkability and discontinuity in addressing specific historical circumstances insofar as prophecy, as Robert Alter argues, 'tends to lift the utterances to a second power of signification, *aligning statements that are addressed to a concrete historical situation with an archetypal horizon.*'[8] A poetics that identifies a target and denounces it as passé or irrelevant can pry open a space for itself distinct from what went before. This effort is in part driven by the horror of what Weber termed 'routinization', the processes that favour the order of everyday life by rules of technical efficiency, economic rationality, or bureaucratic consistency.[9] Routinization is itself the mark of the expected and the banal, it is a future foreseen as a continuation of the patterns of the present, and so the growth of the individual is really an illusion if it's already predetermined by scientific or economic rationality. Put into Bourdieu's framework of struggles within cultural production, a poetics that *names, asserts,* or *demands* is part of a larger struggle 'in conservation, that is, routine and routinization, or in subversion, that is, a return to sources, to an original purity, to heretical criticism and so forth.'[10] Marinetti's poetics and manifestoes do not merely describe a new future, but declaim a prophetic, de-routinized impossible future against the apparent future of what *will be*.

One of Marinetti's innovations for the manifesto form was the opening narration, which sought to inscribe the movement into a self-authored drama between the future and the Ideal — the latter being Marinetti's description of the decadent nostalgia of his Symbolist predecessors. The *Manifeste et fondation du futurisme*, for example, begins with a long narration of the Futurists in the city reaching a point in which they witness the birth of the new era:

> Allons, dis-je mes amis! Partons! Enfin la mythologie et l'Idéal mystique sont surpassés. [...] Voilà bien le premier soleil levant sur la terre!... Rien n'égale la splendeur de son épée rouge qui s'escrime, pour la première fois, dans nos ténèbres millénaires.[11]
>
> [Let's go, my friends, I say! Depart! Finally, myth and the mystical Ideal have been surpassed. [...] There it is, the first sun rising over the land! ... Nothing rivals the splendour of its red sword which duels, for the first time, in our millennial shadows.]

In this, as in other cases, the thrust of the narrative dramatizes the Futurists' escape from a 'prison' of nostalgia and idealism. 'Tuons le Clair de Lune!!' [Let's Murder the Moonlight!!] (described by Marinetti as the second Futurist manifesto) is an allegorical narrative recounting the Futurist poets' flight from the city of Paralysis to attack the city of Gout:

> Nous sortions de la ville, d'un pas souple et précis qui voulait danser et cherchait des obstacles. [...] — Lâches! Lâches!... criai-je en me retournant vers les habitant de Paralysie, qui s'amoncelaient en contre-bas, masse de boulets irrités pour nos canons futurs...[12]
>
> [We leave the city, with a supple and precise step that wanted to dance and was looking for obstacles [...] — Cowards! Cowards!... I cried as I returned to the residents of Paralysis, who clustered below, a pile of annoyed bullets for our future cannons...]

La Conquête des étoiles, subtitled as *poème épique*, another highly allegorical work, establishes the poet as a witness and instigator of a battle between the stars and the ocean — the former representing the Ideal, the latter standing in for matter. The story concludes by overcoming the dichotomy between materiality and idealism, which, as Cescutti says, 'induit dans le vers une dynamique autonome qui vise à la création d'un espace transitoire entre les deux pôles de la représentation' [induces in the verse a dynamic autonomy that aims towards the creation of a transitory space between the two poles of representation].[13] In the same way that biblical prophets re-narrate and re-describe the political or national dilemma (i.e., Israel's defeat at the hands of Assyrian or Babylonian empires) into one of a spiritual dilemma of Israel's relationship to God, the poet achieves the prophetic voice by dramatizing an encounter with an 'archetypal horizon'. For the prophet, that horizon is the history of divine salvation; for the Futurist poet, it's an apotheosis of humanity as structured by modern technology. Significantly, Marinetti's allegorical mode, what Cescutti terms the 'je narrant', conveys the internal revolution of the poet as a message coming from without, rendering 'Ce "mystère" original, à vocation messianique, [...] lisible sous la forme d'un "savoir" crypté dans la texture du poème qui est ainsi élevée au rang de présage, de parole révélée' [This original 'mystery', according to the messianic vocation, [...] legible in the form of an occulted 'knowledge' in the texture of the poem which is elevated in this way to the level of premonition, of revealed word].[14] As Cescutti states of the narrator of *Conquête*, 'le "je narrant" souligne, dès les premiers vers, l'investiture extraordinaire qu'il s'accorde lui-même' [the 'narrating I' underlines, from the first verses, the extraordinary investiture that he accords himself].[15]

In *Monoplan*, the 'je narrant' takes the form of the Pilot describing the struggle against the confines of his daily life:

> Horreur de ma chambre à six cloisons comme une bière!
> Horreur de la terre! Terre, gluau sinistre
> à mes pattes d'oiseau!... Besoin de m'évader!
> Ivresse de monter!... Mon monoplan! Mon monoplan!
>
> Dans la brèche des murailles brusquement éclatées
> mon monoplan aux grandes ailes flaire le ciel.
> Devant moi le fracas de l'acier
> déchire la lumière, et la fièvre cérébrale
> de mon hélice épanouit son ronflement. (*MP*, 7)
>
> [Horror of my six-sided bedroom like a coffin!
> Horror of the earth! Earth, sinister glue
> on my bird's feet!... Need to escape!
> Intoxication of rising!... My aeroplane! My aeroplane!
>
> Into the breach abruptly exploded in the walls
> my aeroplane with great wings sniffs the sky.
> Before me the crash of steel
> rips up the light, and the cerebral fever
> of my propeller unfolds its whirring.]

From the very start, the 'je narrant' of the Pilot inscribes itself into a context of a larger drama of modernity. The technique adopted by Marinetti is to speak as both himself and another simultaneously, reminiscent of Pound's personae, fostering a productive ambiguity. The dramatization of the pilot from earthbound to airborne, from human to machine, is also the transformation of Marinetti from non-Futurist to Futurist. The Pilot's vision enlivens the flight even beyond what might be expected from an aeroplane, and casts it as the inauguration of a number of conflicts between freedom and civilization, reality and sensation, and life and death. Like a coffin, the bedroom does not merely stifle the Pilot, but entombs him as one who is dead. In fact, he adopts a resurrection narrative — the Pilot starts at the point of death only to leap out of his own coffin like a new Christ. In the way that death brings the individual in contact with everything that transcends earthbound life, the individual returned from the dead, now bearing that transcendence, is no longer entirely individual, but speaks and acts as an embodiment of the Italian or Futurist ethos. Similarly, the Futurist, in the first manifesto, is placed in a dark — even musty — setting at the very beginning, only to break out of it upon hearing a car. If these Futurists are to be thought of as representatives of a 'new' Italy, then both the manifesto and *Monoplan* are driven by resurgent imperial aspirations and industrial development. Both senses — the Futurist ethos and Italian nationalism — are possible given *Monoplan*'s explicit description as a Futurist work and its vociferous Italian nationalism, but the point is that, abetted by modern technology, a new life for artist and nation is possible.

The 'je narrant' then dramatizes the tone and form of the manifesto from the 'archetypal horizon' of Italy becoming a sublimely experienced imperial power and, at the same time, Futurism becoming a world-historical movement. But the manifesto, existing in the future anterior, needs an act of revelation precisely because it speaks of the *will have been*. Martin Puchner has extensively detailed the struggle that manifestoes engage in to establish principles that are apparently non-extant and impossible, unlike other political tracts. Contrasting the Futurist manifesto to the American Declaration of Independence and the French Declaration of the Rights of Man, Puchner writes that

> These rights, no matter how radical, are not presented as being created, enacted, constituted, or made, and consequently their declaration is not something that is in need of a *poesis*. All that is required is an innocuous mention of rights whose natural authority rests solely in themselves. Nature does not need to be revealed; it is not in need of a manifesto.[16]

Necessarily, the 'horreur' of the bedroom, the 'gluau' of the earth, the improbably exploded wall: these impediments simultaneously acknowledge, only to flamboyantly deny, the Pilot's inability to break beyond himself. Analogously, the opening of *Monoplan* is set against a background in which an Italian empire and Futurist cultural dominance are, at first glance, absurd. The aggressive rhetoric and stylistic extravagances of the manifesto, as Martin Puchner argues, agonize against the manifesto as *mere* manifesto, constituting its 'theatricality':

> Saying that the manifesto is theatrical means that its speech acts occur in an unauthorized and unauthorizing context [...] the manifesto does not rest comfortably in this unauthorized space; indeed, it tries to exorcize its own theatricality by borrowing from an authority it will have obtained in the future.[17]

What is embedded in the 'je narrant' is the struggle against the distinction between dream and reality itself: the first line, locating the Pilot in his bedroom, initiates a dream-space in which everything subsequent occurs. The Pilot asserts not so much the achievement of flight (which had been accomplished almost a decade prior in any case), but the possibility of a new, completely unknown freedom and power to make dream reality by claiming to have achieved that reality already.

★ ★ ★ ★ ★

The manifesto's lack of correspondence to reality presents the barrier to its own message that must be crossed, engendering its prophetic nature, for the manifesto is itself a definitive *form* of faith in its own future realization. The Futurist manifesto was a stand against the predictable, ordered rationality that was the common sense of industry and technology. Futurism insists on irrationality over and against that common sense, particularly as it relates to technology as 'the archetypal form of human alienation' with its impersonal calculations and abstract, interchangeable components and forms. As J. W. Burrow writes, 'the Futurists' solution was simple: complete the alienation and become whole again by identifying with it in Dionysian rupture.'[18] In *Conquête*, the poet experiences a series of strange, waking visions that anticipate this resolution of the world into myth and, 'La vision de *La Conquête des Étoiles*', explains Cescutti, 'est tout d'abord le produit d'un rêve qui, de par sa nature irrationnelle, assure le lien avec un univers invisible au-delà du réel' [The vision of *Conquest of the Stars* is from the outset the product of a dream which, through its irrational nature, assure a link with an invisible universe beyond the real].[19] For instance, the first chapter concludes with a possible allusion to Baudelaire's 'Les Phares': 'Je ne crois plus qu'en mon grand Rêve illuminant de phare!' [I now only believe in the bright lighthouse of my grand Dream!].[20] Several sections in *Monoplan* defy rationality as a standard of 'order' in which a hierarchy of values predominates. As a dream of flight, *Monoplan* dramatizes the achievement of height and speed as the defeat of a sense of 'measurement' by a uniform, external standard that grounds the idea of rationality in the first place. In this sense, Marinetti opposes the strictures and constrained realism of measurement to a disordered sense of possibility: 'Au déterminisme sceptique et pessimiste, nous opposons en conséquence le culte de l'intuition créative, la liberté de l'inspiration et l'optimisme artificiel' [To sceptical and pessimistic determinism, we oppose accordingly the cult of creative intuition, the freedom of inspiration and artificial optimism].[21]

Chapter 10 of *Monoplan*, entitled 'Les Licous du Temps et de l'Espace' [The Halters of Time and Space], describes the Pilot escaping the most basic structures of the human condition: the spatial and temporal limits of corporeal existence. This chapter contains one of several visionary interludes, and it strongly foregrounds the potential of the Futurist aesthetic in the sense of Rimbaud's famous *dérèglement de tous les sens* in the form of mechanized power. While the Pilot watches the Italian preparations for war against Austria, he begins to feel himself capable of confronting, and breaking out of, the restrictive weight of time and space. After describing the army moving towards the front, the Pilot comes to a certain kind of cusp or point of no return: 'Je passe en ce moment le seuil | du terrible Palais du Mauvais Temps!...' [At this moment I pass the threshold | of the terrible Palace of Bad Weather!...] (*MP*, 245). This 'Palace of Bad Weather' describes a sacred construction where a kind of divine presence dwells — the archetype of which is the temple of Jerusalem. This passage in *Monoplan* marks several elements that we find in more fantastic descriptions of the temple, such as the threshold crossed by the Pilot, which is a significant dividing line between the divine presence and world, and where, in Ezekiel, the 'glory of the Lord' departs the temple to join the exiled Israelites in Babylon (Ezekiel 10. 4, 18). Moreover, the images of clouds behind the threshold that are described by Ezekiel's epiphany are suggestive of the Pilot's experience. Ezekiel writes of 'a cloud filled the inner court. Then the glory of the Lord rose up from the cherub to the threshold of the house; the house was filled with the cloud, and the court was full of the brightness of the glory of the Lord' (10. 3–4). But given Marinetti's ambivalence towards religion, it's not surprising that his 'temple' is much gloomier, more enshrouded in shadow:

> Palais majestueux du Mauvais Temps
> dont les murs gris qui fuient
> se voilent çà et là de la fumée sinistre
> d'invisibles encensoirs!... (*MP*, 245)

> [Majestic Palace of Bad Weather
> whose grey leaking walls
> are veiled here and there with sinister smoke
> from invisible censers!...]

The temple, as described in Hebrews 9. 3–4, describes an 'earthly sanctuary' (9. 1) similar to the desert tabernacle of Exodus, after which the temple was modelled: 'Behind the second *curtain*[22] was a tent called the Holy of Holies. In it stood the golden altar of *incense* and the ark of the covenant' (emphasis added). In particular, the Pilot's visual awareness — normally so wide-ranging in *Monoplan* — is obscured in the Palace. The walls are 'gris', enclosing his view of the earth or horizon, and they are themselves further obscured by the 'fumée sinistre' coming from the incense. However, within the Jerusalem temple or desert tabernacle, the Holy of Holies, blocked from view by a curtain, is precisely where the High Priest would encounter God — an encounter that placed ordinary individuals at mortal risk (see Isaiah 6. 5). References to veiling ('se voilent') and incense ('la fumée sinistre', 'encensoirs') that envelop this scene in mystical or occult connections are also found at the beginning of the first Futurist manifesto. And while this atmosphere draws parallels to Decadent art, it's not quite the putrid rot of the 'Atmosphère empestée' (*MP*, 115) of the Vatican that Marinetti describes earlier in the novel (and to which I will return).

The Pilot then makes a supplication to the storm to assist Italy, which has the effect of waking up his plane as well:

> Je glisse avec angoisse
> sur tes profonds tapis de brume violette,
> en suppliant tes fantômes armés d'éclairs
> d'être propice à l'Italie!...
> Tiens! Tiens! L'orage a réveillé mon moteur! (*MP*, 245–46)

> [Anxiously I glide
> over your deep carpets of violet fog,
> imploring your armed phantoms of lighting
> to be favourable to Italy!...
> Hold on! Hold on! The storm has awoken my motor!]

Flying over the fog that obscures his sight, he begs the phantoms — that is, beings that exist to a certain extent only as constructions of faith — for their aid in battle.

The palace, like the temple, is the space where the Pilot is in the presence of a non-visible power, whose existence is paradoxically confirmed by the obstructions to viewing it. The relationship between vision, supplication, and the temple might be explicated with reference to the book of Jonah, where, lying in the belly of the fish, the prophet's prayer makes explicit reference to the Temple and sight: 'Then I said, "I am driven away from your sight; | how shall I look again upon your holy temple?["]' (Jonah 2. 4). Faith, for Jonah, is a function of his ability to maintain a visual connection to the temple. Furthermore, when Jonah's prayer reaches God, it is through the temple: 'I remembered the Lord; | and my prayer came to you, into your holy temple' (2. 7). Both Jonah and the Pilot are in positions of danger: Jonah under the sea, and the Pilot in the midst of a storm. Not seeing the temple or God is, for Jonah, a challenge to his faith and an occasion for reaffirming that faith, whereas the Pilot's inability to see presents a similar occasion for strengthened faith. The Pilot's authority, similar to the many Futurist manifestoes, is taken from precisely what cannot, and perhaps should not, be seen or directly experienced by the senses. But Marinetti makes a series of reversals on this supplication motif that are necessary to maintain the scandal of Futurism.

Perhaps, then, the ambiguity of the word 'Temps', in the 'Palais du Mauvais Temps', between 'weather' and 'time', becomes a little more apparent — while I've translated it as 'Bad Weather', it might also be rendered as 'Bad Time', or an unsanctioned time that subversively exists within and against our more standard notions of time. Technology has opened spatial and temporal vistas, abetting the vision of the Futurist poet to penetrate what typically cannot be seen by escaping a singular space and perspective. In one of the few moments when he refers to himself as an artist or poet the Pilot states:

> Je suis l'artiste, l'être nombreux et fourmillant,
> la rixe pullulante,
> la soirée de première,
> la salle comble où tout est pris (MP, 254)

> [I am the artist, the numerous and swarming being,
> the proliferating fight,
> the opening night,
> the full stands where everything is taken]

The poet imagines himself as a multiplicity, as was common in much of the pre-war avant-garde — the artist as a dynamic and uncontrollable collection — and is a subtle nod to Romains's Unanimist thought. He is the show ('la rixe pullulante') as well as the spectator ('la salle comble'), creator as well as the work. But the following three lines open up the idea of spectacle: the boxing match, the opening night, the full-house. The vision of the Pilot or artist is as much about seeing and asserting what is fabricated, imagined, or staged. The poet's will is dramatized as an oppositional moment to that which is expected through rationality or routine, especially if the artist is the summation of that oppositional moment.

The motif of the temple also establishes the opposition between the prophetic and the priestly as one over a space of legitimacy. Situating the prophetic sphere against the priestly sphere creates a tension between the two, but historically prophets and priests often act as two sides of the same coin, shifting position to respond to different circumstances and to each other. Marinetti, in the guise of the 'prophetic' Pilot, enters the 'priestly' space of the palace as a space he's familiar with and, to some extent, sympathetic to and nostalgic for (as will be explored below, the Futurist poet ridding himself of his youthful nostalgia is a recurring theme in *Monoplan*). As with biblical prophets such as Amos, criticism of the functionaries of the temple cult (see Amos 5. 21–24) is not necessarily a rejection of the temple itself, but of the hypocrisies of the priesthood. Isaiah and Ezekiel are strongly associated with the temple — the latter as a prophet of the temple's *re-establishment* after its destruction in 587 BCE. Like the opening of the first Futurist manifesto, where Marinetti critiques the clouded visions and remote idealism of aestheticist movements such as Symbolism and Decadence and their quasi-spirituality, the attack is leveraged by the poet's own credibility as a one-time acolyte of these movements. The 'Palais du Mauvais Temps' can also be read as the re-establishing or re-purposing of the temple's Futurist spirit as air, smoke, or cloud in an anticipation of Futurist *aeropoesia*'s requirement to evoke atmospheric phenomena. The 'Palais du Mauvais Temps' reads as a similar Futurist scandalizing of the Christian tradition, appropriating the image, stripping it of its sanctity, and positioning it for the new moment.

★ ★ ★ ★ ★

This new moment presents not just an accelerated view of history, but an effort to defeat or triumph over time itself. Prophecy, especially in its most poetic modes, is the metaphorical means by which the reader 'rises' with the Pilot; that is to say, prophecy asks the reader to continually consider a widening array of identities within history or the material world, so that the reader feels themself at the centre of a universal present that carries the stakes of destiny. The Pilot turns his ire against the 'licous des temps et de l'espace' [halters of time and space]:

> O Temps, je te conspue, ô toi le plus haï
> et le plus redoutable de tous nos ennemis!
> Je sais que ma vitesse et ma fièvre t'irritent!...
> C'est pourquoi j'accélère le pouls de mon moteur. (*MP*, 261)

> [O Time, I shout you down, O you most hated
> and most formidable of our enemies!
> I know that my speed and my fever annoy you!...
> That's why I accelerate the pulse of my motor.]

In the 1916 manifesto entitled *La Nouvelle Religion-morale de la vitesse*, Marinetti explicitly proclaims the apotheosis of speed, insisting that the synthesis of forces he associates with speed is pure, whereas slowness and lassitude are impure or unclean. The stagnation, both moral and physical, that the Pilot finds in the Vatican is the polar opposite of speed's purity. This spiritual division of speed and slowness is taken to an extreme conclusion: 'L'ivresse des grandes vitesses en auto est l'ivresse de se sentir fondu avec l'unique divinité' [The intoxication of great car speeds is the intoxication of feeling melded with the only divinity].[23] The Pilot condemns time itself, equating it almost entirely with slowness and decay — a slackening of life. Moreover, measurements of time and space are static and constricting. He taunts it with the speed and acceleration of his motor in the manner of a defiant young man, as if to suggest that he thinks he can outrun time. And in a moment when he feels more at one with his plane, the Pilot refers to the motor's 'pouls' [pulse] in a comparison to a heartbeat. Marinetti employs the cliché of time as a devourer, but just as soon as he establishes the image, he dismisses it:

> O Temps rapace!
> Tu prétends dévorer tout le temps qui me reste!
> Fi des journées solaires, chronomètres faussés! (*MP*, 262)

> [O rapacious Time!
> You claim to devour all the time that remains to me!
> Fie on solar days, false chronometers!]

Time is Poe's great Conqueror Worm eating away at the finite moments of an individual's life, and its instruments — clocks, watches, calendars — convince people that they are already dead. In contrast, Marinetti proposes that time be understood as experience, as 'le temps qui me reste', claiming the sensuous and subjective nature of time. This proposal echoes the influence of Henri Bergson (1859–1941) and Georges Sorel (1847–1922), both of whom influenced Marinetti. Walter Adamson states that: 'In his *Reflections on Violence*, which appeared in 1908 and which Marinetti very likely read', Sorel developed a notion of myth that 'drew upon Bergson's notion of intuition, which points us to a "self" that knows in time as lived duration, that lives, as it were, internal to the world.'[24] For Futurism, transience and mutability, within modern life, are opposed to the absolute permanence of the divine and the nostalgia of history, both of which exist outside of lived time.[25] 'The contrast term [to myth] is intellect,' writes Adamson, 'which views the world from the outside, inspects it, dissects it, analyzes it, describes it.'[26] Upon denouncing the rational, intellectual descriptions and dissections of time, the Pilot understands it as malleable, for time exists through him and his actions, his various experiences, without which time itself would be empty:

> Je puis doubler ma montre en montant dans le ciel,
> toujours plus haut afin que le soleil
> frappe encore mes regards de son heure élastique... (*MP*, 262)

> [I then double my altimeter while climbing into the sky,
> always higher so that the sun
> still strikes my view with its elastic hours...]

The Futurist aesthetic's embrace of the machine age is grounded in the belief that the speed, perspective, or distance that can be achieved through the merging of the aeroplane, the train, or the car with the human being will obviate prior understandings of time, as Marinetti wrote in the first manifesto: 'Le Temps et l'Espace sont morts hier. Nous vivons déjà dans l'absolu, puisque nous avons déjà créé l'éternelle Vitesse omniprésente' [Time and Space died yesterday. We are already living in the absolute, since we have already created the eternal, omnipresent Speed].[27] Nearly three decades later, in the manifesto entitled *La matematica futurista immaginativa qualitativa* [*Futurist qualitative-imaginative mathematics*] (1941), Marinetti (writing in the third person) still seemed to maintain this view: 'Thirty years ago in Marinetti's poem *The Pope's Airplane* one finds longer and shorter kilometers and longer and shorter hours'.[28] This manifesto uses the term 'qualitative' rather than 'quantitative', for if time, space, or mathematics are *qualities* rather than discrete, standard units of measurement, then the quality of time itself becomes amendable and changeable according to the life that lives in it. This subjectivizing of time brings it back to the human level of experience and draws it out into a continuity of relationship and change.

One cannot read *Monoplan* without being struck by Marinetti's obsession with spatial dimensions, rising and falling, moving back and forth and side to side. As the quotation above indicates, space is also distorted and malleable from the viewpoint of the Pilot in his cockpit, seen through the paradigm of decay and disease: 'l'Espace, vieux vautour podagreux' [Space, old gouty vulture] (*MP*, 266). However, the strictures of space are only limited to the Pilot's visual field, that is, what exactly he can see from his ever-shifting vantage point in the sky:

> Espace! tu m'as mis autour du cou,
> comme un licou,
> cet horizon changeant
> hérissé de montagnes, de plaines
> et de villes chevelues!... (*MP*, 267)

> [Space! you placed around my neck,
> like a halter,
> this changing horizon
> bristling with mountains, plains
> and hairy towns!...]

The constrictive horizon, no matter how high the Pilot goes — thus increasing his visual field — is still always that spatial limit bounded by the limit of his sight. But through the increased freedom of movement, the Pilot feels an increased control over space:

> Espace, je t'oblige en volant
> à me mettre autour du cou
> sans répit, sans repos, à chaque instant
> un nouvel horizon! (*MP*, 270)

> [Space, as I fly I compel you
> to place around my neck
> without relief, without pause, every instant
> a new horizon!]

Flight gives the Pilot a sense of freedom and control over space as he creates or, rather, forces space to create a new horizon at every moment, loosening its ability to confine the Pilot or define his physical limitations. Every 'nouvel horizon' is, for the Pilot, another challenge for him to surpass. The next lines read:

> Licous toujours divers et de plus en plus sombres!
> C'est bien la Voie Lactée
> qui m'embellit en cet instant (*MP*, 270–71)

> [Halters always changing and always darker!
> It's even the Milky Way
> that adorns me in this moment]

As the Pilot ascends higher, he escapes one horizon only to find another one, each 'licou' containing a wider view but never providing complete liberation. As the Pilot approaches outer space, the darkness fades into the circular shape of the Milky Way galaxy. Cescutti points out that in Marinetti's early poetry an attention to vertical movement, like the prophet ascending a mountain, is a metaphorical movement towards revelation or, as Frye terms it, 'intensified consciousness and experience'.[29] Of the chapter in *La Conquête des étoiles* called 'La Montagne fatidique', she writes that 'Au pied de la "montagne fatidique" [...] l'objet de la quête se précise comme l'hypothèse d'une révélation' [At the foot of the 'fateful mountain' [...] the object of the quest is clarified as the hypothesis of a revelation][30]. As the Pilot ascends to greater heights, the revelation becomes simultaneously more apparent and more obscure. Space becomes vaster, less focused, but never fully transcended.

There is a striking definition of infinity in Marinetti's memoirs of the Futurist era, which he attributes to the 'Futurist aviator' Fedele Azari (1895–1930): 'a sphere whose center is nowhere and whose circumference is everywhere'.[31] It seems as though this definition plays on a much older axiom of medieval philosophy that describes God as a sphere whose centre is everywhere and whose circumference is nowhere. Blaise Pascal (1623–1662) later described nature in the same terms and added, as well, that the 'visible world is merely an imperceptible speck in nature's ample bosom'.[32] Marinetti's inversion of this philosophy and his claiming of the non-visible through the experience of the machine expresses the boldness, even arrogance, of the Futurist ethos, always just about to push beyond the boundary of divinity or nature. At the conclusion of his revelation, the Pilot switches into the future tense, predicting what can or will happen in days to come and stating:

> Vous serez forcément devancés, Temps, Espace!
> Espace, tu perdras chaque fois
> un peu de ton ami, le Temps...
> Mon licou est au moins cent fois plus large
> que celui de ce train dépassé!...
> Tu devras dans une heure allonger
> à l'infini
> la laisse dont tu me tiens encore!... (*MP*, 271)

> [You will be forcibly outpaced, Time, Space!
> Space, you will lose each time
> a little of your friend, Time...
> My halter is at least one hundred times larger
> than that of this outdated train!...
> In one hour, you must lengthen
> into infinity
> the leash you still hold me on!...]

As a matter of sheer faith or radical belief, however haunted it may be by doubt, the Pilot insists that time and space can and will always be overcome. What is more, the close relationship between time and space, that is, the necessity to *take* time in order to *cross* space, will itself be severed with ever greater achievements of speed. Within the vision of the poet, time and space are pushed beyond the routine structures by which they are measured. They achieve an infinity defined by the experience of the poet, through the act of writing or narrating, overtaking space and time, or even creating a new space and new time. The goal is to fill out the empty measurements of chronology with a sense of difference, a genuine change from one state to another, recalling a phrase by Bourdieu: 'Introduire la différence, c'est produire le temps' [Introducing difference produces time].[33] Bourdieu of course refers to a *social* sense of space and time, the experience not just of individuals, but collectives. But is it really the case that Marinetti's Pilot, this lone explorer, sees time and space in the purely physical or psychological sense, and not a broader, more social, sense as well? As the Futurist figure, the break to a new position is allegorically inscribed in this chapter and throughout *Monoplan*, allowing such a transition to be mapped onto art, religion, politics and national life.

Message of the Motor-Heart

The intent of the prophetic mode of discourse, that of *calling to* as well as *being called*, be it Futurist or on some other basis, is to present it as a cultural practice that ought to be taken up by an implied audience, or that it dares the audience to refuse. Maria Pia De Paulis-Dalembert writes of the Futurist manifestoes that 'C'est dans l'optique d'un dialogue réel avec le public que le manifeste accentue son caractère déclamatoire' [It's within the optic of a real dialogue with the public that the manifesto accentuates its declamatory character].[34] The manifestoes engage with contemporary politics, refer to specific Italian cities, and challenge Italian culture. By doing so, they provide a certain level of 'realism' to Futurist writings, but largely to the extent that such a sense of reality is present as a challenge to be met and an ideal to be satisfied. This declamatory mode of discourse engages the reader or listener, challenging them to take sides in Futurism's agenda of condemning 'passéisme' — the Futurists' epithet for anybody deemed their enemies — and promoting the new age. Conversely, a Futurist is not merely one who embraces the ethos of Futurism, but one who achieves an affinity with the author of a Futurist text that transcends 'conventional' or complacent relationships such as politics, family, or religion. The narrator of *Monoplan*, for example, calls to his side the island of Sicily, the city of Trieste, students, and the military, each of which has demonstrated sufficiently the aggressive attitudes towards art, culture and politics that Futurists and, later, their fascist counterparts, found appealing.

The first location mentioned in *Monoplan* was likely the most politically pertinent to Marinetti's readership. He dedicated this free-verse novel to the city of Trieste: 'A Trieste notre belle poudrière!' [To our beautiful powderkeg!]. Prior to Austria's defeat in World War I, Trieste was a part of the Austro-Hungarian Empire but, sharing the North-Eastern border with Italy, much of its population was Italian-speaking and thought of itself as culturally and nationally Italian. The city was a rallying-point for irredentism, an Italian nationalist movement that advocated the forcible recovery of formerly Italian areas from Austria. Trieste was also the site of several early Futurist *serate*, some of which ended in strident denunciations of Austria. The dedication is clearly a reference to these anarchic evenings that provided an origin-myth for Futurism. In choosing Trieste, Marinetti politicizes the aesthetic, but historicizes it as well, grafting the relevance of *Monoplan* to a particular moment in Italy's self-becoming in the twentieth century, striking at the nerve of the issue that drove much Futurist work, but also anticipating the ephemerality of that work, anticipating — as he does in the first manifesto — the supersession of events eventually antiquating the most modern of arts.

The second location, Sicily, is first visited in the second chapter of *Monoplan*, entitled 'Les Conseils du volcan' [The Volcano's Counsel], where the Pilot speaks to Mount Etna. While the majority of the dialogue is taken up by the Pilot, it is the volcano's voice that dominates here. In this scene, Marinetti makes a point of emphasizing the voice and words of the volcano by setting-off its side of the dialogue with headings as in a theatre script. Moreover, the Pilot is particularly pre-disposed to hear those words, stating before the volcano first speaks:

> O Volcan, j'entends depuis longtemps
> le roulement continu de ta voix turbulente
> qui frémit dans la rauque cheminée de ta gorge.
> Je m'oublie tellement à contempler
> l'éruption de tes paroles chauffées à blanc
> que je n'ai pas encore démêlé l'écheveau
> fulgurant de ta pensée! (*MP*, 42–43)

> [O Volcano, I've heard for such a long time
> the continuous rumbling of your turbulent voice
> that simmers in the stony chimney of your throat.
> I have forgotten so much to contemplate
> the eruption of your white-hot words
> that I haven't yet untangled the lightning skein
> of your thought!]

In this state of awe, the Pilot is at first unable to understand the volcano's meaning, though he can hear the voice and receives inspiration from its power:

> Oh! la maîtrise et l'inspiration
> que le tonnerre éclatant de ta voix manifeste
> sur les torrides parois de ton atelier!... (*MP*, 43)

> [Oh! the mastery and inspiration
> that the exploding thunder of your voice manifests
> over the blistering walls of your studio!...]

In this sense, at least, mastery and inspiration are emotions or feelings that operate not on the level of rational thought or abstract reasoning, but at the level of instinct or intuition. The Pilot seems to find this acceptable even though it can hardly constitute an answer to his query, which is stated just after he enters the volcano:

> Mets donc en branle tes muscles buccaux,
> ouvre tes lèvres rocailleuses encroûtées de granits,
> et crie-moi quelle est la destinée
> et quels sont les devoirs qui s'imposent à ma race. (*MP*, 31)

> [Set in motion your mouth's muscles,
> open your rocky lips encrusted with granite,
> and call to me what is my destiny
> and those duties that are imposed upon my race.]

The Pilot comprehends the volcano's power, which elicits an emotional, intuitive drive to go beyond the traditions holding the Italian nation back.

Before examining what those specific traditions are, and why Marinetti chooses them, it's useful to dwell on how he formulates a Futurist camaraderie, because that formulation shows how even the most ardent Futurists must pause and seriously engage with familiar cultural fundamentals. The avant-garde, as a social movement, is in a continuous process of segregating from the general public an audience that is familiar but singular, novel but also connected to something transcendent. Marinetti's Sicily stands in for a sense of the past that cannot be equated with a traditional character but, rather, a more elemental one — durable and explosive, like the volcano that formed Sicily. Before flying into Mt Etna, the Pilot salutes the Sicilians as his Futurist comrades:

> Siciliens! vous qui luttez depuis les temps brumeux
> nuit et jour, corps à corps avec la rage des volcans
> j'aime vos âmes qui flamboient
> comme les fous prolongements du feu central,
> et vous me ressemblez, Sarrazins d'Italie,
> au nez puissant et recourbé sur la proie que l'on mâche
> avec de belles dents futuristes!... (*MP*, 24)

> [Sicilians! you who struggle night and day,
> since time shrouded in mist, body to body with volcanic rage
> I love your souls that flame
> like the mad tendrils of a single fire,
> and you resemble me, Saracens of Italy,
> by a nose strong and bent over the prey that it eats
> with beautiful Futurist teeth!...]

The Sicilians are aggressive, even predatory, organically connected to the power of the volcano. The Pilot also compares Sicilians to himself in a way that is reminiscent of Apollinaire's use of the language of resemblance in poems such as 'Vendémiaire'[35] or Pound's identification of one's 'kin' (discussed in the following chapter). Furthermore, the reference to Saracens, a medieval term for Arabs, may allude to Marinetti's own upbringing in Egypt, placing both the Pilot and Sicily in an intermediate place between Futurist Italy and 'ancient' or 'primordial' Africa. The character of the Sicilian elect, like any avant-garde, is paradoxical as it extends back to 'les temps brumeux' as well as forward in time, and whose strong sense of the past enables it to alter the present and future or, more specifically, continually re-establish values that exist 'beyond' time in the 'absolute' where history is dissolved into a constant and ungroundable experience.

To the extent that the Sicilians are an inspired people, their inspiration emanates from their 'âmes qui flamboient'. Milan also receives accolades from the Pilot in terms of its culture and, especially, its industry, but not, as with Sicily, in terms of any particular attributes of the Milanese; in fact, Milan seems to be Futurist in spite of itself — an ambivalence that Marinetti captured in the title of one of his posthumously published memoirs, *La grande Milano tradizionale e futurista* [*The Great Traditional and Futurist Milan*][36] — a title that invokes the dual nature of the city. The first mention of Milan in *Monoplan* is a reference to the smokestacks of factories, the first thing the Pilot sees over the horizon as he flies towards the city: 'comme des trompes soulevées d'éléphants, | les puissantes cheminées milanaises!...' [like the raised horns of elephants | the powerful Milanese chimneys!...] (*MP*, 155). But upon reaching Milan, the Pilot finds competing factions of politicians, students, and activists, divided over the question of Italy going to war with Austria. Concluding his call to Milan, he has decided to shake it into wakefulness:

> O Dôme de Milan, je viens de t'effrayer
> [...]
> Je suis, dis-tu, un Milanais qui va trop vite...
> Car c'est bien ta tendresse épouvantée
> qui colore de jaune et de rouge et de noir
> et de vert et de blanc
> la peau transparente de tes vitraux caméléons.
> C'est bien moi qui t'agace chaque soir, en lançant
> le boulet de mon cœur plus haut que ta madone!... (*MP*, 233–34)

> [O Dome of Milan, I have just frightened you
> [...]
> I am, you say, a Milanese that goes too fast...
> For it's really your terrified tenderness
> that colours yellow and red and black
> and green and white
> the transparent skin of your chameleon windows.
> It's really me that annoys you every evening, launching
> the cannonball of my heart higher than your Madonna!...]

The Pilot confronts the 'Dôme de Milan' (or *Duomo di Milano*), the largest cathedral in Italy other than St Peter's Basilica at the Vatican, positioning Futurism as a potential 'spiritual' rival to Catholicism, aspiring not only to aesthetic, but moral and theological value. The Pilot's Futurist principles are contrasted to Milan's, which are indulgent and tender and, by that measure, weak. The description of the cathedral's stained glass concludes one line in 'noir' and the very next ends in 'blanc', but this chameleon-like changeability — normally a credit to Futurism — suggests an effort to hide itself. Ultimately, it is transparent, adopting positions that suit it at whatever is the most opportune moment. However, because 'Prophets are not without honor, except in their hometown, and among their own kin, and in their own house' (Mark 6. 4), this milieu of opportunism and fear is where Futurism finds the fertile soil of struggle. It is, again, within the moment or place of the least likelihood — Jeremiah imprisoned in the cistern, Jonah in the belly of the fish, Daniel in the lion's den — that the prophet finds the expression of faith. Like an alarm clock waking a startled sleeper, the birth of Futurism is announced in Milan:

> Il faut sonner encore... 'Réveillez-vous! Courez!
> La terre nous enfante!
> C'est nous, les nouveaux-nés!... Milan accouchera
> d'un nouveau futuriste!' (*MP*, 231)

> [Let's sound the alarm again... 'Wake up! Go!
> The earth gives birth to us!
> Here we are, the newborn!... Milan will mother
> a new Futurist!']

Marinetti has no reasonable justification for his belief that Milan will be mother to the 'nouveaux-nés' [*sic*] Futurists — especially given the frequent descriptions of a sclerotic political class and a culture defined by cowardice and passéism. But like many of the salvation prophecies of the Bible, which come from a place of complete despondence and political defeat, Marinetti emphasizes his own powers as a prophet by embedding his predictions and visions in the most apparently unlikely context. The tactic is meant to establish credibility through its adherence to a doctrine that's not applicable to any contemporary context. This rhetoric is not simply an isolated *cri de cœur*, but an attempt at social mobilization, seeking allies and naming enemies. As Bourdieu writes, the prophetic doctrine is a persuasive action:

> Le pouvoir du prophète a pour fondement la force du groupe qu'il mobilise par son aptitude à *symboliser* dans une conduite exemplaire et/ou dans un discours (quasi) systématique les intérêts proprement religieux de laïcs occupant une position déterminée dans la structure sociale.[37]

> [The prophet's power is founded on the group that he mobilizes through his ability to *symbolize* in exemplary conduct and/or (quasi) systematic discourse the properly religious interests of lay people occupying a determined position in the social structure.]

The position of the Futurists, in this respect, is constituted by their ability to marshal culture without access to its orthodox institutions. The prophetic position is at its strongest when the prophet's faith seems most definitively unjustified. It is when Jonah is in the belly of the fish that his prayer to God is uttered and, ironically, when God's promise to Nineveh is fulfilled that Jonah feels his faith to be hollow (Jonah 4. 1–3). The prophetic position raises the stakes of Futurism: by claiming a mandate without respect to and even against the traditional institutions through which power is legitimated, the change on offer is all the more radical.

★ ★ ★ ★ ★

Any industrial advancement such as Milan's at the beginning of the twentieth century will raise the question of financial interests and the relationship between

the productive and monetary goals of capitalism. Finance may frequently be represented as a parasitic and non-productive appendage to manufacturing, construction,
or even agriculture, all of which retain a notional connection to earlier forms of
artisanal or manual labour. As one prominent means of routinizing, calculating,
and measuring, Marinetti treats finance as cynically, or even dishonestly, evaluative
without being productive, reflecting a wider view amongst the avant-garde — a
judgment that reaches its apex in Pound's numerous polemics against usury 'age-old
and age-thick'.[38] To establish, in Bourdieu's words, Futurism's 'intérêt désintéressé'[39]
[disinterested interest], the Pilot's encounters in Milan single out and disparage
economic and financial interests, and the Milanese population's apparent lack of
principle is particularly evident in the realm of politics and finance. In chapter 6,
entitled 'Les Moucherons politiciens' [The Political Flies], the Pilot's question to
the politicians assumes that the parliament has been irreparably corrupted by a base
desire for profit:

> Pourquoi vous prêtez-vous ainsi
> aux intérêts retors des financiers
> qui vous trépanent le crâne
> avec leurs froides menaces
> et leurs doutes aiguisés? (*MP*, 136)
>
> [Why lend yourself in this way
> to the cagey interests of financiers
> who trepan your skull
> with their cold threats
> and their sharp doubts?]

Marinetti also engages in antisemitic conspiracy, accusing the politicians of being
controlled by the Rothschild family: 'Ce grandissant murmure nasillard | c'est la
voix de Rothschild' [This great nasal murmuring | is the voice of Rothschild]
(*MP*, 136). The term 'murmure'[40] may allude to the murmuring motif in the story
of the Exodus, as the paradigmatic example of the Jews' recalcitrance before the
divine, an attribute that ultimately results in their exile in the desert and their
characterization as a 'wandering people'. Furthermore, the connection of Judaism
with international finance, the branch of capital that is the purview of 'rootless
cosmopolitans', racializes the distinction between national, 'productive' capital and
trans- or non-national banking or 'unproductive' capital. Decisions that are made
and life that is ordered in the context of financial risk and reward, monetary value,
and capital accumulation are inherently suspect, being formed without respect to
the national spirit. Marinetti extends this polemic to the Vatican as a 'vieil agent de
change à la Bourse des âmes' [old broker at the exchange of souls] (*MP*, 128) — even
the centre of religious life has been corrupted by the calculus of profit. And indeed,
the criticism strongly recalls Jesus' overturning of money-changers' tables in the
temple. By contrast, the students (a group perennially light in economic capital)
laud the social outcasts as being freed from the order of money:

> Voici les courtisanes et les grues loqueteuses,
> les gentilles tapettes, les repris de justice,

ex-assassins, ex-voleurs, mendiants brévétés [*sic*]
et pouilleux de toute sorte.
[...]
La révolte, la lutte et le guet patient,
la guerre cauteleuse et l'assaut corps à corps,
voilà bien leurs métiers. Ils n'ont plus rien à perdre!
D'où leur complet désintéressement. (*MP*, 139–40)

[Here are the courtesans and the tattered hookers
the nice fags, the convicts,
ex-assassins, ex-thieves, certified beggars
and vermin of every kind.
[...]
The revolt, the struggle and patient look-out,
the cunning war and the body-to-body assault,
those are their means. They have nothing left to lose!
Hence their complete disinterestedness.]

Marinetti's use of the terms 'intérêts' and 'désintéressement' both have distinctly financial connotations. 'Intérêts retors' is drawn from the field of bankers, clerks, and Rothschilds, ordered along the lines of economic rationality, reducing human relations to their monetary quantifiability, stabilizing one's identity in relation to another system in contradistinction to Futurist dynamism, transience, and mutability.

The antipathy towards quantification and calculation is further expanded in Marinetti's formulation between the machine and time. In the chapter 'L'homme multiplié et le règne de la machine' [Multiplied man and the reign of the machine], of *Le Futurisme*, Marinetti envisions a time when man will extend his will like 'un immense bras, le Rêve et le Désir, qui sont aujourd'hui de vains mots, régneront souverainement sur l'espace et sur le temps domptés' [an immense arm, Dream and Desire, which are vain words today, will reign sovereign over domesticated space and time]. Though the will is Dream and Desire, this man is 'inhumain et mécanique' [inhuman and mechanical], having merged with the machine. But as chapter 10 of *Monoplan* demonstrates, the erasure of difference between the plane and the Pilot is never quite complete, for, at this moment, an antagonism arises between the Pilot and the motor. After the Pilot laments his loneliness as a poet (the only time he actually alludes to himself as such), the motor takes up its own discourse:

MON MOTEUR
Tais-toi donc, imbécile! Veux-tu mieux respirer?...
Tu n'as qu'à sortir de ce Moi empesté
où tu t'ennuies lugubrement (*MP*, 255)

[MY MOTOR
Quiet, imbecile! Do you want to breathe better?...
You only have to depart that stinking Me
where you dismally bore yourself]

It's an obvious point that if the motor is driving the Pilot, then the normal relationship between man and technology has been reversed, which had the effect of subduing the anxiety of that relationship by implicating it as the motive force of a greater purpose as yet unknown to the Pilot. The Pilot, in a moment that recalls a certain 'crisis of faith', laments time as a form of slow loss, in contrast to the motor, that knows only speed:

> Nous ne serons jamais les gavroches sans cœur
> et sans mémoire,
> qui crachent de très haut sur les balcons à femmes,
> volant à tire-d'aile hors de l'histoire et de l'anatomie (*MP*, 253)

> [We'll always be newsboys without heart
> and without memory,
> who spit at women from high up on the balconies
> swiftly flying outside of history and anatomy]

Marinetti sees the individual as constituted both bodily and historically, and the goal of Futurism, for him, is to do an end-run around those basic constraints. The reference to the heart and memory, in particular, suggests the strictures of the individual experience increasing over time, and that the body is constituted in a doubly historical sense: both of its personal history, and history proper. Habits, cares, and traditions — which are neither strictly personal nor social, being conditioned by the latter but often rendered by the former — become weights around the neck of the Pilot, who wishes to fly outside of 'l'histoire et de l'anatomie'.

The will of the Pilot, working in conjunction with the machinery that makes a poetry of speed and change conceivable, releases the Futurist's heart from the confines of its cage in an apocalyptic or era-defining change of character:

> Enfin mon cœur, mon grand cœur futuriste
> a vaincu sa rude bataille millénaire
> contre les barreaux du thorax (*MP*, 20)

> [At last my heart, my great Futurist heart
> has conquered its harsh millennial battle
> against the cage of my thorax]

> Mon cœur-moteur m'entraîne avec l'élan
> de trois cent fox-terriers tenus en laisse. (*MP*, 67)

> [My motor-heart drags me with the momentum
> of three hundred fox-terriers held by a leash]

As his heart physically guides, even drags, the Pilot through the air, his will is externalized; it's an entity that, like the aeroplane itself, is not entirely *of* him, and draws him outside of himself. Like the Catholic image of the sacred heart situated over the breast of Christ or the Virgin, it's a spiritual image that recalls the resurrection, the power of God, and the faith of the believer. More importantly, despite the Futurist trappings, it's an ironically classic indication that the poet is *guided by* a force outside of himself, bolstering his credibility based on a sincere belief in art and speed as values in and of themselves. Marinetti, casting himself as disinterested in material wealth or political power, implies that traditional, consecrated art is sclerotic, and 'popular' art is cynical; whereas, he is guided by something 'purer': his heart, his belief in the dynamic potential of the individual, his genuine embrace of his own death and of the openness of the future.

Therefore, much of the conflict in *Monoplan* rests in the contrast between the mercenary values of bourgeois culture on the one hand, which restrict life to the quantifications of time and space, money and profit, and Futurist values on the other, which give the Futurist command over those very concepts at the cost of their command over the self, which will be joyously subsumed into the vibrant change of modernity and technology. The storm that the Pilot braves in 'Les Licous du temps et de l'espace' jolts or jump-starts the mechanics of the aeroplane, which seem to behave according to its own will. Whereas the Pilot feels anxiety and doubt, the motor is revived, pulling the plane away from the depths of the fog: 'Tiens! Tiens! L'orage a réveillé mon moteur! | Cent, mille, dix mille kilomètres...' [Hold on! Hold on! The storm has awoken my motor! | One hundred, one thousand, ten thousand kilometres...] (*MP*, 246). Where one aspect of the Pilot has lost its nerve, another aspect has found its will, and he contends with this fragmented character throughout the work, much like Apollinaire's 'Cortège' ('Les peuples s'entassaient et je parus moi-même' (*ŒP*, 76)) or 'Vendémiaire' ('Mondes qui vous ressemblez et qui nous ressemblez' (*ŒP*, 153)), where the speaker's identity must be worked out through a fragmented body or consciousness. Marinetti understands the Pilot as a multiplicity, divided between internal desires and external forces, where unity between the person and technology is something to be achieved. Through most of the poem, the exact point where the body of the Pilot begins and the mechanics of the plane end is ambiguous, but a distinction, however subtle, is maintained. For example, clearly the Pilot cries out at one point, 'Je suis fondu avec mon monoplan' [I have merged with my aeroplane] (*MP*, 20), but the fact that a conceptual separation between 'Je' and 'mon monoplan' is asserted suggests that a true identity between the two has not yet been achieved and still remains for the future.

The fracturing of the Pilot's identity, between his body, his will, and the machine that he engages, rather than undermining his prophetic legitimacy, is meant to bolster it: the Pilot, as prophet, acts neither in his own interests, nor entirely with his own power. Between the semi-deified machine and the Futurist will, the Pilot is a mere proxy. He identifies his own heart with Futurism and the machine in fairly quick succession at the beginning of *Monoplan*: 'mon grand cœur futuriste' [my great Futurist heart] (*MP*, 20) and 'forte hélice de mon cœur monoplan' [strong propeller of my aeroplane heart] (*MP*, 21). Elsewhere, the Pilot frequently refers to his 'cœur-moteur' [motor-heart] (*MP*, 67, 70, 73, 197). Furthermore, the 'cœur futuriste' is counterpoised against the Pilot's own chest, which is described as 'les barreaux du thorax' [the bars of the thorax] (*MP*, 20). The metaphor of the heart, as the physical embodiment of an ideal, bears a relationship to prophetic literature in the structure of the metaphor, but also in the dynamics of a divided body that acts as vessel for a will not one's own. In particular, a prophecy of Ezekiel speaks of a spiritual 'heart transplant' on the people of Israel: 'I will give them one heart, and put a new spirit within them; I will remove the heart of stone from their flesh and give them a heart of flesh' (11. 19; see also 18. 31; 36. 26). The transformation from stone to flesh works to make Israel more fully human in inhuman circumstances. Technology is regarded by Futurism as assisting the human to transcend the limits of modern society, and the 'cœur-moteur' is a truer rendering of the reality of the Pilot's character than any other aspect of his body. But the surgical metaphor in Ezekiel, however, is altered in two ways by Marinetti. First, while Ezekiel is clearly looking towards a future condition ('I *will give* them one heart'), the Pilot speaks of the 'cœur futuriste' or the 'cœur-moteur' as essentially a *fait accompli*, the future is written and the only thing left is to complete it. Technological advances, the image asserts, have reached a point where the 'heart' of the human and the motor, as 'heart' of the aeroplane or automobile, no longer need be distinguished *at the same time* as they become less identifiable with any one individual. The second way in which Marinetti re-characterizes the heart metaphor is through the different emphasis on the material of the organ. Ezekiel's metaphor refers to 'that which is unconscious, immobile, and so unresponsive to God' being replaced by 'that which is tender, yielding, and responsive'.[41] Marinetti, on the other hand, once claimed that Futurists ought to think with 'la sensibilité et les instincts des métaux, des pierres et du bois' [the sensibility and instincts of metal, stones, and wood],[42] so it would seems that tenderness and responsiveness were precisely the types of attributes that a 'cœur-moteur' was meant to preclude. Rather, to be fully human, in the Futurist sense, was to break through the constraints of tradition as well as the quantifying and stabilizing strictures of modernity, and to think with a single-mindedness that would not be caught up by the intellectualizing tendencies of the theologian or the academician, or with the sentimentality of the Christian or, indeed, the poet.

★ ★ ★ ★ ★

In *La Nouvelle Religion-morale de la vitesse* Marinetti attempts one of the more direct attacks on Christianity, claiming that its usefulness has run its course and lacks any real purpose: 'La morale chrétienne a développé la vie intérieure de l'homme, mais elle n'a plus raison d'être aujourd'hui, puisqu'elle s'est vidée de tout le Divin' [Christian morality has developed the interior life of man, but has no *raison d'être* today, since it has been entirely emptied of the Divine].[43] We've seen that Futurism has little use for a highly developed interior life. The heart must break out of its cage, the writers must break out of their den, and discover divinity in the experience of speed and motion. Exclusive attention to interiority, be it mental or physical, leads to stagnation and rot, and Christianity's apparent domination by priests and theologians seems to have forced out any sense of living divinity, and the Catholic Church is the major culprit.[44] 'La Pêche du Grand Phoque verni' [Baiting the great varnished seal] is the chapter where the Pilot enters the Vatican, characterizes the church as a swamp and its pontiff as an absurd seal:

> C'est dans les vastes marécages du Vatican,
> que je vais dénicher le grand Phoque verni
> de candeur ivoirine et de lumière,
> la pape! (*MP*, 114)

> [It's in the vast Vatican swamps
> that I hunt the great varnished Seal
> of bright ivory and light,
> the pope!]

The atmosphere of the Vatican is stifling to the Pilot, who is accustomed to flying in the open skies:

> Atmosphère empestée! C'est ton haleine,
> ô vieux phoque asthmatique, car tu respires
> à grand'peine hors de l'eau purulente!... (*MP*, 115)

> [Poisoned atmosphere! This is your breath,
> O old asthmatic seal, for you wheeze
> with great effort out of purulent water!...]

The Pilot loses patience searching the 'swamp' and dives into the centre of the Vatican to snatch the Pope with hooks lowered from a spring-loaded crane, as if on a fishing expedition:

> C'est bien simple, voyez, le piège se referme,
> et je tire, oh lentement je tire,
> ce lourd, très lourd ballot de chapelets,
> de crucifix, de scapulaires...
> Un pape, un vrai pape, le Saint-Pontife lui-même! (*MP*, 119)

> [It's quite simple, you see, the trap closes,
> and I pull, oh slowly I pull,
> this very, very heavy bundle of rosaries,
> crucifix, and scapulars...
> A pope, a real pope, the Holy Pontiff himself!]

Despite the Pilot's obvious objections, however, he isn't blind to Catholicism's enticement particularly for a young man. The moment of kidnapping the Pope is bracketed by two sections where the Pilot experiences a nostalgic seduction in his encounters with religion. As he flies towards the Vatican over Rome, the Pilot has a vision of clouds that bring to mind romantic or religious sentimentality comparable to Apollinaire's own religious reminiscences in 'Zone'. However, the comfort provided by religion is doubly rejected by Futurism as an attraction to lassitude and rot. The first clouds he encounters bear the resemblance of a young religious child, followed by another, more ominous figure that recalls an overbearing priest. The sympathy that the Pilot shows for the first cloud in the image of an 'enfant de chœur' (*MP*, 109) indicates a naïve, youthful predilections towards religion, but the second image turns on a lumbering, domineering inertia:

> Qu'a-t-il donc à se presser ainsi,
> ce nuage élégant, svelte et blond enfant de chœur,
> soutane rouge et blanc surplis?
> [...]
> ce grand nuage noir, bedonnant et solennel
> qui sème dans la brise ses faux airs bénisseurs
> et son sourire doucereux.
> Ce n'est plus qu'une lourde idole obèse (*MP*, 109)

> [Why has he hurried so,
> this elegant cloud, slim and blonde choirboy,
> red cassock and white surplice?
> [...]
> this large black cloud, potbellied and solemn
> who seeds the breeze with his false benedictions
> and his sweet smile.
> He's just a heavy, obese idol]

Clouds, in Marinetti's earlier works, were associated with immaterialism and spirituality, to be later developed into a representation of sentiment and memory — not entirely negative in their own right, but in the dangerous presence of nostalgia. For example, in *La Conquête des étoiles* clouds are described in extensive detail. Cescutti, drawing from the frequent cloud imagery in the book of Exodus, particularly when Moses ascends various mountains, points out that the cloud is 'l'archétype biblique de l'oubli et de l'abandon de toute attache matérielle ou humaine' [the biblical archetype of forgetting and abandoning every material or human attachment].[45] Isaiah, as well — whose vision in the temple contains copious smoke (Isaiah 6. 4) — uses the image of a cloud as a symbol of God's forgetting of the people's sins and accepting them after their period of wandering: 'I have swept away your transgressions like a cloud, and your sins like mist; | return to me, for I have redeemed you' (Isaiah 44. 22). The instability of clouds is surely one of their attractive features to Futurism, but as representations of religious sensibility, they lack coherence and solidity which leads to Marinetti's advocacy of thinking with the sensibility of metal, stone, and wood.

After capturing the Pope and struggling to escape, the Pilot is confronted with another wave of sentiment: that of his own memories of youth in terms that connect piety and sensuality. Three times in this section, in the most striking similarities with 'Zone', he repeats the phrase 'Je ne suis plus l'adolescent', recalling memories of being a proudly pious young man, enamoured of the symbolism and ritual of the church:

> Je ne suis plus l'adolescent tout fier de sa piété
> qui s'agenouillait sensuellement
> pour prier au hasard les chauds parfums errants,
> le reposoir en feu, la Madone élégante
> et bien moulée dans sa robe de plâtre (*MP*, 123)

> [I am no longer the adolescent so proud of his piety
> who sensually kneeled
> at random for prayer to the hot, drifting perfumes,
> the tabernacle aflame, the Madonna elegant
> and well-shaped in her plaster robe]

But he also expresses a certain regret at his youthful self-denial, lost in 'l'odeur de l'encens et des hosties sucrées' [the odour of incense and sugared hosts] (*MP*, 122), where, as in the opening of the first manifesto, such symbolic voluptuousness leads, ultimately, nowhere. While sensual pleasure is frustrated by spiritual duty for the young Pilot, spiritual desire is no less frustrated by the physical body, and ultimately

Futurism aims towards overcoming the dichotomy. The final stanza relates this vision shifting from the ethereal and unattainable to the carnal:

> Je ne suis plus l'adolescent au cœur flottant,
> aux mains inquiètes, qui pleurait de n'avoir
> qu'un corps acide à donner à personne,
> à Jésus-Christ, à la langue éclatante
> des cierges que torture la folie de monter,
> à la fureur caressante des roses (*MP*, 124)

> [I am no longer the adolescent with the floating heart,
> with nervous hands, who cried at having only
> an acidic body to give to someone,
> to Jesus Christ, to the exploding language
> of candles that torment the madness of rising,
> to the caressing fury of roses]

His adolescent body is 'acide', corrosive, or impure — a view reflecting the asceticism and self-denial of the body, so the pious desire of the young Pilot turns to religious objects. The implication, from the perspective of the adult Pilot, is that only with the advent of technology can such desire be consummated, and the body avoid the failings of biology and physics.

Clearly, it is not the youthful inclination to religion that Marinetti finds problematic, as youth itself was prized by Futurism, whose first manifesto declares that

> les plus âgés d'entre nous ont trente ans; nous avons donc au moins dix ans pour accomplir notre tâche. Quand nous aurons quarante ans, que de plus jeunes et plus vaillants que nous veuillent bien nous jeter au panier comme des manuscrits inutiles!...[46]

> [the oldest of us are thirty; therefore we have at least ten years to make our mark. When we are forty, younger and more valiant ones than us should want to throw us into the bin like useless manuscripts!...]

The decadent emptiness of the church, where youthful spirituality is smothered in its crib, is the target for Marinetti in this section of *Monoplan*. There is also a broader critique here of formal education that instructs the youth to idolize traditional culture, be it religious or artistic, at the expense of their own growth and development. In this sense, the Futurist adoration of youth is placed in contrast to 'the "criminal" connection between an art of museums and religious belief' which was 'doubly to be rejected because it fostered unquestioning veneration for timeworn dogmas and habits [...], and because it induced passive forms of contemplation.'[47] It is here that an ambivalent relationship to youth emerges rather than the more common, full-throated alliance that the Futurists felt they had with students and the young. Clearly it was the youthfulness of the young poet that caused the Pilot to 'fall prey' to the sentimentality of Catholicism. But he also sees adolescence as being a source of energy that is so important to Futurist thought. The Pilot's own stifled adolescence is redeemed in the nationalism and enthusiasm of the students encountered later in the novel, who are most fervently and vocally in support of war with Austria. Students in particular formed a core constituency for the Futurists, and Marinetti's *Le Futurisme* makes the bold claim that 'j'ai l'orgueil de déclarer ici que tous les étudiants d'Italie sont aujourd'hui avec nous' [I am proud to declare here that every Italian student is with us today].[48]

Le Futurisme is also dedicated not to Italian, but to Parisian students, who, it seemed, led the way in providing a model for melding aesthetics, spirituality, and national politics. As Adamson explains, many in Italy in particular were 'heavily inspired by European, especially French, avant-garde Modernism, that is, by counter-cultural movements arising after 1900 which aimed at "cultural regeneration" through the transformative power of art and a secular-religious quest for "new values"'.[49] Only after the war would this stance lend itself to the politics of fascism, for as Adamson also notes, 'what is at stake in fascism is a religious problem: the need somehow to respond to the secularization of Western societies since the eighteenth century.'[50] In this way, Futurism and fascism were parallel responses, particularly in Italy, to the issue of secularization in Europe: both proposed modernity and Italy as a spiritual principle around which society could be re-organized. This prospect necessitated a serious re-evaluation of humanity's relationship to technology and aesthetics, psychology and materiality, space and time. *Monoplan* scandalizes biblical myths, inflecting them with Futurist, anti-traditionalist or anti-Christian sentiments, as one method of unsettling basic religious themes of resurrection and prophecy in *Monoplan*. Marinetti hoped to become something of a Joshua, leading the Italians into the conquest of the Promised Land. The title of the final chapter of *Monoplan* is 'La Bataille de Monfalcone ou le tombeau des papes' [The Battle of Monfalcone or the fall of the popes], which encapsulates both the supplanting of Christianity as well as the sense of leading Italy into the Promised Land. A shipping and manufacturing port near Trieste, and controlled by Austria, Monfalcone was one of the flashpoints for Italian irredentism. Marinetti was, at least regarding this city, 'profetico': in 1915 Italy captured Monfalcone from Austria, and the Futurist architect Antonio Sant'Elia was killed there the following year.

Notes to Chapter 2

1. Somigli, *Legitimizing the Artist*, p. 176.
2. Ibid., p. 164.
3. This study will refer to the narrator as the 'Pilot'. Marinetti never uses either 'pilote' or 'aviateur' in reference to the narrator, nor is the narrator ever named, denoted using only personal pronouns ('je' or 'moi'). Like many of Apollinaire's speakers, the narrator is an allegorized version of the poet himself.
4. Bourdieu, 'Une Interprétation de la théorie', p. 12; emphasis added.
5. A precise accounting of Futurist manifestoes is probably impossible, due to the difficulty of defining the form. Marinetti described a particular *tone* and *technique* for manifestoes, and many works deemed such lack the word itself. When Marinetti's allegorical conquest narrative, 'Tuons le Clair de Lune!!', was first published in 1909, it lacked either an explicit description as a manifesto in the title or the stated principles or theses common to the form. Yet, when the same text was included in the *Le Futurisme* in 1911, Marinetti subtitled it as the 'Second Manifeste futuriste'. Given this difficulty, Marjorie Perloff figures around 50 manifestos published during Futurism's early period of 1909–1915 (Marjorie Perloff, *The Futurist Moment: Avant-Garde, Avant-Guerre, and the Language of Rupture* (Chicago, IL: University of Chicago Press, 1986), p. 90).

6. De Paulis-Dalembert points out that the 1914 Italian translation does attempt, with partial success, to adhere to the principles of the manifesto, suggesting occasional efforts to see through the possibilities of these declarations (De Paulis-Dalembert, 'La Réécriture de l'imaginaire symboliste', pp. 24–26.

7. Perloff, *Futurist Moment*, p. 84.

8. Robert Alter, *The Art of Biblical Poetry* (New York: Basic Books, 2011), p. 182.

9. See H. H. Gerth and C. Wright Mills, 'Introduction: The Man and His Work', in *From Max Weber: Essays in Sociology* (London: Routledge, 1948), pp. 51–52.

10. Pierre Bourdieu, *The Field of Cultural Production: Essays on Art and Literature*, ed. by Randal Johnson, trans. by Claud Du Verlie (New York: Columbia University Press, 1993), p. 183.

11. F. T. Marinetti, *Le Futurisme* (Paris: E. Sansot & Cie., 1911), pp. 142–43.

12. Ibid., pp. 155–56.

13. Cescutti, *Origines mythiques*, p. 133.

14. Ibid., p. 30.

15. Ibid., p. 45.

16. Martin Puchner, *Poetry of the Revolution: Marx, Manifestos, and the Avant-Gardes* (Princeton, NJ: Princeton University Press, 2006), p. 19.

17. Ibid., p. 25.

18. Burrow, *Crisis of Reason*, pp. 246–47.

19. Cescutti, *Origines mythiques*, pp. 49–50.

20. F. T. Marinett, *Scritti Francesi*, ed. by Pasquale A. Jannini (Milan: Mondadori, 1983), p. 58.

21. Marinetti, *Le Futurisme*, p. 91.

22. The King James translation is even closer to Marinetti here, using the 'veil' rather than 'curtain'.

23. F. T. Marinetti, 'La Nouvelle Religion-morale de la vitesse', in *Futurisme: Manifestes — Proclamations — Document*, ed. by Giovanni Lista (Lausanne: L'Age d'homme, 1973), pp. 366–70 (p. 368).

24. Walter L. Adamson, 'How Avant-Gardes End — and Begin: Italian Futurism in Historical Perspective', *New Literary History*, 41 (2010), 855–74 (p. 860).

25. See Somigli, *Legitimizing the Artist*, p. 149.

26. Adamson, 'How Avant-Gardes End', p. 860.

27. Marinetti, 'First Manifesto', p. 87.

28. F. T. Marinetti, et al., 'Qualitative Imaginative Futurist Mathematics', in *Futurism: An Anthology*, ed. by Lawrence Rainey, Christine Poggi, and Laura Wittman (New Haven, CT: Yale University Press, 2009), pp. 298–301 (p. 298).

29. Frye, *Words with Power*, p. 229.

30. Cascutti, *Origines mythiques*, p. 32.

31. F. T. Marinetti, *Marinetti: Selected Writings*, ed. by R. W. Flint, trans. by R. W. Flint and Arthur A. Coppotelli (New York: Farrar, Straus and Giroux, 1972), p. 269.

32. Blaise Pascal, *Pensées and Other Writings*, trans. by Honor Levi (Oxford: Oxford University Press, 1995), p. 66.

33. Pierre Bourdieu, 'La Production de la croyance: contribution à une économie des biens symboliques', *Actes de la recherche en sciences sociales*, 13 (February 1977), 3–43 (p. 39).

34. De Paulis-Dalembert, 'La Réécriture de l'imaginaire symboliste', p. 27.

35. 'Mondes qui vous ressemblez et qui nous ressemblez' (ŒP, 153)

36. Originally published in 1969. After leaving Alexandria, Marinetti settled in Milan to study law. From there, he travelled frequently to Paris to pursue his literary career. In 1905, he founded the journal *Poesia* in Milan with a group of poets who would later become the early Futurists.

37. Bourdieu, 'Une Interprétation', p. 14.

38. Pound, *Personæ*, p. 188.

39. Bourdieu, *Les Règles de l'art*, p. 300.

40. Although modern translations often render the Hebrew לוּן, *lūn*, as 'complain', 'murmur' was popularized in English in the King James Bible, while the French Ostervald and Segond versions also use 'murmure'.

41. Leslie C. Allen, *Ezekiel 1–19* (Dallas, TX: Word Books, 1994), p. 165.

42. F. T. Marinetti, 'Manifeste technique de la littérature futuriste', in *Futurisme: Manifestes —
Proclamations — Documents*, ed. by Giovanni Lista (Lausanne: L'Age d'homme, 1973), pp. 133–37
(p. 135).

43. Marinetti, 'Nouvelle Religion-morale', p. 366.

44. There is a political basis for Marinetti's opposition to Catholicism, as well. Austria, as a
predominantly Catholic nation, was an ally of the Vatican, which opposed war against the
Austro-Hungarian Empire, setting it at odds with Italian irredentism.

45. Cescutti, *Origines mythiques*, p. 52.

46. Marinetti, 'Fondation et Manifeste du Futurisme', in *Futurisme: Manifestes — Proclamations —
Documents*, ed. by Giovanni Lista (Lausanne: L'Age d'Homme, 1973), pp. 85–89 (p. 88).

47. Poggi, *Inventing Futurism*, p. 233.

48. Marinetti, *Le Futurisme*, p. 3.

49. Perhaps the irony of Futurism looking to Paris, in particular, for inspiration in national politics
is that so many of the French avant-garde — especially Apollinaire — lacked French nationality
and had an ambivalent relationship to their adoptive country. Walter L. Adamson, 'Fascism and
Culture: Avant-Gardes and Secular Religion in the Italian Case', *Journal of Contemporary History*,
24.3 (July 1989), 411–35 (p. 421).

50. Ibid., p. 415.

CHAPTER 3

❖

Sledge and Drill

In 1905, Ezra Pound wrote to his mother, enumerating some formative influences on his poetry: 'I shall continue to study Dante and the Hebrew Prophets.'[1] Louis L. Martz argues that what captured Pound's imagination in his reading of the Hebrew Prophets (and Dante, for that matter) was the prophetic dialectic between searing criticism and utopian aspirations. Martz's understanding of the definitive style of prophetic literature, which 'oscillates between denunciation and hope, between the abyss and the ideal, [...] held together by the prophetic voice',[2] is prevalent in much of Pound's poetry. The prophet provides an alternative history for the national body, allowing it to see itself in the light of the ideal that the prophet proclaims, but this ideal is part of the disorienting nature of much prophetic rhetoric, where the prophet never seems to be looking at the nation *as it is*. Or, to put it another way: the prophet is revealing an aspect of the nation that is unacknowledged by official national histories but is no less real for that. But this unacknowledged aspect is not necessarily a negative viewpoint, as Pound, Apollinaire, and Marinetti all present aspects of the nation whose valuation is explicitly bound to how the audience responds to the avant-garde project more broadly. Whether one sees Apollinaire's presentation of France as a cosmopolitan nation, or is sympathetic to Marinetti's advocacy of Italian dynamism and industry is, in some senses, predetermined by the construction of an audience these writings imply. The prophetic view that rejects context, nuance, or balance is due mainly to the prophet's alienation from the cultural, political, or economic centres of power that maintain the status quo, and will necessarily seek out social homologies with its audience. The prophet has no interest in capturing the realistic viewpoints and justifications of those who are members of such centres of power, because the prophet has no stake in their maintenance. Therefore, Martz argues that Pound acts as a prophet-in-exile in one way or another: 'Wherever the location of the writer, "exile" describes a state of mind always searching for "home".' And for the prophet, the meaning of this home extends 'into the deepest recesses of the self, in search of abiding values that will redeem the troubled present'.[3]

Martz follows a general consensus in studies of biblical prophecy that regard prophets as social critics and reformers rather than foretellers of future events: 'The Hebrew prophet is a reformer: his mind is upon the present.'[4] To the extent that prophets engage with the hopes and anxieties of the future, predictions are usually non-specific and broadly fall into general categories of condemnation or redemption. Although they are reformers, they are not normally *reformists* in the sense that institutions should be corrected. Instead, those institutions need to be radically refashioned at their most basic levels or abolished altogether. The prophet's vocation as a social critic predisposes him or her to the oscillation of prophetic rhetoric that Martz describes because the world *as it is* is an existential threat to the survival of the people: 'No words are too harsh for the biblical prophet to use in denouncing these "abominations" (Ezekiel's word); no words of promise are too idyllic for the prophet to use in his exhortations of redemption.'[5] In speaking of the *Cantos*, Martz states that

> the term *prophetic poem* or *prophetic voice* will do, since violent denunciation
> of evil forms an essential part of the prophetic voice. Seeking the ideal for
> his people, the prophet reacts with fierce revulsion from what he sees as the
> corruption of his people [...] but always with the indestructible ideal in mind.[6]

The prophet's own voice balances or unifies the alternating sense of condemnation and redemption by providing a sense of continuity and outlook, and speaking to a deeper concern held by the audience. Martz emphasizes that this voice lies at the nexus between the prophet's place in society and that which the prophet speaks for, be it God, truth, beauty, or even all these at once. Describing Walt Whitman's sense of prophecy, which is 'based upon the vistas of the biblical prophets', Martz states that, 'This prophet desires to speak for all Americans, diverse as they are: he desires to bind them all together by the power of his voice.'[7] At his most effective, the prophet can confirm to an audience that a common, collective outlook exists between them. In order for the prophet to describe *possible* futures and *potential* histories in reference to the present, it is as if the prophet must first encompass or embody society and history, in its vast multiplicity, before expressing judgment on it. A similar technique can be found in Pound's early use of poetic personae, divorcing his personality from his writing to step into that of an honoured or admired figure. In the personae, Pound adopts the mode of speaking 'on behalf of' without fully identifying with the chosen persona, writing neither from his own context nor that of his personae, but from an intermediate position that improbably speaks both from and against his time.

Based on this description of the prophet, Pound's interest in social critique and biting satire, as well as his ideal of a transhistorical beauty, separates him from the prophetic figures of Apollinaire and Marinetti. The two latter poets are optimistic — sometimes cautiously, sometimes enthusiastically — about the potential for the technical and cultural innovations of modernity to realize the broadest and most dynamic expressions of human intelligence and creativity, provided that artists appropriately embrace this future. Pound, on the other hand, deeply felt that modernity was a particular cultural 'vortex', a concentration of energies unique to the epoch,[8] a particular configuration of a universal tradition of beauty that could only be uncovered by the few intelligent artists and writers that were sufficiently critical of modernity.[9] Without such a critical distance from modernity, the moment would inevitably emphasize, and even drive, social and national decline. Pound was the consummate exile in regards to his native America and even to his adopted home of London. America was, in Pound's view, a cultural wasteland that he was only too happy to leave in 1908, at the age of twenty-two. But London hardly fared better, filled as it was with bourgeois morality and small-minded critics. Of the selection of poems that this study will examine, one of the few constants is Pound's pessimism and sense of loss, his feeling that the cultural values of modernity, whatever positive effect they might have, were inevitably supplanting traditions that emphasized artistic values (beauty, the sublime, the tragic), and that there was no place for a poet 'in a society that ignored private strength and passion in favor of assumed public rectitude and morality.'[10] This is perhaps why writers such as Martin Puchner have described as 'rearguard' the acceptance of the revolutionary rhetoric of Modernism in order to 'reduce and contain the consequences' of it by 'restrict[ing] the true revolution to some neatly confined elite'.[11] Pound's relationship to the prophet is of the constant Jeremiah, an outcast surrounded by an ignorant public who mocked his calling as the advocate for a now-derided tradition. This chapter will examine Pound's relationship to prophecy as a self-nominated inheritor of a poetic tradition, the 'it' in Pound's famous dictum of 'Make it new'. In doing so, I hope to shed some light on William Marx's question of the arrière-garde: 'For is the past to which all reactionary movements profess devotion, really just the past? Is it not in principle something irrevocably new?'[12]

The American Poet and the Prophetic Tradition

The figure of the poet is a figure alienated by his adherence to an ideal, an order, or to a calling that is radically separate from the contemporary society. But, crucially, Pound does not present himself as the originator of an order that cannot but pre-exist his writing, that is, without which he is no poet at all. A very early poem entitled 'Masks', published in Pound's first collection *A Lume Spento* (1908), begins with a meditation on the ways earlier poets might have adopted the personae, as Pound now does:

> These tales of old disguisings, are they not
> Strange myths of souls that found themselves among
> Unwonted folk that spake an hostile tongue,
> Some soul from all the rest who'd not forgot
> The star-span acres of a former lot
> Where boundless mid the clouds his course he swung,
> Or carnate with his elder brothers sung
> Ere ballad-makers lisped of Camelot? (*CEP*, 34)

But Pound writes of 'These tales of old disguisings', looking back onto poets who adopted the personae of a 'former lot', even occasionally using an archaic diction ('spake', 'carnate') that throws the poem back into an invented tradition. This 'former lot' is also treated as superior, as suggested by the description of their 'star-span acres' that are 'boundless mid the clouds'. Furthermore, at the end of the poem, it's shown as distant from the earth, but at the same time, quietly considering it — perhaps even judging it — as they 'Ponder in silence o'er the earth's queynt devyse?' (*CEP*, 34). Pound uses the words 'tales' and 'myths' to describe the custom of poets adopting the personae of older practitioners who are described in the poem as:

> Old singers half-forgetful of their tunes,
> Old painters color-blind come back once more,
> Old poets skill-less in the wind-heart runes,
> Old wizards lacking in their wonder-lore (*CEP*, 34)

But rather than 'tales' or 'myths', this custom could be termed as 'tradition', which is a way to legitimate the contemporary speaker; or, perhaps more precisely, what Pound is describing is a tradition in the midst of being constructed, a retrojection of Pound's own current psycho-aesthetic complex. These 'souls' feel that their ideals are expressed by a tradition of beauty, music, or even magic, so they choose to cast their lot in with the singers, painters, poets, and wizards. Pound's point is that tradition is not something passively existing in relation to the present, but is actively summoned in relation to or in open contention with the present. It's 'relived' with every new act of creation that cannot be entirely identified with its contemporary historical context. Tradition is not simply 'the past' — it is a particular understanding of the past 'carnate' in active dialogue or confrontation with the present. This point is driven home in Pound's juxtaposition in the final two lines of the first stanza. While the poet's 'elder brothers' have 'sung', the current 'ballad-makers lisped of Camelot', and the tradition is embodied in the 'brothers', the 'former lot' who are both of the speaker and precede him. The temporal arrangement of the poem therefore speaks to how Pound conceives of his own relationship to the poetic tradition. Pound constructs 'Masks' as a conversation of three different eras. The 'old' singers, poets, painters, and wizards lie at the furthest point in the past and provide the basis for how the tradition is constructed by later, like-minded artists who live in their own times as outcasts. Finally, the speaker himself expresses sympathy with the poets who adopt the personae of the original founders of the tradition, and thereby continue that tradition. By providing an answer to the implied question of who these poets are and why they adopt the personae provided by the tradition, this poem acts as a kind of negative apologia of a technique that needs no justification.

Prophecy in biblical literature grounds itself in the lineage or tradition of prophets that is set out in the book of Deuteronomy, where Moses himself is presented as that archetypal 'mask' that other prophets must wear. The 'appropriate' criteria are laid out for identifying true prophets from false ones, which is to say that Deuteronomy establishes the way in which the Israelites might distinguish a prophet who truly serves God from a prophet whose interests are greed, false gods, or other nations. Simply (and tautologically) speaking, true prophets of God speak the truth: 'If a prophet speaks in the name of the Lord but the thing does not take place or prove true; it is a word that the Lord has not spoken. The prophet has spoken it presumptuously' (Deuteronomy 18. 22). Of even more importance, the model for the prophet of God is Moses himself, who claims that, 'The Lord your God will raise up for you a prophet like me from among your own people; you shall heed such a prophet' (Deuteronomy 18. 15). Throughout the Bible, prophets are described in terms clearly meant to cast them in the tradition of Moses, such as Elijah's ascent

up Mount Horeb to receive the word of God (1 Kings 19. 8) in the manner of Moses'
ascent up the same mountain in his encounter with the burning bush (Exodus 3.
1). The parallels confirm 'the impression that Jeremiah is being presented from the
beginning of his career as a prophet after the manner of Moses'.[13] The opening
of the book of Jeremiah is also at pains to place the eponymous prophet within
the Mosaic tradition. For example, both Jeremiah and Moses express a reluctance
to accept the prophetic call (Jeremiah 1. 6; Exodus 4. 10); both are accompanied
by the word of God (Jeremiah 1. 8; Exodus 3. 12); both focus on the imagery of
the prophet's mouth as surrogate for God (Jeremiah 1. 9; Exodus 4. 12). Indeed,
Jeremiah is the latest iteration of a tradition of prophetic liberation begun by Moses:
'From the day that your ancestors came out of the land of Egypt until this day, I
have persistently sent all my servants the prophets to them, day after day' (Jeremiah
7. 25). And finally, his placement within the Mosaic tradition is further highlighted
by his conflicts with rival prophets in language reflecting the criteria for a 'true'
prophet in Deuteronomy: 'Thus says the Lord of hosts: Do not listen to the words
of the prophets who prophesy to you; they are deluding you. They speak visions of
their own minds, not from the mouth of the Lord' (Jeremiah 23. 16). The constancy
of God's relationship to Israel, rooted in the Exodus and the law, is not so much
spoken by the true prophet, but repeated with reference to a changing historical
context.

Pound's awareness of prophecy as a tradition which the prophet establishes
by adopting the language and concerns, or recalling notable events, of a notable
forebear is evident in his relationship to his favoured poets. Hugh Witemeyer states
that, from the age of fifteen, Pound 'knew that he was to be a poet. Moreover, he
was to be a national epic poet, *on the model* of Homer, Dante and Whitman.'[14] Just
as Moses provided the model for biblical prophets like Jeremiah, Pound looked to
the canonized poets of ancient Greece, the Renaissance, and an emergent America.
But his tradition was wider than even this, including an encyclopaedic array of
poets from the medieval troubadour tradition, the Roman Empire, and nineteenth-
century England. Yet, when speaking specifically of the tradition *as prophecy*, Pound
appealed to his closest American forebear, as in his essay of 1909, 'What I feel about
Walt Whitman', where he writes: 'I honour him for he prophesied me while I can
only recognize him as a forebear of whom I ought to be proud.'[15] What Pound
is referring to is the tradition of the national epic, the dramatic aetiology of the
nation's character, that he felt himself destined to write. The concerns of Whitman
are Pound's concerns as well, but his phrase 'ought to be proud', noting the pull of
a responsibility that he nonetheless questions, complicates the matter. On the one
hand, Pound is somewhat reluctant to claim Whitman as a forebear,[16] although
he admits that, 'when I write of certain things I find myself using his rhythms'.[17]
On the other hand, Pound feels that he is compelled by his own temperament,
birthplace and history to acknowledge Whitman's place in the tradition: 'Personally
I might be very glad to conceal my relationship to my spiritual father and brag
about my more congenial ancestry — Dante, Shakespeare, Theocritus, Villon, but
the descent is a bit difficult to establish.'[18] This crucial point describes a tension not

between tradition and modernity, but competing traditions that exist, on one hand, within the poet's social and artistic upbringing and, on the other, the tradition of which the poet subjectively feels himself to be a part. Both bear some truth, and Pound cannot choose one over the other. There is a higher ideal to which Pound must attend, and if honouring Whitman is the way to attend to it, then so be it.

Pound writes in the same essay, 'It seems to me I should like to drive Whitman into the old world. I sledge, he drill — and to scourge America with all the old beauty. (For Beauty *is* an accusation)'.[19] The aggressive tone and use of the word 'scourge' sharpens and elevates Pound's rhetoric, echoing, perhaps, the sentiment of Isaiah when describing God's anger as a scourge (Isaiah 10. 26).[20] Whereas Whitman is a force for exploration and discovery, Pound is one of chastisement, using the 'old beauty' of the 'old world' to strike or 'sledge' his modern contemporaries. But Pound distinguishes himself from Whitman, as well:

> This desire is because I am young and impatient, were I old and wise I should content myself in seeing and saying that these things will come. But now, since I am by no means sure it would be true prophecy, I am fain set my own hand to the labour.[21]

Hebrew prophecy was formed by the urgency of repentance and so designed to elicit immediate changes in behaviour. Pound felt that Whitman, somewhat ironically dubbed the 'old and wise' poet, was too confident in America's ability to naturally understand his message. The nation was too clogged with cheap culture and poor morals to adhere and adapt to Whitman's view of a blossoming democracy. Pound, as will be examined below, was sceptical that democracy was universally possible or desirable, and so quarrelled with what he felt was the falseness and superficiality of Whitman's optimism.[22] Pound accuses Whitman in *The Spirit of Romance* (1910) of 'pretend[ing] to be conferring a philantropic [*sic*] benefit on the race by recording his own self-complacency.'[23] Whether or not Whitman might have had an appropriate message, he was content with simply prophesying its future occurrence, whereas Pound, adopting his own language of prophecy, hopes to 'scourge' America with beauty, and thereby actively creating or willing history into existence.

★ ★ ★ ★ ★

In describing Whitman's relationship to prophecy and America, Martz has an insight that informs not only Pound's relationship to Whitman, but potentially Pound's relationship to the use of personae in general: 'A prophet is one who speaks for another.'[24] This definition is, broadly speaking, coherent with the mediational function of prophets given by Wilson and Overholt and examined in the introduction to this study, but would require, for our purposes, an elaboration for how a prophet is chosen by the force or entity on whose behalf he or she speaks, how the public identifies a trusted prophet, and how the prophetic message is rhetorically tailored to signal his or her legitimacy. Whereas Whitman wanted to commune with America, to be the collective voice of America, Pound summoned the tradition for the purpose of setting himself against America. In 1913, several years after Pound has relocated to London, he sent a poem containing an explicit address to America entitled 'From Chebar' to Harriet Monroe (1860–1936), the founder of the long-running journal *Poetry*, and although not published at the time, the poem describes the arts as the medium or tradition through which the new order will be expressed. The arts retain their autonomy, and so are best positioned to reconfigure the tradition: 'The order does not end in the arts, | The order shall come and pass through them.' (*CEP*, 271). Other institutions are sclerotic, lacking the mutability of art that comes from adhering to a dynamic sensibility of beauty and become the source of change in the world:

> The state is too idle, the decrepit church is too idle,
> The arts alone can transmit this.
> They alone cling fast to the gods,
> Even the sciences are a little below them. (*CEP*, 271)

Political and spiritual orders are beyond hope; the arts, on the other hand, might recover what has been lost. The arts are, then, allies of the gods or mediums through which the gods are manifest. In a brief and enigmatic piece of writing, 'Religio or, The Child's Guide to Knowledge' (1918), Pound again lays out this relationship between the beauty expressed in the arts, and the divine. At several points in this piece, he states that divine knowledge is the 'tradition', but more significantly, divinity is found within the division of form and content. Written in a question-and-answer style, he asks, 'When is a god manifest?', answering, 'When the states of mind take form.' Further along he asks, 'By what characteristic may we know the divine form?', answering, 'By beauty.'[25] Exhibiting itself not by a set of ideas or themes, the divine is a formal rendering of aesthetics and psychology, both of which found a diachronic differentiation across peoples and history.

As an advocate for the arts, the speaker in 'From Chebar' is the proxy for divinity (being the guise of tradition), which is rendered primarily through formally artistic means, and he need not advocate any one particular agenda beyond beauty itself. The speaker is lost in a self-referential loop, in which his own antagonism against a flawed world is the means and motive of his prophecy, repeating himself in an objectified manner, attributing to the arts his own beliefs. Both the speaker and the arts aspire to the highest ideal: 'I am "He who demands the perfect"' (l. 39); 'They [the arts] are "Those who demand the perfect"' (l. 66). In order to proclaim this ideal, both the speaker and the arts represent a kind of fearlessness, braving the dangerous or obscure aspects of life: 'I am not afraid of the dark, | I am he who is not afraid to look in the corners.' (ll. 24–25); 'They are "Not afraid of the dark"' (l. 67). The speaker sees himself as both part of America and at the same time transcending America. The arts also transcend time, seen as eternal and eternally present: 'I came with the earliest comers, | I will not go till the last.' (ll. 41–42); 'They are after you and before you.' (l. 68). Finally, the arts, as well as the speaker, set themselves apart from the common language, which is given to undignified pandering: 'I do not join in the facile praises, | In the ever ready cries of enthusiasms.' (ll. 35–36); 'They have not need of smooth speeches, | There are enough who are ready to please you.' (ll. 69–70). The final six lines of the poem bring these disparate comparisons together in an alliance between the speaker and the arts:

> It is I, who demand our past,
> And they who demand it.
>
> It is I, who demand tomorrow,
> And they who demand it.
>
> It is we, who do not accede,
> We do not please you with easy speeches. (*CEP*, 271–72)

'From Chebar' refers to the book of Ezekiel, where the prophet receives his first revelation from God while on the banks of the Chebar River: 'the word of the Lord came to the priest Ezekiel son of Buzi, in the land of the Chaldeans [Babylonians] by the river Chebar' (Ezekiel 1. 3). The book of Ezekiel was composed after the destruction of Jerusalem in 587 BCE and the Chebar river is the symbolic place of arrival for the exiles into Babylon. For Pound, then, Ezekiel is specifically a prophet of exile: 'I came to the exiles at Tel-abib,[26] who lived by the river Chebar. And I sat among them, stunned, for seven days.' (3. 15). Ezekiel's experience of prophesying from Babylon is one of traumatic alienation and loss, presenting the divine as the only foothold in this diaspora. The speaker of 'From Chebar' is likewise in a place apart from his home, calling back to it to reform itself, to aspire to the same ideal that the poet aspires to, and thereby open up the possibility, however remote, of homecoming or rapprochement. Like the divine spirit that has departed from Jerusalem, the national spirit has gone into exile with the poet.

The speaker's credibility is grounded in his self-presentation as a member of the nation but simultaneously as one apart, sympathetic but distant, as the quintessential voice of the prophet-in-exile. Pound begins 'From Chebar' with the lines:

> Before you were, America!
>
> I did not begin with you,
> I do not end with you, America. (*CEP*, 269)

Although America is but one manifestation of the speaker's voice, his distance from the nation speaks to the choice to write about his native country and a need to struggle with questions of national origin, how deeply engrained national character is, and to what extent the nation is the product of a few guiding lights:

> You are the present veneer.
> If my blood has flowed within you,
> Are you not wrought from my people! (*CEP*, 269)

Paradoxically, the nation is the product of those who are also much more than the nation and those who can draw it out of itself and into a more transcendent tradition. In this respect, Witemeyer provides an important detail in Pound's early understanding of the poet's role in society: 'Pound followed the neo-classical ideal of the epic poet as a man of no less learning than imagination.' An ideal that

> emphasized a cosmopolitan internationalism of intellect and culture, a transcendence of provincial, monolingual perspectives, and an awareness of the best that has been thought and said (at any rate by Europeans).[27]

Pound therefore reverses the relationship of the individual to his nationality, which is to say that the individual is not so much *of* a nation, but the nation is formed in the image of select individuals. It takes the Walt Whitmans of the world (however few there might be) to truly create an America, even if America might not exactly live up to the inspiration of its creator.

The Prophetic Elsewhere

Exile allows the poet to establish a critical distance from the nation, to judge it while excusing himself from the judgment of his peers. In his view, the only true 'judges' transcended specific national cultures even as they are firmly associated with a quintessentially national tradition that provides them with a singular viewpoint; Robert Browning (1812–1889), Villon, or Dante are examples that Pound frequently cited, insofar as they are unmistakeably English, French, and Italian, respectively, even as they came to represent, not unproblematically, the literary basis of 'European' or 'Western' civilization. They were the eyes through which he hoped to judge both himself and the national culture from which he came, prompting him to adopt, from an early age, the conceit of the poetic persona. Pound's use of personae is described by Witemeyer as 'not so much impersonations as momentary reincarnations of the great souls of the past'.[28] These souls aspired to something more 'true' or more 'pure' than Pound saw in his contemporary society; but they also acted as surrogates for Pound's own aspirations to render a universal beauty in poetic art. Yet, the use of personae is a further indication of Pound's sense of exile and isolation, as identified by an early critic of his 1909 publication of *Personae of Ezra Pound*, who writes that the collection is 'the battle with the world of a fresh soul who feels himself strong but alone'.[29]

Among the many personae that Pound adopted in his poetry, the troubadour, accepting only the judgment of a deified lady, was one of the earliest and most prominent. In *The Spirit of Romance*, Pound related troubadour love to the realm of the spiritually ascetic in a chapter entitled 'Psychology and Troubadours': 'The "chivalric love," was, as I understand it, an art, that is to say, a religion.'[30] Chivalric love represented a discipline rather than simply a free expression of erotic feeling, and so, like art, was a *re-ligio*, or binding of oneself to a practice or ethic. Moreover, the love-object is so highly symbolized that chivalric love is inevitably practiced from a place of distance or exile, just as one attempts to make contact with the divine. Chivalric love and religion both ordered life, as a general goal, around the attainment of that divine knowledge, be it intellectual, mystical, or erotic. But like many religious practices, especially of the more ascetic sort, the consequence of the troubadour's quest for contact with his love was an inevitable break between himself and the everyday lives of the people around him.

In 'Marvoil' (1909), Pound adopts the persona of the twelfth-century troubadour Arnaut de Mareuil, who 'possessed a Poundian capacity for abuse',[31] hiding the truth of his life and his love. Arnaut travels to Beziers where he initiates a romance with the wife of the Vicomte of Beziers:[32]

> The Vicomte of Beziers's not such a bad lot.
> I made rimes to his lady this three year:
> Vers and canzone, till that damn'd son of Aragon,
> Alfonso[33] the half-bald, took to hanging
> *His* helmet at Beziers. (*P*, 21)

Alfonso arrives and, jealous, conspires to have Arnaut exiled, condemning him to work as a clerk and write poetry for his lost love. The current poem is written as a final witness:

> As for will and testament I leave none,
> Save this: 'Vers and canzone to the Countess of Beziers
> In return for the first kiss she gave me.' (*P*, 22)

In the end, Arnaut hides the poem inside a hole in the wall, perhaps hoping that some sympathetic soul in the future will find it and finally know the 'real' Arnaut.

'Marvoil' places presence and absence in a self-reinforcing relationship. More than half of 'Marvoil' is taken up with Arnaut lamenting the loss of his Countess Beziers, and her absence makes her more real to him. And as each counterpart of the relationship becomes apparent through their exclusion, Arnaut's exile brings him to his 'proper' place as a poet and chivalric lover. The key image in the poem, the hole in the wall, establishes this dialectic between fullness and lack in Arnaut's life after he is sent away, becoming the place for his poetry for some future revelation of who he 'really' is:

> And if when I am dead
> They take the trouble to tear out this wall here,
> They'll know more of Arnaut of Marvoil
> Than half his canzoni say of him. (*P*, 22)

These lines also indicate that Arnaut is doubly exiled inasmuch as his inner life can never be truly communicated to his contemporaries. Furthermore, that Arnaut doubts that he can speak for himself renders all the more poignant that Pound, through the use of this persona, speaks on Arnaut's behalf. Arnaut's silent exile is doubled just as Pound's presence is doubled, being both the writer Pound and mediator of Arnaut. This tactic draws on the book of Jeremiah, in which the prophet is in hiding, so he summons the scribe Baruch to prophesy in his place (Jeremiah 36. 4–10). Baruch writes Jeremiah's words on a scroll and reads them in the temple but, significantly, the words of the prophecy are not related to the biblical reader (vv. 13–15). Jeremiah 36. 4 states only that Baruch wrote 'all the words of the Lord that he had spoken to' Jeremiah, so that the specific message is only related to the audience to which it was intended: the court of King Jehoiakim. Jeremiah is resurrected in his conspicuous absence in the temple, and the description, but not transcription, of his words. Much like the 'vers and canzone' of Arnaut, which are equally absent, the reader must intuit what such words might say. The court officials become frightened and tell Baruch himself to join Jeremiah in hiding: 'Then the officials said to Baruch, "Go and hide, you and Jeremiah, and let no one know where you are"' (Jeremiah 36. 19). The point is that while the scribe can bear a power equal to that of the original word, the officials, startled by the prophecy, are incapable of making a distinction between the prophet and the emissary. That both Baruch and Jeremiah must suffer exile and go into hiding, even though the former is not considered a prophet, but a scribe, confirms that the 'authority of the word does not fade as the scrolls pass from hand to hand'.[34] Indeed, the force of the tradition seems to increaase the further it gets from the source, expanding beyond its specific context to capture in metaphor the meaning of events across generations.

This image of the hole where Arnaut hides his poem bears connotations of unfulfilled desire or want, emphasizing the absence, and the unlikely return, of the Lady in the life of the poet. Robert Casillo states that the ever-deferred consummation of the troubadour's love '*credits* [the Lady] with the highest spiritual and aesthetic powers, and hopes for the ultimate realization of his *investment* of time and emotion'.[35] Casillo, picking up on the language of finance across Pound's work, presents art and love as an alternative system of credit, investment, and return. The longer that Arnaut remains exiled from Beziers, the greater his emotional 'investment' in the Countess Beziers and the greater the 'spiritual and aesthetic' returns. By depositing — to extend Casillo's metaphor — the poem into the hole in the wall, Arnaut expresses the hope for a future, even a future beyond his own lifetime, in which he 'returns' from exile. The image of the hole occurs immediately after Arnaut speaks that he is not in the place where his desire resides:

> And may I come speedily to Beziers
> Whither my desire and my dream have preceded me.
>
> O hole in the wall here! be thou my jongleur (*P*, 22)

The juxtaposition of the two locations allows Pound to stretch Arnaut, figuratively speaking, across southern France, from Arnaut's residence in Avignon to his Lady's in Beziers. Arnaut's 'desire' and 'dream' are in the latter location, whereas 'here' (in Avignon) there resides only the hole, the lack, and the wind, which Pound includes in three separate instances relating to the hole in the wall:

> O hole in the wall here! be thou my jongleur
> As ne'er had I other, and when the wind blows
> [...]
> Wherefore, O hole in the wall here,
> When the wind blows sigh thou for my sorrow
> [...]
> O hole in the wall here, be thou my jongleur,
> And though thou sighest my sorrow in the wind (*P*, 22)

There is a hollowness represented in these lines: the hole in the wall as the space, and the wind as the motion or sound of unfulfilled desire. That Arnaut uses the phrase 'So is my heart hollow' (*P*, 22) raises the stakes, for the heart is a key metaphor in the language of prophecy, as well.

In his analysis of Jeremiah's use of heart-language, Timothy Polk connects the word to the construction of the self in the book of Jeremiah. Jeremiah frequently uses the word 'heart' (לֵב, *lēḇ*) to express the formation of the individual through a telos and orientation, constituted by the individual's actions as expressions of their faith (or lack of faith) in God. Polk describes this heart-language as that 'which in summary fashion characterizes the basic shape and direction of a person's life',[36] but more specifically, the metaphor is 'used in addressing and characterizing people as moral agents responsible for what they make of themselves through their exercise or neglect of the capacities proper to and constitutive of human subjects.'[37] Polk refers to Jeremiah 4. 4, and its image of the uncircumcised heart, to describe how the individual with a particular telos is formed in the book:

> Circumcise yourselves to the Lord,
> remove the foreskins of your hearts,
> O people of Judah and inhabitants of Jerusalem

Jeremiah translates the literal act of circumcision as a practice of cultic purity into a metaphor of emotional fidelity to God. Polk writes: 'The use of "heart" here in 4. 4 focuses attention on the moral agency of human subjects. It is a way of addressing or representing people in their capacity as creatures profoundly responsible for what they do and who they are, and what they make of themselves. This is to bring to the fore yet again the teleological aspect of selfhood.'[38] The directionality of heart-language in Jeremiah is reinforced even further in the image of walking after the imagination of one's own heart:

> At that time they shall call Jerusalem the throne of the Lord; and all the nations shall be gathered unto it, to the name of the Lord, to Jerusalem: neither shall they *walk any more after the imagination of their evil heart.* (Jeremiah 3. 17; emphasis added)[39]

Differing versions of this phrase occur several times in the book of Jeremiah, all with the intent of representing the heart as the essential emotional or religious direction of one's life.

A lack of direction, a wandering reminiscent of the exodus, also serves as an opportunity to right the way and demonstrate God's power or love. Jeremiah 4. 1, which serves as an opening for the circumcised heart of verse 4, contains the lines: 'if you remove your abominations from my presence, | and do not waver', suggesting that Israel lacks determination in its direction toward God. But, as Polk states, vacillation is not an option: 'The verb [תָנוּד, *tānûd*] suggests "wandering" between motion and action, indicating a confusion about one's telos, an indecisiveness which precludes clear action and in which the self thereby forfeits definition and is truncated.'[40] But as this verse only relates to the heart-language three verses later, Polk refers to Jeremiah 5. 21 to emphasize the connection: 'Hear this, O foolish and senseless [וְאֵין לֵב, *vᵉ'êyn lēḇ*, literally, "without heart"] people, | who have eyes, but do not see, | who have ears, but do not hear.' The heart is the locus for the senses of sight and hearing, and the means by which physical perceptions are ordered and directed, thus even connecting it to the intellect and the capacity for judgment. Perception of the physical or external world is possible, but without the heart, a sense of understanding or a perception of the divine, supernatural, or 'true' world is lacking: 'By ignoring the heart and its resident powers, the self remains amorphous, undirected and in danger of dissolution.'[41] Likewise, Arnaut's lament about the heart is directly connected to its status as medium between the rational senses and the beauty of the Countess:

For even as thou art hollow before I fill thee with this parchment,
So is my heart hollow when she filleth not mine eyes,
And so were my mind hollow, did she not fill utterly my thought. (*P*, 22)

Pound, like Jeremiah, connects the image of the heart to the senses and perceptions insofar as the hollow mind is a consequence of the hollow heart. But Pound qualifies Arnaut's description of his heart by stating that the feeling of hollowness is 'before I fill thee with this parchment'. In *Monoplan*, Marinetti externalizes his 'cœur-moteur' (*MP*, 155), which guides the Pilot at a point that his will might fail, and likewise Arnaut's externalization of his heart into the hole in the wall re-establishes that telos for personhood. Pound employs a similar comparison a second time at the end of the poem when comparing the hole in the wall to the heart: 'Keep yet my secret in thy breast here; | Even as I keep her image in my heart here.' (*P*, 23). By placing the parchment into the hole for a future reader, Arnaut's telos is re-established, his desire for the Countess is given a direction as a form of redemption that he himself will not live to see. In this way, art and poetry inscribe and justify his exile into a lasting tradition. This commitment to her, which he consecrates in the act of placing the poetry into the hole, maintains his identity and the direction of his life and saves him from the amorphous 'elsewhere' of his life as a clerk in Avignon.

Yet Pound concludes the poem with an enigmatic phrase in Latin: '*Mihi pergamen deest*' (*P*, 23), translated as 'I do not have the parchment'. If this line is Pound speaking (it is italicized in the text, unlike every other line in the poem), then it suggests that Pound himself has yet to find his own 'Countess'. He certainly has beauty in his mind as his telos, but that does not necessarily mean that he has discovered *his* particular aesthetic in the way that Arnaut or the other troubadours may have found theirs. The personae allow Pound to explore tendencies and devotions that are distinct from the modern world, but, as images of the past, they cannot provide a full framework for existing in the present moment. Pound feels like an exile in the world, but he is not necessarily fully aligned with his personae. The personae are models of prophetic exile insofar as they cling to a vital ideal that sets them apart from their world, but the impetus or goal for that vital ideal is, for Pound, not entirely relevant to his own world. Pound's sense of exile is most apparent when he reflects on his contemporary society of increasing individualism, constantly longing for kindred souls which were almost always lacking in the world around him, and which he occasionally finds in his avant-garde movements. In fact, one reason he adopted his personae was to commune with long-dead poets that he felt he had more in common with than his contemporaries. 'In Durance', an early poem from the 1909 publication of *Personae*, uses the term 'soul-kin' to describe those who 'feel | And have some breath for beauty and the arts' (*P*, 20). The 'breath for beauty and the arts' anticipates Pound's self-identification with the arts several years later in 'From Chebar', but 'In Durance' stresses how the poet's alignment with the tradition marginalizes him in contemporary society. The poem begins with a lament for the lack of these kindred spirits:

> I am homesick after mine own kind,
> Oh I know that there are folk about me, friendly faces,
> But I am homesick after mine own kind. (*P*, 19–20)

The poem was written in 1907, when Pound was still resident in America, a place filled with 'friendly faces'. As we can perhaps surmise from Pound's famous short poem, 'In a Station of the Metro', which characterizes faces as 'apparitions' (*P*, 111), 'friendly faces' are in Pound's view transient, almost ghostlike. Looked at more cynically, they might even be called shallow or dishonest. They lack the credibility of a Dante, Whitman, or Jeremiah, who read their worlds and their histories through the lens of a theological or aesthetic ideal.

'In Durance', to the extent that it locates any 'place' in which the poet's home might be, locates the poet's own heart as the place in which the poet's 'soul-kin' reside:

> But reach me not and all my life's become
> One flame, that reaches not beyond
> My heart's own hearth,
> Or hides among the ashes there for thee.
> 'Thee'? Oh, 'Thee' is who cometh first
> Out of mine own soul-kin (*P*, 20)

Once again, as in 'Marvoil', Pound locates the vital drive within the heart, but with a greater isolation insofar as it 'reaches not beyond | my heart's own hearth'. However, the 'Thee', one of the 'soul-kin', connects with Pound in a way that he could not with those around him. Pound moves on from the heart to the soul, but the intention seems the same: to provide a telos for the individual based on a tradition that has now been lost: 'Well then, so call they, the swirlers out of the mist of my soul, | They that come mewards, bearing old magic' (*P*, 20). Just as the flame hides in the ashes of his heart, the 'soul-kin' arise from 'the mist of my soul' while simultaneously coming 'mewards', as if from outside himself. Pound keeps these 'soul-kin' within himself, but they are not entirely of himself. Like the personae, they are, in a sense, a practical tool for gaining a particular perspective on the world, without requiring Pound to fully commit or identify with them, dividing and destabilizing the self in its modern, autonomous form. Nonetheless, they are figures of the past coming 'mewards, bearing old magic', allowing the poet to approach reality in a new manner. But it is a temporary magic, ecstatically experienced:

> And yet my soul sings 'Up!' and we are one.
> Yea thou, and Thou, and THOU, and all my kin
> To whom my breast and arms are ever warm (*P*, 21)

And yet, like 'Marvoil' an aspect of the kin will remain hidden until discovered at the right moment, by the right people:

> My fellows, aye I know the glory
> Of th' unbounded ones, but ye, that hide
> As I hide most the while (*P*, 20)

The glory, normally hidden away, cannot be expressed by the poet except in the language provided by the 'soul-kin'. But that language is necessarily elusive, concealed, ripening from its conception in the past. Pound states in 'In Durance' that 'Beauty is most that, a "calling to the soul"' (*P*, 20), but that call, like a prophetic call, elicits an overall direction for the life of the poet, and ultimately leaves him alone in the world. Here, Pound and Apollinaire dwell on the experience in a similar manner: the call resolves itself upon the poet in the uniqueness of their individuality as modern subjects, and draws them out of that individuality, fracturing it or aligning it with proper surrogates, but failing to truly dissolve it.

Rascality and Wangle

Two aspects of Pound, as a poet in the modern world, can be re-iterated: he presents himself as the inheritor of a tradition in which society and history are evaluated through aesthetic criteria — the tragic, the dramatic, the beautiful — that were once the purview of religion; and as an inheritor of this tradition, which is only revealed through a particular discipline, he is inevitably isolated from society. But because the poet sets aside his own personality to speak on behalf of the tradition, he garners a credibility that allows him to judge his contemporary world from the place of exile. Pound's personae allowed him to view the world through the eyes of one whose active life was based on the ideal of beauty that he felt was lacking in the contemporary world. In this respect, Weber has a suggestive note on court romance in his own discussion of religion and the rejection of the world, writing that 'The conception of the "lady" was constituted *solely and precisely by her judging function*.'[42] The poet, devoting himself entirely to the transcendent figure of the lady, does not judge on his behalf, but on hers or, more precisely, on behalf of the tradition. Making specific reference to troubadours, Weber writes furthermore that, 'Therewith began the "probation" of the man, *not before his equals* but in the face of the erotic interest of the "lady".'[43] In just this way do prophets acquire their authority to judge the world by withdrawing their interest in the 'worldly'. It is not the prophet *per se* who is judging the world, but the prophet in the guise of the word of God. But the prophetic attitude, as Pound understood it, was not a democratic viewpoint, and it judged the world based upon an ideal that was essentially inaccessible to the general public.

In 1912, Pound travelled to France where he met the poets around the Unanimist group as well as the journal *Mercure de France*, and he felt that they were ahead of the English in waging a war 'against the reign of general stupidity'.[44] And the following year, he wrote that English poetry was essentially a history of English poets learning their craft from the French.[45] He felt that the Unanimists were at the cutting edge of literature, not just in France but potentially in all of Europe. However, the most important continental avant-gardist to whom Pound responded was Marinetti, who first began giving lectures on Futurism in London from 1910.[46] In fact, as Lawrence Rainey relates, on 19 March 1912, the evening of a major lecture on Futurism by Marinetti in London, Pound gave his own lecture on Provençal poetry.[47] His lecture was intended for a small, erudite, and relatively wealthy audience. Marinetti, on the other hand, gave his lecture in a large auditorium, tickets were cheaply priced, and the lecture was widely advertised. The following day, Marinetti's lecture was prominently covered in the London press, whereas Pound's lecture received no mention. It was, in part, a response to Marinetti's ability to capture a wide audience that informed, negatively in some cases, Pound's own avant-garde engagement with the poets of Imagism, F. S. Flint (1885–1960), H. D. (1886–1961), and Richard Aldington (1892–1962). As Somigli explains, Pound couldn't simply ignore the mass marketing techniques Marinetti used, as it became a force for cultural legitimation whether he liked it or not, but he did attempt an

> ultimately unsuccessful *mediation* between high and low culture, utilizing select techniques of publicity of mass culture to carve a position and an audience for his poetic project *without simultaneously redrawing the boundary* between high and low culture or questioning the autonomous status of the aesthetic.[48]

The avant-garde collective, as Pound understood it, is best expressed in his relationship to Imagism,[49] which was not described as a 'movement' but a 'school': 'something more informal, more casual, more individualistic, the fortuitous outcome of "two or three young men agree[ing], more or less, to call certain things good".'[50] Rather than the meetings, collective manifestos, and sense that the movement would penetrate every aspect of daily life, Imagism was conservative by comparison. However, this casual language obscures Pound's prominent role in deciding what 'certain things' were allowed to be called 'good'. When the American poet, Amy Lowell (1874–1925), suggested that decisions in the group be made democratically, Pound balked: 'He wasn't going to waste his time, he told her, pretending that "a certain number of people" were his "critical and creative equals". That would only lead to "dilution" of the essential principles, "floppy degeneration", the end of *Imagisme*.'[51] If Pound saw himself as a prophet, it was as a prophet against society, one who was sceptical of the more overtly collective ethos expressed by movements such as Futurism. Pound 'would speak of the unique *virtu* of the serious artist. Believing that "the life of the race is concentrated in a few individuals", those rare truly original makers of reality, he was [...] opposed [...] to the democratic idea which would subject individual genius to a species of mob-rule.'[52] Pound believed that the aesthetic principles he promoted were accessible only to a very few — anybody else was derided as a fraud. The approach to the world, judging it and its people based on a narrow and inaccessible ideal, will be examined in two poems: 'And Thus in Nineveh', and a brief selection from *Hugh Selwyn Mauberley*.

Like 'From Chebar', 'And Thus in Nineveh' alludes to the prophet separated from his home and raises the question of whether or not the public is discerning enough to understand true poetry or prophecy. First published in 1909 in *Personae*, the title recalls the book of Jonah, where the Bible relates one of the rare instances that the prophet's message to repent is treated seriously by his public. After Jonah is sent by God to the Assyrian capital of Nineveh to pronounce doom upon it, his prophecy — in a notable departure from much prophetic literature — is enthusiastically heeded: 'Jonah began to go into the city, going a day's walk. And he cried out, "Forty days more, and Nineveh shall be overthrown!" And the people of Nineveh believed God; they proclaimed a fast, and everyone, great and small, put on sackcloth' (Jon. 3. 4–5). Studies of Jonah have noted that it can be read as a satire on false-prophecy,[53] and it seems clear that Pound was sensitive to that reading. 'And Thus in Nineveh' mocks the way in which a poet is regarded as exceptional by the public when, indeed, so many poets are entirely conventional. Pound begins his poem by portraying the poet as an honoured individual:

> Aye! I am a poet and upon my tomb
> Shall maidens scatter rose leaves
> And men myrtles, ere the night
> Slays day with her dark sword. (*P*, 23)

The poem is 'a fanciful reconstruction of the obsequies accorded to poets in ancient Nineveh',[54] and indeed, this is hardly the scorned poet — genius of the beautiful, spurned by the public that ignores or misunderstands him — prevalent in Pound's work. The reader who is aware of the biblical tradition would, like Jonah (4. 2), probably expect Nineveh to disregard his prophecy of doom and carry on in its sinful ways. While the speaker in 'And Thus in Nineveh' is likewise an honoured figure within the city, his attitude towards the public is much more ambiguous precisely because he places himself in a tradition of poetry that the public does not understand, unlike the public in Jonah, which clearly understands what the prophet is attempting to convey. He is compelled to compare himself with the greatest of that tradition, and so is subject to bouts of self-effacement and self-criticism, for shortly after describing his own honour, he states:

> And many a one hath sung his songs
> More craftily, more subtle-souled than I;
> And many a one now doth surpass
> My wave-worn beauty with his wind of flowers (*P*, 23)

Although his tomb is swiftly praised ('ere the night | Slays day'), the poet is unsure that he is doing justice to his predecessors or that there are no contemporaries greater than himself. A parallel to the tomb imagery in 'And Thus in Nineveh' occurred about five years later in 'Salutation the Third' (1914), a poem Pound published in the Vorticist journal *Blast*:

> Perhaps you will have the pleasure of defiling my pauper's grave;
> I wish you joy, I proffer you all my assistance.
> It has been your habit for long
> to do away with good writers,
> You either drive them mad, or else you blink at their suicides (*P*, 75)

Both poems are clearly satirical takes on the reception of the poet by a particular public. The irony occurs in how each poet is honoured in a way not necessarily befitting their place, so each poem throws into question the judgment of the public. The 'good writers' of 'Salutation the Third' will have their poor graves defiled, while in 'And Thus in Nineveh', the poet whose grave is treated with respect is, at least with respect to the poetic tradition, not clearly presented as the most 'subtle-souled'. Pound saw himself as the condemned poet whose grave was defiled by mediocre critics in 'Salutation the Third'. But it does not necessarily follow from there that the crowds who honour the grave of the speaker in 'And Thus in Nineveh' are any more perceptive about good poetry. Like the visionary audience inside Mount Etna in Marinetti's *Monoplan*, who seem to cheer and applaud at any spectacle, the people of Nineveh demonstrate an enthusiasm that lacks any critical discrimination.

Pound makes a distinction here between custom and tradition, the former being the public treatment of poets. And he strikes a tone of ambivalence about custom, suggesting that he must tolerate it regardless:

> 'Lo! this thing is not mine
> Nor thine to hinder,
> For the custom is full old['] (*P*, 23)

The custom is a kind of critical consensus, neither bad nor good, and has the benefit of stabilizing tradition but sometimes at the cost of rendering it more or less neutral. On the other hand, Pound's tradition, in its full force, freed from the critical consensus, exists in *living tension* with the world around it. This 'consecration' of custom safely tucks the great poets away where they will not disturb the society itself:

> And here in Nineveh have I beheld
> Many a singer pass and take his place
> In those dim halls where no man troubleth
> His sleep or song. (*P*, 23)

Nineveh is obsequious, ready to praise everyone who 'hath sung his songs'. The problem, as Pound understands it, is that every poet is rendered as good as the last or as good as the next, in a 'custom' that levels the strengths and weaknesses of each. Every time a poet is consecrated in the halls of Nineveh, the consecration itself means increasingly less, it is left to this poet himself to point out that the poets who have come before were superior to him. He ends by claiming:

> It is not, Raana,[55] that my song rings highest
> Or more sweet in tone than any, but that I
> Am here a Poet, that doth drink of life
> As lesser men drink of wine. (*P*, 23)

Life, for this poet, is not about rendering inert the tradition through an uncritical praise of every singer who passes through society, but about resurrecting a vibrant, and even dangerous, tradition. This reformulation of traditions requires the poet, like much avant-garde art, to collapse the distinction between art and life somewhat, to be a poet that has lived life in accordance with his or her art. This effort to blur the distinction between art and life might explain some of the didactic and discursive nature of Pound's early poetry, but it also draws art out of the social world, and into the poet as an individual increasingly estranged from his time.

Therefore, the poet of 'And Thus in Nineveh' recalls Jonah's ambivalence about being so easily accepted by the people of Nineveh: 'But this was very displeasing to

Jonah, and he became angry. He prayed to the Lord and said, "O Lord! Is this not what I said in my own country?" That is why I fled to Tarshish at the beginning; for I knew that you are a gracious God and merciful, slow to anger, and abounding in steadfast love, and ready to relent from punishing' (Jonah 4. 1–2). Jonah's attempt to flee from his call is based on the possibility of the repentance of the people of Nineveh. In stating, 'for I knew that you are a gracious God', Jonah is effectively saying, 'I knew that if Nineveh repented, then you would relent in your anger.' But it is not immediately clear why that would have prompted Jonah's flight, or his anger at being heeded by Nineveh. A note of satire can be detected here: on the one hand, Israelite prophets are rarely heeded by their public 'in [their] own country'; on the other hand, Nineveh — a pagan nation — has proven itself more faithful to God than Israel. The criticism points in two directions: towards the prophet who assumes his rejection, and the unfaithful nation. Jonah, from his place of exile, has criticized Israel by prophesying to another nation.

Given Pound's interest in satire, he was surely sensitive to the same elements of the book of Jonah.[56] John C. Holbert points out that in Hebrew, Jonah son of Amittai, can be translated as 'dove, son of faithfulness',[57] a name that contrasts with Jonah's disobedience as well as his churlish attitude. In contrast, the extent to which the king of Nineveh repents after hearing Jonah's pronouncement of doom is absurd, going so far as to instruct the animals to participate in the ritual: 'By the decree of the king and his nobles: No human being or animal, no herd or flock, shall taste anything. They shall not feed, nor shall they drink water. Human beings and animals shall be covered with sackcloth, and they shall cry mightily to God. All shall turn from their evil ways and from the violence that is in their hands' (Jonah 3. 7–8). It is not clear what evils the livestock might have committed so that they must repent, but the exaggeration of repentance is apparent. Furthermore, Jonah's anger when Nineveh is spared from destruction seems to arise partly from the failure of God and Nineveh to adhere to the formula for biblical prophecy — the prophet is ignored, the people are punished — suggesting that the author of the book was aware of the literary conventions of prophetic histories. But through the satiric images of Jonah's adventure, the author raises serious critiques of the entire institution of prophecy.[58] Holbert argues that the book is meant to attack the 'prophetic hypocrisy' of those who 'claim great insight and unique callings, but who ultimately are found empty of substance, save their real anger at those who do not agree with them'.[59] However, this view assumes that Jonah's behaviour was grounded in a lack of faith, when it was, instead, his faithfulness taken to a ridiculous conclusion. Jonah's rather uncharacteristic behaviour, but all-too-characteristic belief, has presented him as an 'anti-hero',[60] 'satirized for behavior thought to be unbecoming to a prophet'.[61]

Writing to his father in 1926, Pound comments upon the heavily satirical style of much of his poetry. In his letter, he writes 'Satire, my dear Homer, [...] SATIRE!!! Wotcher mean by satire?!? [...] what I am trying to give is the STATE of rascality and wangle.'[62] The emphasis on the state of things describes a key element in the aspect of Pound's satire and, more broadly, satire as a literary form. Although

Pound, as we will see, is not shy about forming his attack around specific *kinds* of individuals, these individuals are symptomatic of more general corruptions of society. Robert Elliott explains satire's widening attack on a specific instance of injustice to a generalized lament of satire as a metonymic transition from the part to the whole: 'The satirist *usually claims* that he does not attack institutions; he attacks perversions of institutions.'[63] But 'an attack by a powerful satirist on a local phenomenon seems to be capable of indefinite extension in the reader's mind into an attack on the whole structure of which that phenomenon is a part.'[64] Pound's attacks on individuals — whether critics, the bourgeoisie, or aesthetes such as himself — are not simply a condemnation of a 'few bad apples', but a measure of the wider 'STATE of rascality and wangle'.

Pound's most important and sustained satire of his London years is certainly *Hugh Selwyn Mauberley* (1920), a sequence of eighteen poems divided into two sections. The first section characterizes Pound's relationships in London and his understanding of how English culture found itself in such a degenerate state; the second section takes the perspective of Mauberley, a failed poet and aesthete who tries to live life according to his ideals, but who ultimately ends in obscurity. In perhaps the most satiric elements of the first section, Pound introduces a number of characters, the Jewish Brennbaum, the acquisitive Mr Nixon, and the aristocratic Lady Valentine, who are specific instances of a generalized malaise in British society at the end of World War I. Section VIII, 'Brennbaum', presenting a dandyish Jewish gentleman,[65] reflects on the experience of exile and explicitly compares it to religious tradition. Brennbaum is portrayed as distinct from the modern world around him in both his dress and physical features:

> The sky-like limpid eyes,
> The circular infant's face,
> The stiffness from spats to collar (*P*, 191)

Brennbaum is a true aesthete, not entirely at odds with Pound's view, seeing the world in its wealth of beauty, but unlike Pound, Brennbaum is unwilling and unable to 'scourge' the world with that beauty. Instead, he seems to use beauty to obscure his identity, leading the reader to suspect anti-Semitic attitudes of the assimilated Jew living in a state of disguise or inauthenticity:

> The heavy memories of Horeb, Sinai and the forty years,
> Showed only when the daylight fell
> Level across the face
> Of Brennbaum 'The Impeccable.' (*P*, 191)

The tragedy of Brennbaum is the individual who 'erases all his inherited traditions in the interests of elegant conformity and acceptance'.[66] Beauty, in this case, is little more than a superficial and decadent aestheticism that masks what cannot, in the end, be truly obscured. It is not the same beauty that Pound attempts to summon in poems such as 'From Chebar' or 'Marvoil'. It is not the beauty of the tradition, but beauty as an escape from tradition. In the end, Pound leaves us with this brief portrait of Brennbaum as someone with little more than the accoutrements of a life lived according to aesthetic values. It's a picture with equal measures of sympathy and contempt.

Mr Nixon, the central figure of section IX, is a portrait of the writer cynically catering to the world of reviewers. Nixon gives the young Pound the advice to 'Consider | Carefully the reviewer' (*P*, 191). This certainly contrasts with Pound's estimation of reviewers in his *Blast* poems, as demonstrated above in 'Salutation the Third'. Nixon's concern is in money and fame, not the production of and engagement with beauty, much less of using art to influence the world in a moral or social way. Nixon's entire artistic practice was informed by his experience of living in poverty, and his effort to escape his penury:

> [']I was as poor as you are;
> When I began I got, of course,
> Advance on royalties, fifty at first,' said Mr Nixon,
> 'Follow me, and take a column,
> Even if you have to work free.
>
> Butter reviewers. From fifty to three hundred
> I rose in eighteen months['] (*P*, 191)

Nixon seems to believe that the poet's real problem is a lack of money, whereas Pound assumes poverty to be a basic condition, if not a form of legitimacy, for the poet. Rather than the search for a relevant aesthetic model for modern art or the ability to live by an ideal of beauty, Nixon searches for notability. Pound was certainly not unfamiliar with the problem of making a living, but took it as a central problem that poetry needed to tackle — that is, asking why poets must live a life of penury and infamy. Eventually, Mr Nixon becomes very candid and effectively renounces the entire literary field:

> [']The tip's a good one, as for literature
> It gives no man a sinecure.
>
> And no one knows, at sight, a masterpiece.
> And give up verse, my boy,
> There's nothing in it.' (*P*, 192)

The final line above is repeated once more at the end of the poem. With echoes of 'And Thus in Nineveh', Nixon has no more regard for reviewers than does Pound — both see reviewers as philistines. Of course, Nixon's understanding of how to identify great art is just as blinkered as the reviewers he mocks: he thinks artistic value is essentially reducible to the amount of money that it brings in, which is another way of denying that art has any inherent value at all. His advice is to 'Butter reviewers', meaning to coddle them, and states that he, 'never mentioned a man but with the view | Of selling my own works' (*P*, 192). Nixon even betrays his own ignorance because he states that, 'no one knows, at sight, a masterpiece', which treats the identification of masterpieces as one of mere vision. By locating the judgment of the masterpiece in sight alone, rather than in the emotions, the intellect, or moral sensibility, Nixon becomes a satire on a social response to art that only values it to the extent that it is a commodity.

Lady Valentine makes her appearance in section XII, which satirizes the salon culture of Edwardian London. There is a touch of T. S. Eliot's Prufrock in this poem, a disjointed hero, out of place in the bourgeois culture that he finds himself in. The speaker is in a well-heeled milieu, yet unsure of his place there:

> [...] In the stuffed-satin drawing-room
> I await The Lady Valentine's commands,
>
> Knowing my coat has never been
> Of precisely the fashion
> To stimulate, in her,
> A durable passion (*P*, 193)

Lady Valentine, also a poet, can be commended for her disinterest in literature for economic gain. But her literary pursuits are viewed by Pound as a cynicism of another kind, interested as she is in garnering a kind of 'cultural capital' that is not immediately tied to her economic and class position. The speaker, accordingly, refers to Lady Valentine's 'vocation' as:

> Poetry, her border of ideas,
> The edge, uncertain, but a means of blending
> With other strata
> Where the lower and higher have ending (*P*, 194)

The reference to 'the lower and higher' is ambiguous, likely referring to the class structure of Edwardian London. Lady Valentine is certainly from aristocratic circles, but poetry is a 'means of blending' with other social classes, providing a false form of social mobility, just as long as such classes remain where they are. For these other classes 'the lower and higher have ending', and Lady Valentine has no particular interest in troubling this system if for no other reason than it would make her mobility meaningless. On the other hand, the 'other strata' may be associated with elite and popular aesthetic forms, and poetry is also said to be, 'A hook to catch the Lady Jane's attention, | A modulation toward the theatre' (*P*, 194). Poetry is used to make Lady Valentine 'of note' to other members of her class, but it also allows her to extend a kind of judgment toward theatre, a more typically popular form of artistic activity. On the other hand, Lady Valentine keeps herself separated from and above those same classes and in this way, poetry becomes a defence against the threat of the 'popular' culture. 'Also, in the case of revolution, | A possible friend and comforter' (*P*, 194). It's a strange use of poetry and not in agreement with Pound's view of beauty as a 'scourge'.

In these three brief portraits, what Pound is not, in the end, so much satirizing Lady Valentine or Mr Nixon or Brennbaum as he is lamenting the culture of Edwardian London, which supports the mediocre and cynical. The ignorance of critics, the avarice of journalists, and the grandstanding of aristocrats are only specific manifestations of the degeneration of aesthetics itself. *Mauberley* is then a poem about a society that has lost its impulse for living by artistic values: the values of beauty, of the sublime, of the tragic. As in 'And Thus in Nineveh', the entire culture has suffocated true beauty, and the poet is praised, but cynically, superficially, hypocritically, or ignorantly. The contradiction, however, is that Pound wishes poetry to be socially effective while acknowledging that there is no formula for such work that the public could automatically respond to. For Pound, living according to aesthetic values represented the possibility for a renaissance in English art and culture to which he felt himself, despite all obstacles, chosen to show the way. Yet, *Mauberley* represents not a proclamation of hope, but the ultimate, and perhaps inevitable, failure of the prophet to turn his people away from the path of decline. A tradition of beauty — from the troubadours to Whitman — is summoned up to declare what the society has lost, but the poet becomes lost with it. *Mauberley* has frequently been thought of as Pound's farewell letter to London: about six months after its publication, Pound moved to Paris, leaving London for good.

Notes to Chapter 3

1. Quoted in Martz, *Many Gods*, p. 44.
2. Ibid., pp. 20–21.
3. Ibid., pp. 135–36.
4. Ibid., p. 3.
5. Ibid., p. 45.
6. Ibid., p. 20.
7. Ibid., p. 7.
8. Reed Way Dasenbrock, *The Literary Vorticism of Ezra Pound & Wyndham Lewis: Towards a Condition of Painting* (Baltimore, MD: Johns Hopkins University Press, 1985), p. 17.
9. Dasenbrock stresses that Vorticism was not detached from modernity, even though it often affected a certain aloofness toward the innovations that were occurring in Continental Europe: 'But it is important to understand that detachment for the Vorticists is not a synonym for indifference: to be in the still point [of the cultural vortex] is still to be in the world, engaged in analytical observation of it' (Ibid., p. 59).
10. John J. Espey, *Ezra Pound's 'Mauberley': A Study in Composition* (London: Faber and Faber, 1955), p. 15.
11. Puchner, *Poetry of the Revolution*, p. 127.
12. Marx, 'The 20th Century: Century of the Arrière-Gardes?', p. 68.
13. Joseph Blenkinsopp, *A History of Prophecy in Israel* (Louisville, KY: Westminster John Knox Press, 1996), p. 137.
14. Hugh Witemeyer, 'Early Poetry, 1908–1920', in *The Cambridge Companion to Ezra Pound*, ed. by Ira B. Nadel (Cambridge: Cambridge University Press, 1999), pp. 43–58 (p. 43); emphasis added.
15. Ezra Pound, *Selected Prose, 1909–1965*, ed. by William Cookson (London: Faber and Faber, 1973), p. 115.
16. In a poem entitled 'A Pact' (1913), Pound writes of Whitman, 'I have detested you long enough' (*P*, 90).
17. Pound, *Selected Prose*, p. 115.
18. Ibid., pp. 115–16.
19. Ibid., p. 116.
20. I refer here to the King James translation of שׁוֹט, *šôt*, 'scourge', due to the relation to Pound's vocabulary, rather than the NRSV, which translates it as 'whip'.
21. Pound, *Selected Prose*, p. 116.
22. Charles B. Willard, 'Ezra Pound's Appraisal of Walt Whitman', *Modern Language Notes*, 72.1 (January 1957), 19–26 (pp. 22–23).
23. Ezra Pound, *The Spirit of Romance* (London: Peter Owen, 1952), p. 168.
24. Martz, *Many Gods*, p. 7.

25. Pound, *Selected Prose*, p. 47.
26. The name of the locale to which the Israelite exiles were assigned in Babylon. See Walther Zimmerli, *Ezekiel 1: A Commentary on the Book of the Prophet Ezekiel, Chapters 1–24*, trans. by Ronald E. Clements (Philadelphia, PA: Fortress Press, 1979), p. 139.
27. Witemeyer, 'Early Poetry', p. 44.
28. Ibid.
29. Quoted in A. David Moody, *Ezra Pound: Poet, A Portrait of the Man and his Work*, I: *The Young Genius, 1885–1920* (Oxford: Oxford University Press, 2007), p. 92.
30. Pound, *Spirit of Romance*, p. 87.
31. K. K. Ruthven, *A Guide to Ezra Pound's 'Personæ' (1926)* (Berkeley: University of California, 1969), p. 169.
32. Ruthven identifies the Vicomte as Roger II Taillefer, whose wife was Azalais de Toulouse (ibid.).
33. Pound mistakenly refers to Alfonso IV of Aragon, but Ruthven points out that Arnaut de Mareuil was actually acquainted with Alfonso II (ibid., p. 170).
34. Pamela J. Scalise, 'Scrolling through Jeremiah: Written Documents as a Reader's Guide to the Book of Jeremiah', *Review and Expositor*, 101 (Spring 2004), 201–25 (p. 215).
35. Robert Casillo, 'Troubadour Love and Usury in Ezra Pound's Writings', *Texas Studies in Language and Literature*, 21.2 (Summer 1985), 125–53 (p. 131).
36. Timothy Polk, *The Prophetic Persona: Jeremiah and the Language of the Self* (Sheffield: JSOT Press, 1984), p. 26.
37. Ibid., p. 49.
38. Ibid., p. 43.
39. The King James translation is used here because the Hebrew לבם, *libām*, 'their heart' is most commonly translated as 'heart' in this verse. The NRSV has translated it as 'will', which, while retaining the metaphorical meaning, loses the common biblical relationship between the physical and mental.
40. Polk, *Prophetic Persona*, p. 39.
41. Ibid., p. 49.
42. Weber, *From Max Weber*, p. 346; emphasis added.
43. Ibid; emphasis added.
44. Moody, *Ezra Pound: Poet*, p. 205.
45. Bohn, *Apollinaire and the International Avant-Garde*, p. 28.
46. Lawrence Rainey, *Institutions of Modernism: Literary Elites and Public Culture* (New Haven, CT: Yale University Press, 1998), p. 13.
47. Ibid., p. 14.
48. Somigli, *Legitimizing the Artist*, p. 209.
49. Pound preferred the French rendering of the term, 'Imagisme' and 'Imagistes', to maintain the connection with the avant-garde groups he had encountered in Paris in 1912 and 1913, but as soon as he parted ways with the Imagists, they reverted the name to the English rendering.
50. Quoted in Rainey, *Institutions*, p. 30.
51. Moody, *Ezra Pound: Poet*, p. 224.
52. Ibid., p. 220.
53. See John C. Holbert, ' "Deliverance Belongs to Yahweh!": Satire in the Book of Jonah', *Journal for the Study of the Old Testament*, 21 (1981), 59–81; David Marcus, *From Balaam to Jonah: Antiprophetic Satire in the Hebrew Bible* (Atlanta, GA: Scholars Press, 1995).
54. Ruthven, *Guide*, p. 37.
55. Ruthven suggests that this name might refer to a Norse sea goddess, or perhaps a descendant of the biblical Noah (*Guide*, p. 37). Ultimately, the reference may simply be too obscure to precisely identify and is possibly inserted by Pound to allude to pagan worship.
56. In fact, this characterization of Jonah goes back some time, and Holbert points out that Thomas Paine (1737–1809) wrote in *The Age of Reason* (1794) that Jonah was intended as a satire. (Holbert, 'Deliverance', p. 76, n. 7)
57. Ibid., p. 63. However, Blenkinsopp regards this translation as a stretch (*History of Prophecy*, p. 241).

58. Consequently, Jonah is generally regarded as a work of late prophetic literature, written by an author knowledgeable of the history and conventions of the genre (see Blenkinsopp, *History of Prophecy*, p. 241).

59. Holbert, 'Deliverance', p. 75.

60. Marcus, *From Balaam*, p. 96.

61. Ibid., p. 158.

62. Quoted in Martz, *Many Gods*, p. 18.

63. Robert Elliott, *The Power of Satire: Magic, Ritual, Art* (Princeton, NJ: Princeton University Press, 1960), p. 271; emphasis added.

64. Ibid.

65. Brennbaum was possibly based on the writer Max Beerbohm (1872–1956), an acquaintance of Pound's whom the latter mistook as Jewish (Ruthven, *Guide*, p. 138).

66. Espey, *'Mauberley'*, p. 15.

PART II

❖

Apocalypse

CHAPTER 4

❖

The Late Arrivals

The following three chapters will explore what David G. Bromley refers to as the 'culture work' of apocalyptic thought and writing. So far, much to the chagrin of innumerable preachers of the new age, and much to the relief of everyone else, the apocalypse still has yet to manifest. In the absence of the fateful event, the new creation is conceived and experienced by apocalyptic groups through culture work, which 'centers on symbolically recasting relationships of time, space, and logic between the transcendent realm and the phenomenal world, primarily through reconstructing sacred texts and narratives. Organizing for the apocalypse calls for de-structuring and separation, enhanced charismatic claims, and extensive dramatization and ritualization of group life.'[1] For Apollinaire, the apocalyptic grouping is variously constituted as his colleagues in the avant-garde, the diverse European cities and countries, and the soldiers he fought with in World War I — all of whose figurations are influenced by his sense of place in the artistic communities of Paris, his feelings of dislocation in France or Europe, and his self-conception as a poet of the modern world. Driven by that tension between alienation and intimacy, Apollinaire is always asking fundamental questions about society and identity within this dynamic moment: What is the nature of community in a future that cannot be known? Are there intimations of this future community in present circumstances? Is the poet's relationship with contemporary society necessarily antagonistic? Can a future that is radically different to the present be communicated to contemporary society? Bromley's description of apocalyptic groups demonstrates similarities with the avant-gardes that Apollinaire frequented, in that they collectivize, and thereby invert, the experience of social liminality, and justify the sensation of existing at the margins of a normative community. Bromley writes that 'apocalyptic organization segregates itself from conventional society. It is a profoundly antinomian form.'[2] These groups actively resist the institutions and ethics that structure day-to-day life for the majority of the public in order to 'create their own space organized as part of the new order.'[3] This new era would succeed the end of the former era, and Bromley describes this attitude toward apocalyptic destruction as 'a cataclysm with meaning, one that has as its final purpose not destruction but creation.'[4]

The Unanimous Life

Though it was largely lost in the shadow of its successors, one of the early avant-garde movements to which Apollinaire attached himself was Jules Romains's (1885–1972) Unanimism, which took the idea of the collective as the basis for its aesthetic outlook. Romains, like Apollinaire, was amenable to the bohemian lifestyle of the avant-garde and sympathetic to the group of poets known as the Abbaye de Créteil. Créteil, situated on an old estate near Paris, was a utopian project, 'an experiment in communal living'[5] and 'strongly influenced by democratic and socialist ideology'.[6] However, urban life played an even larger role for Romains, who conceived the city as a singular living organism. Denis Boak describes Romains's epiphany of Unanimism during

> one evening in October, 1903 [...] walking up the crowded Rue d'Amsterdam, Romains had the sudden vision that the whole city, shops, passersby, cabs, formed a vast unity, with its own collective consciousness, to which he himself had intuitive access.[7]

Romains's theory presented an optimistic vision of the ways that individuals, as a part of crowd or group, intuit the behaviours and thoughts of the other individuals of the group. Whereas earlier social scientists like Gustave Le Bon saw individuals reduced to primitive and base instincts in the crowd, Romains saw a heightened capacity for cooperation and sensibility. For example, in an early, brief piece of fiction entitled *Le Rassemblement* (1905), Romains describes the spontaneous birth and slow death of a crowd that meets on the street. The novelty of this story lies in its perspective, taking the crowd as its single protagonist: 'a group, seen, say, from above — and Romains adopts a kind of bird's-eye perspective — might well form, move about, and disperse in precisely the way described.'[8]

Unanimism also attempted to replace the loss of religious experience in modernity, asserting the value of collective ecstasy, and growing, as Boak states, 'directly out of Romains's religious crisis in his teens, and in essence provided a defence against metaphysical solitude, even a substitute religion.'[9] Advocating not so much a series of aesthetic techniques as an overall approach to and outlook on life, Romains saw the modern world as containing 'vast collective sentiments, which created a flux of uncanny physical and spiritual relationships voiding classic concepts of space and time'.[10] He was inclined to express a distinctly urban experience that was 'an intuitive concept rather than the product of rational analysis' and 'requires the active consciousness of the observer'.[11] At the end of *La Vie unanime* (1908), Romains proclaimed, with a forward-looking, almost eschatological expectation, that 'Il faudra bien qu'un jour on soit l'humanité' [It's necessary that some day, we are one humanity], expressing the future vision of Unanimism.[12] The idea was to merge identities until 'the group has a single soul, the *unanime*, and once created, it becomes, explicitly, a *dieu*.'[13] Compared with Jesus's discourses on unity in the Gospel of John, perhaps Unanimism can be seen as a form of secular Christian communalism where individual identities were lost in the figure of Jesus and the institution of the early church:

I ask not only on behalf of these, but also on behalf of those who will believe
in me through their word, that they may all be one. As you, Father, are in me
and I am in you, may they also be in us. (John 17. 20–21)

Throughout this entire discourse, Jesus's focus is on eliding the distinction between
the present, partial community and the future, universal community. The phrase
'on behalf of these' refers to Jesus's contemporary disciples, as opposed to the
Christian community 'who *will believe*', whose identity is characterized by a unity
between it, Jesus, and God.

A similar combination of Unanimism's future-orientation and collective outlook
served as a model for many poets across Europe, including Marinetti and Pound.
Marinetti likened the Créteil community to a 'convent' for the avant-garde,
whereas Pound found inspiration for Imagism and Vorticism among the theories
of Romains. Apollinaire formed a personal friendship with Romains, alluding to
the Unanimist concept of collectives — where the poet struggles with an ecstatic
merging of the self into the population on the one hand, and the effort to maintain
his individual integrity on the other — at several points in *Alcools*, such as in
'Cortège' (1912), where he writes:

> Le cortège passait et j'y cherchais mon corps
> Tous ceux qui survenaient et n'étaient pas moi-même
> Amenaient un à un les morceaux de moi-même
> On me bâtit peu à peu comme on élève une tour
> Les peuples s'entassaient et je parus moi-même
> Qu'ont formé tous les corps et les choses humaines (ŒP, 76)

> [The procession was passing and I looked for my body there
> All those who appeared and were not myself
> Brought one by one the pieces of myself
> They built me little by little as if raising a tower
> The people piled onto each other and I appeared
> All the bodies and the human things having formed me]

The poet's identity is diffused throughout the population, and, in turn, the individual
members of the population construct the poet's identity 'comme on élève une tour'.
The 'tour' may be a sly allusion, entirely coherent with Unanimism, to the tower
of Babel, and the association would imply a unity within the heterogeneity of the
crowd. But Romains's project is characteristic of a belief — evident in avant-garde
and modernist writing that favours collectively signed manifestoes, varying forms
of stream-of-consciousness writing, or the belief that the artist was speaking from
the point of view of a tradition — that the distinction between a world that was
individually experienced and one that was collectively experienced was illusory. By
engaging, to the extent possible, in collective experience, the poet objectifies and
makes self-evident new attitudes and dispositions seen as 'fit for purpose' for the
increasingly urbanized modernity. In this way, Unanimism resembles the 'culture
work' of apocalyptic social organization described by Bromley: the tendency
towards collective ideas and ideals that re-symbolize the external world in terms of
a transcendent reality.

* * * * *

Two poems from *Alcools*, 'Les Fiançailles' (1908) and 'Vendémiare' (1912), were written at the height of Apollinaire's pre-war interest in an avant-garde community and both reflect apocalyptic themes and concerns of friendship and loneliness, destruction, and creation. But crucially, as I will show with reference to the Gospel of John, these poems employ a common technique of apocalyptic language, as they invert the terms of community and affect, describing a poet who is alone because he loves or finds company in rejection — a standard trope of avant-garde movements. They also reflect the sense of a new creation that drew Apollinaire to such movements in the first place. To the extent that the poet in 'Les Fiançailles', for example, confronts and associates with others, dropping numerous clues that the poem is largely inspired by his connections to the avant-garde, he resists identifying a definitive individual or group. Rather, the poet presents the struggle for a new reality that's offered as an opportunity or possibility, conceived somewhere between the external reality of the poet and his imagination. Stanza 2 opens with an image that recalls the affection between the Virgin and Christ, but quickly shifts to an eschatological association:

> Une Madone à l'aube a pris les églantines
> Elle viendra demain cueillir les giroflées
> Pour mettre aux nids des colombes qu'elle destine
> Au pigeon qui ce soir semblait le Paraclet (*ŒP*, 128)

> [A Madonna at dawn picks dog-roses
> She will return tomorrow to collect wallflowers
> To place in doves' nests that she destines
> For the pigeon that tonight seemed like the Paraclete]

These lines present an image of an imminent future: a figure of the Madonna will return tomorrow to line a doves' nest for a pigeon that, today, resembled the Paraclete or the Holy Spirit. The creation of the dove's nest by the Virgin is an indication of the messianic pretensions of the image, which the remainder of the poem will undercut. However, the broad and indeterminate language — '*Une* Madone', '*semblait* le Paraclet' — frustrates the reader's confidence in the poet's vision and ability to accurately identify the image. As Susan Harrow describes, the indeterminacy of the poet's vision prevents the reader from really discerning a concrete reality in these lines, and Apollinaire retreats into the safety of an outmoded Symbolist abstraction:

> On se sent glisser dans une pénombre symboliste. Évasion, abstraction, connotation: l'expression fuit le réel pour se réfugier dans l'imprécis, dans l'insaisissable. [...] Ainsi se développe une rêverie d'amour idéal qui, faute de réaliser ses espoirs de transcendance, aboutit à l'évocation d'une certaine stérilité, de l'inertie des cœurs 'suspendus'.[14]

> [We feel ourselves slide into a Symbolist twilight. Evasion, abstraction, connotation: expression escapes the real to take refuge in the imprecise, in the intangible. [...] So a reverie of ideal love is developed that, failing to realize his hopes of transcendence, concludes with the evocation of a certain sterility, of the inertia of 'suspended' hearts.]

The image takes on the sense of the tragically incongruou with the figure of the Madonna creating a doves' nest for the pigeon, and the reader is caught by the poet's lack of clarity in envisioning the future. Carrying this misfortune a step further, the specific vocabulary contains a few telling double-entendres: 'le pigeon', aside from referring to the bird, can also mean a dupe or a fool; and the Madonna collects 'giroflées', which may refer to wallflowers or to a slap to the face. The pigeon is therefore a despised and abused figure — perhaps even a martyr.

The biblical term, Paraclete, is the strongest indication in this stanza of an eschatology. The Paraclete, a significant feature of Jesus's prophecy in the Gospel of John, is associated with the Holy Spirit. Apollinaire describes it in his story 'L'Hérésiarque' (1902), where the main character, Benedetto Orfei, states that one of the two thieves crucified with Jesus 'était le Saint-Esprit, le Paraclet' [was the Holy Spirit, the Paraclete].[15] The identity of the Paraclete is somewhat obscure, and variously translated in the Bible as Advocate, Comforter, Councillor, or Helper, and is not a contemporary figure, but a promise made by Jesus to his disciples: 'If you love me, you will keep my commandments. And I will ask the Father, and he will give you another Advocate [παράκλητος, paraklētos], to be with you forever' (John 14. 15–16). But as Andreas Hoeck describes, it maintains an eschatological function as either the guarantor of the Christian community until the apocalypse, or as the signal of the apocalypse itself: the Paraclete is

> the unequivocal sign of the arrival of the Messianic age. The Divine Spirit represents the eschatological *continuum* in which the work of Christ, initiated in his ministry on earth and awaiting its termination at his Parousía, is wrought out.[16]

However, when Jesus predicts the coming of the Paraclete, he also predicts the inability of the world outside of his disciples to comprehend the Paraclete, indicating a substantial cognitive break between the before and after of its revelation: 'the world cannot receive' the Paraclete (whom this verse refers to as the 'Spirit of truth') 'because it neither sees him nor knows him. You know him, for he abides with you, and he will be in you' (John 14. 17). The Paraclete maintains a presence within the community, but not in a sense that can be registered by anybody outside of that early church, presenting it as both actuality for a contemporary community and potentiality for the future. The invocation of the Paraclete positions the poet in a particular moment where he can experience the past, present, and future as densely intermingled in a single, fortuitous moment.

'Les Fiançailles' takes on the character of a 'message in a bottle', written for a community that does not yet (and may never) exist, but without whom the new reality cannot be manifested. The following stanza shifts from the overtly religious references to a group that has arrived late: 'Au petit bois de citronniers s'énamourèrent | D'amour que nous aimons les dernières venues' [In the little lemon grove the late arrivals | Enamoured each other with the love that we love] (ŒP, 128). Like Pound's 'former lot', of whom the poet is an inheritor of tradition, the poet in 'Les Fiançailles' looks forward to those who might inherit his own sensibilities in the 'dernières venues'. In 'L'Hérésiarque', Apollinaire identifies the Paraclete with love when Benedetto Orfei calls the former 'l'éternel Amour',[17] which suggests that these 'dernières venues' are those to whom the Paraclete is finally revealed. These circular references to love bear a peculiar resemblance to John 14. 21, where Jesus explains the meaning of the arrival of the Paraclete: 'They who have my commandments and keep them are those who love me; and those who love me will be loved by my Father, and I will love them and reveal myself to them.' However, the revelation of love in the gospel verses necessitates a loss of personal identity within the unity of the Christian community. Ernst Haenchen writes that 'the one with great love wears a mask of nothingness. [...] It is precisely because Jesus has so completely rejected his own importance that he can stand in fully for the Father.'[18] Does, like Pound's personae, the poet stand in for another, or a loss of identity occur between the 'nous' and the 'dernières venues'? Perhaps if the logic of metaphor — one image always slipping into another — is read as the logic of love and creation. After their arrival, it is said of the 'dernières venues' that 'parmi les citrons leurs cœurs sont suspendus' [among the lemons their hearts are suspended] (ŒP, 128), calling forth the creative effect of love and shedding of the divisions of this or that, them or us, or me and you. As Harrow states, love becomes the juncture between the real and the imagined: 'la présence de l'"amour" charge le sens créateur supérieur du potentiel simultaniste par lequel s'opèrent les grandes synthèses poétiques' [the presence of "love" fills the superior creative sense with the simultanist potential by which great poetic syntheses are effected].[19]

The lemon-hearts are, fundamentally, an act of poetry, completing an imaginative reverie on springtime begun in the first line with the 'fiancés parjures' [perjured betrothed], whose name suggests an erroneous or dishonest betrothal. Springtime, that is the act of poetry, 'laisse errer' [lets wander] these men and women. Rees suggests that the adjective 'parjures' 'refers perhaps both to the deceptions of art and of life from which the poet strives to emerge'.[20] Timothy Mathews writes that this 'perjury' may be read as a failed promise of the messianic imagination, and 'calls into question the power of image itself to impose contours in time and space; and it is the fact of relation that is presented as a silence and a broken contract.'[21] Poetry becomes a union or marriage within the vision of the poet, recalling William Blake's grand synthesis in *The Marriage of Heaven and Hell*; however, the marriage is always undermined by the very fact of art existing as something of a deviation from the real world, a measure of the poet's desire that cannot be fulfilled in the world. But in Jesus's discourse on the Paraclete, he contrasts love and hate as analogous to separation and union: 'If you belonged to this world, the world would love you as its own. Because you do not belong to the world, but' because of Jesus's love, 'I have chosen you out of the world — therefore the world hates you' (John 15. 19). For Apollinaire, love likewise singles out from the world and mingles or identifies object with subject in the act of creative or poetic 'deception'. 'Le matériau poétique [...] se situe par-delà le vrai et le faux' [Poetic material [...] is situated beyond the true and the false],[22] momentarily enacting a new world that confuses the divisions of the real world and the desire of imagination.

It's for this necessity to blur the line between the real and the false, the present and the future, that the groups of the first three stanzas of 'Les Fiançailles' are so abstract, presented as symbolic cyphers for art and love, rather than specific or historic individuals. These communities live *in* and *for* the future, in the way the disciples of Jesus live *in* and *for* his expression of love. And this life utterly separates these groups from the world. However, in the following part of 'Les Fiançailles', Apollinaire brings the poem back to the real world and real people, to express a series of contrasts with the above stanzas. He writes that: 'Mes amis m'ont enfin avoué leur mépris' [My friends have declared their contempt of me] (ŒP, 129). Jesus's use of the term 'friend' (φίλος, *philos*) occurs three times in a brief speech in John 15. 13–17:

> No one has greater love than this, to lay down one's life for one's friends. You are my friends if you do what I command you. I do not call you servants any longer, because the servant does not know what the master is doing; but I have called you friends, because I have made known to you everything that I have heard from my father.

The definitions of friendship here entail the substitution of one life for another, the carrying forward of an action from one to another, and, most significantly, the mutual understanding of a rarefied knowledge. Moreover, Jesus makes a clear distinction between friends and servants. The gospel uses δοῦλος, *doulos*, for the latter term, which is generally used to refer to a slave, and this figure lacks the soteriological knowledge of the divine love that Jesus preaches. Jesus emphasizes friendship with the attributes of sacrifice and trust, but now Apollinaire is in a place of shame and contempt:

> Une ange a exterminé pendant que je dormais
> Les agneaux les pasteurs des tristes bergeries
> De faux centurions emportaient le vinaigre (ŒP, 129)

> [While I slept an angel exterminated
> The lambs the shepherds of sad sheepfolds
> Some false centurions carried away the vinegar]

Apollinaire once again brings the reader the image of the shepherd and the flock, but the shepherds fail to protect their flocks and even themselves. There's a guilt to the poetic reverie that the poet has indulged in, allowing him to 'sleep' while the exterminating angel lays waste to the community. The last line above is a clear reference to centurions giving Jesus wine mixed with gall (Matthew 27. 34) or sour wine (Luke 23. 36) as a form of mockery. Apollinaire feels shame not in the promises he has made regarding the power of art, but his inability to truly fulfil those promises in the real world. As L. C. Breunig writes, 'His failure was a failure not of weakness, but of excessive strength, a feeling of plenitude which in the final version of "Les Fiançailles" will be expressed by the line: "Je buvais à pleins verres les étoiles" [I drank right down glasses of stars]'.[23]

The sense of community given in the first two sections is essential for Apollinaire's belief in the ability of art to renew the world. Bromley argues that apocalyptic thought is always to some extent social in order to justify the marginalization of that thought: 'The [apocalyptic] community they create is specifically constructed, both to be part of an order that does not yet exist and to be distanced from the existing social order.'[24] Without the 'fiancés parjures' or the 'dernières venues', the poet is living a disjointed life in the order of the *as yet*, alone in his belief in the future and unable to convince friends to accept the falsehood of art that would allow them too to act as though they were living in the next world. The knowledge of the creative potential of the poet and his art strikes that note of affection and knowledge that is both communal and distinguishing found in the verses from the Gospel of John cited above. Bourdieu also characterizes this eschatological worldview of art as two mutually exclusive universes that succeed one another, divided by the idea of love. In order to truly succeed 'dans l'au-delà' [in the beyond], 'on y a intérêt au désintéressement: l'amour de l'art est un amour fou [...] C'est à travers l'homologie entre les formes de l'art et les formes de l'amour que la loi de l'incompatibilité entre les univers s'accomplit' [one has a disinterested interest in it: the love of art is a mad love [...] Across the homology between the forms of art and the forms of love the law of the incompatibility between the universes is achieved].[25] By the second section of 'Les Fiançailles', it seems that love and friendship have been lost and the poet is left to find a new form to replace 'l'ancien jeu des vers' [the old game of verse] (ŒP, 132).

★ ★ ★ ★ ★

An early draft of 'Les Fiançailles' addressed the apocalyptic sense more explicitly than the version published in 1908. The following stanza recalls lines 7 to 9 in section III of the latter, though with an extra line underscoring the capacity for renewal, and a slight adjustment to the final line. Apollinaire writes in the early draft:

> Jadis les morts sont revenus pour m'adorer
> Car ma vie avait le pouvoir de faire renaître tout l'univers
> Et j'espérais la fin du monde
> Mais la mienne arrive en sifflant pareille à l'ouragan glacé (ŒP, 1059)[26]
>
> [Long ago the dead returned to adore me
> For my life had the power to renew the universe
> And I hoped for the end of the world
> But only mine arrived whistling like an icy storm]

The second of these lines was eventually removed, but it clearly pairs the final apocalyptic cataclysm with a renewal of the entire universe. The dead once returned to adore Apollinaire because his life had the power to make the world anew, perhaps even to bring them back to life.[27] The dead likely have a dual point of reference: they represent the poet's past and memory, which is reiterated in the second line of part 4: 'Les cadavres de mes jours' [The cadavers of my days] (ŒP, 131); on the other hand, they represent 'l'ancien jeu des vers', closely associated with Apollinaire's youthful adherence to the Symbolist aesthetic.[28] There, an emphasis on the self-referential autonomy that poetry and language increasingly divorced from external relation is enticing to the poet even as he confronts the anxiety of its apparently bloodless (lack of) connection to life. In this sense, the poet believed that he could somehow renovate the old aesthetic, a hope characterized as no less than an apocalyptic change in the world. What Apollinaire expects is an overall, world-historical end ('*tout l'*univers', 'la fin *du* monde'), but it finally comes down to 'la mienne' — his end, his life, his world. What he believed was influencing and impacting the world was, to borrow from Ecclesiastes, 'chasing after wind' (1. 14). Secondly it seems to have been far less spectacular than expected. The early draft presents this end as 'sifflant pareille à l'ouragan glacé', adding the feeling of a chill to what apparently ought to have been a more vibrant, fecund rebirth. Relative to the frequent images of fire as a symbol of poetic inspiration in Apollinaire's work, the image of ice is something of a rarity and so likely connotes a lack of inspiration. The expected end is never quite the final end; Apollinaire's words 'se sont changés en étoiles' [have changed into stars] (*Œ*P, 130), evoke a Symbolist image of inspiration but, in this context, it also signifies a distant beauty and overwrought ambition, as it is accompanied by an image of Icarus.[29] Both the deadness and distance invoked by the Symbolist style create an anti-climactic experience. Breunig suggests that 'Les Fiançailles' roughly follows a 'Christian progression' from innocence to salvation, with an intermediate state of sin and confession;[30] if this is the case, then his disappointment in the 'fin du monde' is only a temporary setback and salvation is always a possibility.

Accordingly, the ninth and final section of 'Les Fiançailles' provides a stark contrast to the hollowness of the apocalypse in section III above, with the poet burning ('brûle') among flaming contemporaries.[31] The first line, 'Templiers flamboyants je brûle parmi vous' [Flaming Templars I burn among you] — recalling the Templars who were burned at the stake for heresy in the fourteenth century — is a potential reference to the avant-garde community suffering for their efforts to modernize their aesthetics, figuring them as martyrs. The second line of section IX begins with 'Prophétisons ensemble' [Let's prophesy together], suggesting, when compared with the apparent disappointment of section III, that the apocalyptic change can only truly occur when the group identifies itself with the collective effort of being modern; but at this point, Apollinaire's loneliness is a sign of courage rather than impotence. '[T]es enfants galants' [Your courteous children], yet another elusive community suggesting a prophetic or avant-garde group, in line 11 build 'le nid de mon courage' [the nest of my courage], returning the image to the state of innocence in which the reader finds the 'pigeon' of the first section. Finally, Apollinaire compares his efforts to a 'oiseau fent pent' [falsely painted bird][32] that is, inasmuch as the 'pigeon' *seems* like the Holy Spirit, is both salvation — the ability to fundamentally change his world — and mere artifice.

Apollinaire's apocalypticism is also expressed in the formal connections of these two sections as well as the thematic connections. The form of section IX is almost identical to section I (with the exception of the absent fourth line of section I). Apollinaire writes the lines of both sections as alexandrines in contrast to the freer lines of the seven central sections. The free-verse of the central sections, where the apocalyptic hopes end in disappointment, finally gives way to the traditional alexandrine metre. This is striking given the reference to poetry in section V — right in the midst of the poet's disappointment and isolation:

Pardonnez-moi mon ignorance
Pardonnez-moi de ne plus connaître l'ancien jeu des vers
[...]
Je médite divinement
Et je souris des êtres que je n'ai pas créés
Mais si le temps venait où l'ombre enfin solide
Se multipliait en réalisant la diversité formelle de mon amour
J'admirerais mon ouvrage (*ŒP*, 132)

[Forgive my ignorance
Forgive me for no longer knowing the old game of verse
[...]
I am divinely meditating
And I smile for beings that I haven't created
But if the time came where the shadow finally made solid
Was multiplied in fulfilling the formal diversity of my love
I could admire my work]

This stanza bears the most explicit connection to the status of poetry and poetic form that Apollinaire confronts. He claims to have forgotten the 'ancien jeu des vers', but as the beginning and end of the piece demonstrates, that's only true within the poetic context of this poem, perhaps even this section. The breakdown of verse, in favour of something new, is always somewhat contingent on the sensibility of the poet. He meditates 'divinement', seeing himself in the guise of godly creator, but only in reference to the beings he did *not* create. Always keeping the eschatology closely allied with a sense of new creation, Apollinaire concludes the stanza by looking to a time when 'l'ombre enfin solide' finds expression in *formal* diversity, meaning that a true change in poetry will occur, whereas, at present, that change has only been intimated by the signs and images such as those found in section I, the 'pigeon' that seems like the Paraclete, the 'citrons' that are also 'cœurs'. The poet returns to his formal origins, but with a newfound confidence that poetry represents an apocalyptic hope. This hope comes at the risk of losing the world one knew and of loneliness; but with courage and love, poetry can point the way to the revelation of the world beyond.

New Wine, Old Bottles

It was not a great leap for Apollinaire to shift from 'mes amis' to cities, nations, and other social formations, and he remained open to the question of what the cost of modernity might be; or, to put it another way, his poetry dwelt on the question of sacrifice, what society would be willing to give up or even destroy. His bottom line was that since science and technology had thrust Western civilization into a new epoch, art and poetry must reflect and consummate the radical break between the past and the future, and there was no obvious institution to which the poet must attach him- or herself. However, Apollinaire sought to be true to his belief that the aesthetic experience of a new epoch could not be brought about gradually or rationally, but was a wrenching and violent break that he often imagined as a large-scale bloodletting. In this respect, the title of Apollinaire's final poem in *Alcools*, 'Vendémiare', recalls the first month of the French revolutionary calendar, and is likely an allusion to the Terror, as well as the French Revolution's resetting of the calendar, in 1793, to Year One. Related to the word for a grape harvest, 'la vendange' (the calendar turned over each autumn), he implies that the harvesting and necessary death of the old world or *ancien régime* (the grapes and the vines being harvested) is the 'wine' of the new era — a concept implicitly drawn from Revelation 14: 'So the angel swung his sickle over the earth and gathered the vintage of the earth, and he threw it into the great wine press of the wrath of God' (v. 19).

The poem was likely written around 1909,[33] along with 'Cortège', as both demonstrate Unanimist themes. 'Cortège', which was originally titled 'Brumaire' (the second month of the Revolutionary calendar),[34] and 'Vendémiare' describe the poet finding himself deeply connected to the multiplicity of life, extending his conscience to every facet of the modern world. The emphasis on European cities, with Paris at the centre, recalls Romains's Unanimist vision of urban life, where 'the modern city [is] a living, positive entity into which the poet's individuality may be merged'.[35] However, the merger goes both ways in 'Vendémiare', where Europe is absorbed — literally, at some points — into the personality of the poet. The mundane and quotidian is a cypher for the transcendence and abstraction of 'musique éternelle' [eternal music] and 'douleur divine' [divine sorrow] (ŒP, 153). This suggests an apocalyptic collapse of the supernatural and terrestrial spheres, where the history of earth is merely the shadow of a cosmic history. Through the unification of sacred and profane achieved within the figure of the poet and the space of the poem, entirely new aesthetic viewpoints are born. Paris is eager for the creative developments of writers and artists, with the towns of Brittany, Rennes, Quimper, and Vannes offering themselves up first to Paris, saying:

> Ces grappes de nos sens qu'enfanta le soleil
> Se sacrifient pour te désaltérer trop avide merveille
> Nous t'apportons tous les cerveaux les cimetières les murailles
>
> [These grapes of our senses that the sun birthed
> Sacrifice themselves to quench your overly greedy wonder
> We bring you all the brains the cemeteries the walls] (ŒP, 149–50)

Revelation 14 presents two harvests that suggest a 'universal ingathering':[36] the harvest of grain (vv. 14–16), and the harvest of grapes (vv. 17–20). The willing sacrifice of the cities cleanses their historically and geographically contingent particularities, clarifying them into a single, common essence. This theme carries throughout the poem to the end, where Apollinaire states:

> Tout cela tout cela changé en ce vin pur
> Dont Paris avait soif
> Me fut alors présenté (ŒP, 153)
>
> [All that all that changed into this pure wine
> That Paris has thirsted for
> Was then presented to me]

The wine is a distillation of the cultures of Europe, offered up to Paris, and more specifically, the poet himself. It might then follow that what comes of this distillation is a jumble, an adulteration of cultures and nationalities, and indeed, it seems to have a disorienting, even inebriating effect on him. Its purity is, like alcohol, an aspect of its headiness. The next lines give some detail as to what has been included in this 'vin pur':

> Actions belles journées sommeils terribles
> Végétation Accouplements musiques éternelles
> Mouvements Adorations douleur divine
> Mondes qui vous rassemblez et qui nous ressemblez (ŒP, 153)

> [Actions beautiful days terrible sleeps
> Vegetation Couplings eternal music
> Movements Adorations divine sorrow
> Worlds that you resemble and where you resemble us]

This hallucination reaches a breaking point of coherence in this moment, where, ironically, the poet becomes fully conscious of being in a consequential place and moment of a historical nexus. But this nexus resolves upon the individuals who are marked by it, producing entire 'Mondes qui vous rassemblez et qui nous ressemblez'.

The eschatological mood of impending catastrophe is also expressed in the imagery of the sacrifice of the towns. The image is of quenching an insatiable thirst: 'J'ai soif villes de France et d'Europe et du monde | Venez toutes couler dans ma gorge profonde' [I am parched cities of France and Europe and the World | Come all flow down into my deep throat] (ŒP, 149). The sense is both of a community feast, sharing in the wealth of the community's bounty, or that of a religious practice in which the sacrifice is consumed in order to gain its powers. Weber himself noted the connection between sacrifice and communal feast, stating that religious sacrifice is 'intended as a *communio*, a ceremony of eating together which serves to produce a fraternal community between the sacrificers and the god.'[37] The apocalyptic community is formed by creating a common stake in the sacrifice, and the towns of Europe are likewise collectively involved in the project of the future. As the poem progresses the sense of communion develops into a chaos where the distinctions between individual and community, distance and proximity, are collapsed:

> Les villes répondaient maintenant par centaines
> Je ne distinguais plus leurs paroles lointaines
> [...]
> L'univers tout entier concentré dans ce vin (ŒP, 153)

> [The cities responded now by the hundreds
> I couldn't distinguish their faraway words any more
> [...]
> The entire universe concentrated in this wine]

The individual contributions, particularly literary ('leurs paroles') of the towns are rendered indistinguishable in the common fund of the sacrifice. But the image of the sacrifice that accompanies so many of the responses of the cities implies that what the avant-garde has gained in Paris leaves the towns wounded, implying a zero-sum view. In stanzas 21 and 22, the German towns, represented by the Moselle and Rhine rivers, and Coblenz, add their contributions, and the sense of violence and loss is more palpable. Sacrifice is the very particular moment where communion and conflict are not easily separated:

> Mes grappes d'hommes forts saignent dans le pressoir
> Tu boiras à long traits tout le sang de l'Europe
> Parce que tu es beau et que seul tu es noble
> Parce que c'est dans toi que Dieu peut devenir (ŒP, 152)

> [My clusters of men bleed profusely in the press
> You will drink in great draughts all the blood of Europe
> Because you are beautiful and only you are noble
> Because God can become within you]

Since the poem was first published in 1912, Apollinaire is likely referring to the history of French and German/Prussian conflict in the nineteenth century. However, Apollinaire still views Paris as the cultural capital, and though the Rhine and Moselle provide the German contribution, the imagery suggests both provision and loss:

> Mais nous liquides mains jointes pour la prière
> Nous menons vers le sel les eaux aventurières
> Et la ville entre nous comme entre des ciseaux
> [...]
> Troublant dans leur sommeil les filles de Coblence (ŒP, 153)

> [But our liquid hands join in prayer
> We steer towards the salt the adventurous waters
> And the town between us as between scissors
> [...]
> Troubling in their sleep the girls of Coblenz]

The two rivers, the French-originating Moselle and the German-originating Rhine, come together like scissors, with Coblenz, and its history of both French and German/Prussian contention, between them. The conflict in 'Vendémiaire' can serve as a figure for any number of intra-European conflicts. The respective contributions of the nations are both entirely essential but mutually destructive, breaking down the self-understanding of any nation involved in the conflict. However, the statement that the 'filles de Coblence' are only slightly disturbed by the waters suggests that this conflict is both a recollection of the past and premonition of the future because, at the moment, it is only playing out on the level of the imagination of the poet or in the dreams of the girls of Coblenz.

While his successors, particularly the Surrealists, made the possibilities of breaching the divide between imagination and reality central to their poetic practice, 'Vendémiaire' maintains, in the last instance, that distinction, asserting that the images are primarily in the imagination of the poet. This remains, on one level, a poem about the practice of poetry as a creative art: 'Tous les fiers trépassés qui sont un sous mon front | L'éclair qui luit ainsi qu'une pensée naissante' [All the proud dead that are under my brow | The flash that shines the way a thought is born] (*ŒP*, 153). The catastrophe that accompanies the apocalyptic event is both a reference to the past history of France and Europe, but also the absolute destruction that results from the 'unanimist terms'[38] of the 'pure wine' in the place of the poem itself. The living traditions of the cities that contribute to Paris's pre-eminence among them are stripped of meaning in the conflict with modernity:

> Des kilos de papier tordus comme des flammes
> Et ceux-là qui sauront blanchir nos ossements
> Les bons vers immortels qui s'ennuient patiemment
> Des armées rangées en bataille
> Des forêts de crucifix et mes demeures lacustres
> Au bord des yeux de celle que j'aime tant (*ŒP*, 153)

> [Kilos of paper twisted like flames
> And those who will know how to bleach our bones
> The fine immortal verses that patiently wait bored
> Armies ranged for battle
> Forests of crucifixes and my lakeside abodes
> At the edge of the eyes of the one that I love so much]

Like soldiers, the 'bons vers immortels', without being deployed for action have lost their sense of purpose; which is to say, that cultural tradition can only mean something when it comes into conflict with alternative traditions. Whilst poetry is a product of imagination, Apollinaire never suggests the kind of isolated autonomy for poetry that reigned over nineteenth-century aestheticism. Tradition is the foundation by which people live their lives, and the avant-garde poet would do well to recognize that; but the bloodletting of the past is also the way in which the avant-gardist distils the transcendent beauty, vitality, or the energy that gave tradition its value in the first place. The next line imagines the 'bons vers immortels' as a forest of crucifixes and idyllic abodes by a lake. The image of crucifixion carries through the sense of martyrdom initially intimated in the previous line of soldiers ready for battle, but the latter image suggests peacefulness. The movement of these images then might lead from action to sacrifice, and finally to paradise in the idyllic 'demeures lacustres', which are brought to mind in the poet's contact with his loved-ones, consolidating the way love and loss are identified in Apollinaire's poetry, or even poetry in general as he sees it. The themes of sacrifice are no more evident than in the poem's references to Catholic communion. The south of France speaks to Paris, asking the city to 'Partagez-vous nos corps comme on rompt des hosties' [Share our body like we break the host] (*ŒP*, 151). Rome's contribution, being the seat of Catholicism, is most explicit about the connection between the communion and the blood. Rome states that the branches of the cross and fleur-de-lys are 'Macèrent dans le vin que je t'offre et qui a | La saveur du sang pur [...]' [Blended into the wine that I offer you and has | The taste of pure blood [...]] (*ŒP*, 152), which recalls the wine of the communion as the transubstantiation into the blood of Christ, itself being a connotation of the radical, even eschatological, change from one state to another.

In 'Les Fiançailles' and 'Vendémiaire' Apollinaire blends time and space, objectivity and subjectivity, and past and future, as a way to intimate how a new creation might be thought. Sacrifice and communion will be essential to any radical change, breaking down and doing away with the distinctions that humans hold on to so dearly. And this nexus is accordingly explored in a largely free-verse form only to revert to the traditional alexandrine. This reversion is a subtle acknowledgement that while the poem can provide a framework for how the apocalypse might be imagined, it is not the thing itself. The final three stanzas read:

> Ecoutez-moi je suis le gosier de Paris
> Et je boirai encore s'il me plaît l'univers
>
> Ecoutez mes chants d'universelle ivrognerie
>
> Et la nuit de septembre s'achevait lentement
> Les feux rouges des ponts s'éteignaient dans la Seine
> Les étoiles mouraient le jour naissait à peine (*ŒP*, 154)
>
> [Listen to me I am Paris's throat
> And I would drink the universe again if it pleased me
>
> Listen to my songs of universal intoxication
>
> And the September night slowly concluded
> The red fires of the bridges extinguished in the Seine
> The stars died the day had hardly been born]

The third standalone line plays with the alexandrine to some extent, as Apollinaire sings his song drunkenly, like Rimbaud's 'Le Bateau ivre' (1883), as a 5/8 division of syllables rather than the standard 6/6. It is a similar technique to one he uses in 'Le Voyageur' (1912) by breaking up the free-verse with four perfect quatrains near the end of the poem. Jean Burgos notes the change from an improvised tone, one that seems suited to exploring the possibilities of the unknown, to the aesthetic dimension itself, which is not truly divorced from its own sense of order: 'ces quatre quatrains d'alexandrins parfaitement rythmés et régulièrement rimés font scandale, qui changent soudain l'allure et le ton improvisé [...]: ils lui imposent une autre dimension' [these four Alexandrine quatrains, perfectly rhythmic and regularly rhymed, are scandalous, suddenly change the allure and the improvised tone [...]: they impose another dimension on it].[39] The standalone line, however, with its suggestion of the 'universelle', opens a view to a reality that is radically separated from this world, which still lies in the future. The avant-garde should not receive that world too easily, but should be prepared to experience great loss for that future.

Slowly Unveiling the Sudden Future

In 'Vendémiaire', the final poem of *Alcools*, Apollinaire's understanding of cultural progress as necessitating conflict and even bloodshed reaches a crescendo. This opposition might take the form of pacifism or violent action, as both, argues Bromley, 'derive their energy from a negative relation to institutions in the existing social order. This means more than simply separation; it entails rejection of and resistance to established institutions.'[40] Whether preaching a pacifistic denial of temporal institutions or active engagement, conflict between Good and Evil or Order and Chaos is a perennial feature of apocalyptic literature. Apocalyptic sects polemically stand as those who live on the side of Order and Righteousness, those who live in and for the *To Come*. Likewise, the term 'avant-garde' suggests a group of comrades in a violent struggle, isolated within enemy territory. In this light, World War I was often welcomed by avant-gardists, and seemed to provide a catalyst for their project of radical modernization and renewal.

'La Petite Auto' (1918) presents the sense of imminent conflict felt by the poet even before war had been declared. The poem describes a road-trip to Deauville at the end of July 1914[41] that Apollinaire took with his friend, the artist André Rouveyre (1879–1962), just as France was preparing for war with Germany. Despite the deep sense of premonition and mystery in the poem, war-fever had been building for some time and the announcement of the draft was expected. This is a different apocalyptic vision from what we find in Apollinaire's pre-war poetry, where the conflicts and contradictions in the poet (self/other, transcendence/ immanence, change/stasis) resolve themselves in an imaginative and unutterable cataclysm. Apollinaire is confronting the evident fact that the conflicts are *emerging* as real-world issues, and his vocation as a poet is to simultaneously inscribe these events into poetic experience. The process from pre-war poetry, where internal experience is ultimately left as such, is reconfigured to one of 'le passage d'une réalité référentielle à une réalité fabriquée par l'écriture à grands coups de ruptures' [the passage from a referential reality to a fabricated reality through the writing of great ruptures],[42] although the process in this particular poem might not be as one-way. In 'La Petite Auto', the conflict is still presented in terms of grand myth as opposed to Apollinaire's more propagandistic poems written during his time on the front, where he regularly praised France or vilified Germany, or the melancholy of his poems of trench-life. Still inexperienced in the realities of war but aware of its imminence, Apollinaire creates a continuity between the idea of conflict as a poetic moment of the death and rebirth of a new, imaginative world, and actually seeing that conflict manifest outside and beyond the will and imagination of the poet.

'La Petite Auto' is not only a simple aestheticization of war, where war is appreciated entirely for its explosive beauty — a style more appropriately applied to Marinetti's description of the Italo-Turkish War, examined in the following chapter — but war as an allegory of a revelatory and transitional experience, unveiling the indescribable future in its own poeticized ways. Apollinaire discerns a meaning in the mundane coincidences of life, for example, amidst the chaos of the war where he perceives an order in the continued repetition of the number three. Lines 4 and 5 read: 'Avec son chauffeur nous étions trois || Nous dîmes adieu à toute une époque' [With his chauffeur we were three || We said farewell to a whole era] (*ŒP*, 207). Apollinaire, Rouveyre, and their driver create a group of three that are fortuitously thrown together to witness the end of an epoch, in the manner of the traditional three Magi in the Gospel of Matthew, who present gifts to the infant Jesus and bear witness to the birth of the Messiah. In his short tale 'La Rose de Hildesheim ou Les

Trésors des Rois Mages', Apollinaire (who acknowledges that Matthew actually says nothing 'quant au nombre et quant à la condition des pieux personnages' [regarding the number and condition of the pious figures])[43] focuses on their possession of gold as a form of glory as well as a symbol of love, the latter of which, as seen in 'Les Fiançailles', is also a symbol of creative power. The travellers of 'La Petite Auto' might then be seen as magi bearing witness to the birth of a new epoch and, as alluded to in the final line, the birth of a new poet, 'chosen' for his creative powers to present the events of the war in a grander, mythological light.

'La Petite Auto' also dwells on the paradox of apocalyptic literature, which presents a gradual *indication* of an event that must, by its nature, come to pass all too suddenly. Recalling the original meaning of the Greek word ἀποκάλυψις, *apokalypsis*, as a revelation of the meaning of history, apocalypse often assumes a gradual or progressive unveiling of the signs' or texts' meanings over time.[44] The number three occurs again in the visual, calligrammatic section, where the image of a large man seated at the back of the car (probably the stoutly built Apollinaire) reads 'O départ sombre où mouraient nos 3 phares' [O sad departure where our 3 headlights died] and the bottom edge of the road reads 'et 3 fois nous nous arrêtâmes pour changer un pneu qui avait éclaté' [and 3 times we stopped to change a flat tyre] (*ŒP*, 208). The repetition of the number three might also be understood as an incitement to presentiment, as when a symbol's recurrence signals a meaning of potentially supernatural significance without revealing precisely what that significance is — as Weber states, 'To the prophet, both the life of man and the world, both social and cosmic events, have a certain systematic and coherent meaning.'[45] However, the understanding of the eschatological future is invariably occluded, as expressed in 1 Corinthians 13. 12: 'For now we see in a mirror, dimly, but then we will see face to face. Now I know only in part; then I will know fully, even as I have been fully known.' As David H. Gill writes, 'the word *ainigma* [translated here as 'dimly'] has a positive as well as a negative signification, that is, as well as meaning "riddle" or "dark saying" or "something which baffles," it may also mean simply "an underlying truth," "a truth clothed in the language of imagery."'[46] Given Apollinaire's occasional fascination with various sorts of spiritualist practices and astrology (expressed most explicitly in the poem 'Sur les prophéties' (1914)), it seems likely that the recurrence of the number three is not so much to engender an identification with a particular legend or myth — such as the Magi or the holy Trinity — but to assert a divine provenance in the course of history, as well as an almost occult or prophetic perception on the part of the poet. The recurrence of the number three represents a coincidence that *must be* more than coincidence. The avant-garde attitude would deny the 'systematic and coherent meaning' of the dominant world-view, given that part of the avant-garde project is to dismantle that world-view, and assert the emergence (however partial) of a new one. Apollinaire brings the sign into the status of mystery or portent, showing a fragment that implies a whole, and by doing so, attempts this double-movement of deconstruction and revelation. As in 1 Corinthians 13. 9–10 ('For we know only in part, and we prophesy only in part; but when the complete comes, the partial will come to an end.'), writes Hans Conzelmann, 'the tone of apocalyptic is followed by its implications for the understanding of the present: the character of the present is — in relation to the future wholeness — broken.'[47]

This refusal to say what the war means is in part due to the problem of being able to comprehend the war from the individual standpoint. J. G. Clark writes of Apollinaire's experience, in contrast to the apotheosized centrality of the poet in 'Vendémiaire', as defined by its partiality and fragmentary understanding:

> Et sauf dans la mesure où la guerre est partout la guerre, elle ne peut être connue dans sa totalité, tant elle est vaste et complexe; le poète ne peut tout embrasser d'un coup d'œil omniscient, il ne peut être omniprésent.[48]

> [And except to the extent that the war is the war everywhere, it cannot be known in its totality, being so vast and complex; the poet cannot embrace it all with one omniscient glance, he can't be omnipresent.]

The lacunae of immediate experience, impossible for the individual to comprehend as a whole, are filled in by the totality of myth and fantasy. Monsters stir in the depths of the ocean, men ascend higher than eagles and, in another nod to the myth of Icarus, fall quickly and violently back to earth. It is not enough to simply describe the new condition of war: mechanized, aerial, accelerated. The poet envisions forces of nature in terms suggestive of instruments of war:

> Des géants furieux se dressaient sur l'Europe
> Les aigles quittaient leur aire attendant le soleil
> Les poissons voraces montaient des abîmes (ŒP, 207)

> [Furious giants rose up over Europe
> The eagles left their eyries waiting for the sun
> The voracious fish climbed from the depths]

Could 'géants furieux' or 'aigles' be metaphors for tanks and aeroplanes — the machinery of modern warfare? The comparison is not so direct (tanks, in any case, had not been invented at the time of this poem's composition), but the images certainly allude to a primordial movement of events that can only occur by invoking the most fundamental and ancient features of the world. Apollinaire elevates the new experiences of the war into a timeless order where they are no longer new, but part of the eternal being reborn.

But it is notable that although these mythic creatures/war machines have made an appearance, they seem to be in a place of tension and suspension. In each line, Apollinaire writes in the imperfect tense ('se dressaient', 'quittaient', 'montaient') stopping before any conclusive actions can be made. These creatures exist in an eerie state of suspension: the giants are 'furieux' but do not battle and the fish are 'voraces' but do not eat. Exactly what the eagles might do when the sun finally appears is not stated, but by the end of the poem it is clear that the morning sun signals a new era. By refraining from showing the beings in these lines in action, Apollinaire further develops the sense of timelessness in this moment, and emphasizes the possibilities of the future inherent in the still presence of these mythical figures. The individual moments of Apollinaire's experience and memory have been recalibrated and

Je n'oublierai jamais ce voyage nocturne où nul de nous ne dit un mot

```
    O              o
   dé            nuit
  part          tendre      o
 •sombre       d'avant     vil      où s e h é t
 où mouraient  la guerre   lages      a i i e  n
 nos·3 phares
```

MARECHAUX-FERRANTS RAPPELÉS

ENTRE MINUIT ET UNE HEURE DU MATIN

```
      v                 ou bien              v
   e  r  s                              e  r  s
   L I S I E U X                        a i l l e
   l a  t r è s                         s d ' o
     b l e u                                r
        e
```

éclaté

un pneu qui avait

et 3 fois nous nous arrêtâmes pour changer

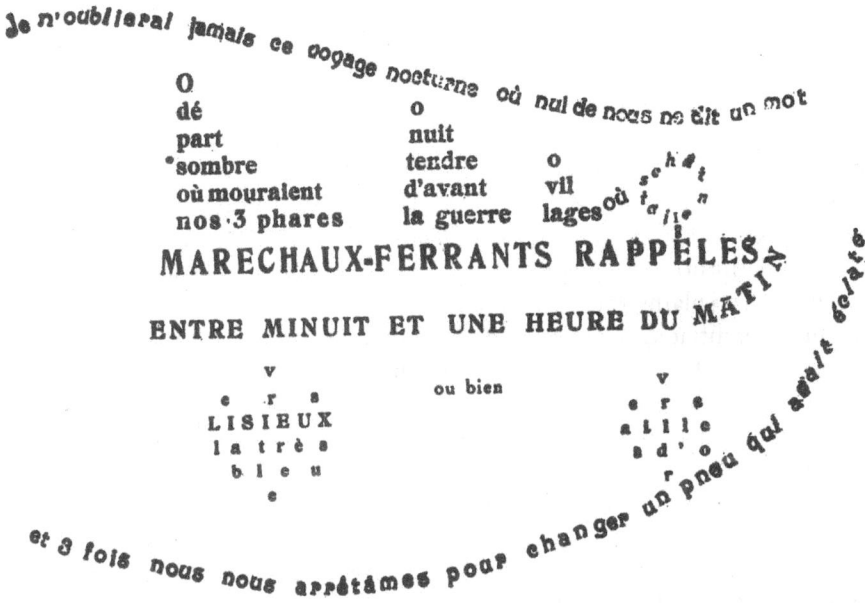

FIG. 4.1. *Calligramme in 'La Petite Auto'*

attuned to a different cosmological time, and the frequent references to time in 'La Petite Auto' betray Apollinaire's heightened sense of the coming of the new and of the passing of history. The journey from Deauville begins 'un peu avant minuit' (ŒP, 207) and ends 'après avoir passé l'après-midi' (ŒP, 208) just at the moment when the draft is being posted in Paris. The fortuitous time of arrival leads Apollinaire to suggest that a new era has arrived, and he and his travelling companions with it. Further references to time are found in the *calligramme* (Fig. 1); in the base of the car, just above the wheels, we read 'entre minuit et une heure du matin', and the middle figure in the car reads 'O nuit tendre d'avant la guerre'. The wheels of the car, while not specifically referring to any particular hour, do suggest the dawn with their colours, the left wheel reading 'Vers Lisieux la très bleue' and the right reading 'Versailles d'or' (ŒP, 208). These chronological references to time, from the 'un peu avant minuit' to 'l'après-midi' imply that the passing of the night was itself a period of tribulation that conceives a new man: 'Et bien qu'étant déjà tous deux des hommes mûrs | Nous venions cependant de naître' [And while both of use were already grown men | We had however just been born] (ŒP, 208). The shift from 'mûrs' to 'naître' clearly reverses the order of a person's life, but within the cosmic vision of the poet, it is a natural movement from the old to the new. Calling up instances of time insinuates the poet into an 'objectified' narrative that he has created by taking fragments of external reality and reimagining them in a myth of recreation in what Bromley terms, as described above, the 'culture work' of apocalyptic thought.

★ ★ ★ ★ ★

Apocalyptic literature such as I have been describing is not simply a challenge to the dominant order of the social world, but rather an assault on the idea of order itself, undermining the categories of perception and experience upon which any common social experience must be founded. If *Alcools*, relative to *Calligrammes*, has a more subdued sense of apocalyptic conflict, both works understand the apocalyptic moment as being something that, in the last analysis, is beyond the bounds of description, being as it is on the far side of 'la frontière du pensé et de l'impensé, du possible et de l'impossible, du pensable et de l'impensable' [the border of the thought and unthought, possible and impossible, thinkable and unthinkable].[49] Malcolm Bull explains the way in which the apocalypse 'describe[s] a process in which undifferentiated chaos is the prelude to a new order [...] The undifferentiated returns, that which was excluded was reincluded, and a new order is created'.[50] And Bromley states that apocalyptic 'culture work' 'challenges official interpretations of reality [...] and promotes de-differentiation.'[51] It's not simply a matter of this poetry upending distinctions, but of viewing that which our normal habits have prevented us from seeing in the first place, and allowing such sights to become part of a new language for structuring thought. The foregrounding of language as the thing that will be renewed in the apocalyptic moment is presented, appropriately, in 'La Victoire' (1917), the penultimate poem of *Calligrammes*. In 'La Victoire', poetic language in particular carries the weight of the past while simultaneously seeking a more modern or 'truer' language. It is always fraught with the meanings that came before while, in its avant-gardist mode at least, stripping such meanings away. This goal is never achieved in the here-and-now but resembles a utopian state of language lying just beyond the horizon of the future, as Apollinaire writes in the future tense: 'O bouches l'homme est à la recherche d'un nouveau langage | Auquel le grammairien d'aucune langue n'aura rien à dire' [O mouths man is searching for a new language | Of which the grammarian of any language will have nothing to say] (*ŒP*, 310). The goal is to create the paradoxical situation of a language that seems to exist outside of meaning and analysis. Moreover, as the next lines imply, it's one where action and conceptualization, body and idea, might be identified, as if Apollinaire recognizes a current disconnect between what somebody says, and what somebody communicates by physically doing. This reformulation of language follows Harrow's observation of 'the broader diachronic shift from romantico-symbolist valorizations of literariness, immateriality, and ideality to fresh, "hard" language more *transparently* communicative of external reality.'[52] Apollinaire posits complete congruence between physical, material reality and the language used to represent it. This would imply that after the apocalyptic moment, word and action would be entirely indistinguishable. After repeating three times in line 32 the desire for 'nouveaux sons', he implores the reader:

> Laissez pétiller un son nasal et continu
> Faites claquer votre langue
> Servez-vous du bruit sourd de celui qui mange sans civilité
> Le raclement aspiré du crachement ferait aussi une belle consonne
>
> Les divers pets labiaux rendraient aussi vos discours claironnants
> Habituez-vous à roter à volonté (*ŒP*, 310)

[Let crackle a continuous and nasal sound
Make your tongue click
Use the muffled noise of someone eating without etiquette
The breathing rasp of spitting would also make a beautiful consonant

Different labial farts would also make your discourse trumpet
Get used to burping at will]

This new language becomes more elemental and eschews politeness and decorum, and returns the mental to the physical. The most significant identification is between the material and ideal, and the revelation is one where what people say and do is a true reflection of who they are.

However, this is not a purifying vision of the apocalypse, as expressed in the 'pur vin' of 'Vendémiaire' where the participants are reduced to a single common essence. Rather, it is the imposition of an irrevocable difference that keeps the avant-gardist at a temporal and spiritual remove from the public. It is, as Harrow states, 'resistance to the aversive effects of material modernity [in] which difference and ambiguity [...] have been factored out.'[53] Accordingly, the anticipation of this victory of the avant-gardist against time itself is tempered by an awareness of the loss of wonder at what is new and novel. For Apollinaire, that is something to fear:

Crains qu'un jour un train ne t'émeuve
Plus
Regarde-le plus vite pour toi
Ces chemins de fer qui circulent
Sortiront bientôt de la vie
Ils seront beaux et ridicules (ŒP, 310)

[Be afraid that one day a train moves you
No longer
Watch it quickly for yourself
These paths of iron that circulate
Will soon exit life
They will become beautiful and ridiculous]

In contrast to 'La Petite Auto', where the instruments of modern technology are almost mythologized, Apollinaire projects the state of the currently 'modern' into a future where it has become antiquated, even quaint. The modern poet cannot keep up with himself, becoming temporally displaced by his own creative impulse. In 'Guerre' (1916), the tragedy of war is an interstitial moment that will lead to greater knowledge and command of the universe. Apollinaire writes:

Ne pleurez donc pas sur les horreurs de la guerre
Avant elle nous n'avions que la surface
De la terre et des mers
Après elle nous aurons les abîmes
Le sous-sol et l'espace aviatique (ŒP, 228)

[So don't cry over the horrors of war
Before it we only had the surface
Of land and seas
After it we will have the depths
Underground and aerial space]

The poet places himself between the 'Avant' and 'Après', speaking from a place of contemporary conflict. But then moves on to say:

> Après après
> Nous prendrons toutes les joies
> Des vainqueurs qui se délassent (Œ*P*, 228)

> [After after
> We will take all the joys
> Of the relaxing victors]

These lines, more specifically oriented towards World War I, conflate the idea of the modern, of discovering greater expanses, with the patriotism of winning the war against the Germans and being at ease, but 'La Victoire' does not rely upon a similar promise of peace, or a final conclusion to the conflict of the modern. Rather, it asserts that the dynamism of the 'modern' has been replaced, and is always being replaced, by a newer, less definable sense of the contemporary or future.

If Apollinaire was jaded about the proliferation of avant-garde groups after his time in World War I, this does not mean that he did not necessarily find the community that he was looking for; it might be that his sympathies were much more aligned to his fellow soldiers. 'A Nîmes' (1917), dated December 1914, when Apollinaire enlisted, is filled with nostalgia for Paris, but includes lines such as:

> Les 3 servants assis dodelinent leurs fronts
> Où brillent leurs yeux clairs comme mes éperons
> [...]
> J'admire la gaîté de ce détachement
> Qui va rejoindre au front notre beau régiment (Œ*P*, 211)

> [The 3 seated artillerymen nod their foreheads
> Where their clear eyes shine like my spurs
> [...]
> I admire the gaiety of this squad
> Which is going to rejoin our beautiful regiment at the front]

The regular rhythm and rhyme suggests that Apollinaire does not feel these fellow soldiers to be akin to a new avant-garde, but when he writes in 'La Jolie rousse', 'Pitié pour nous qui combattons toujours aux frontières' [Pity us who always battle at the borders] (Œ*P*, 314), the echo of the war is certainly apparent, which signals a possible shift in his thinking: the soldiers and artistic avant-garde both, in very different ways, are participating in the construction of a radically new reality. The bulk of *Calligrammes* was written during the war, and while there are poems in *Alcools* that are clearly looking for an ideal, unreachable artistic community, in *Calligrammes* there are names that are largely lacking in the earlier collection. 'La Petite Auto' names André Rouveyre, who is directly addressed in several other poems in the collection; *Calligrammes* is dedicated to René Dalize, who makes a significant appearance as Apollinaire's childhood friend in 'Zone', and who was killed in combat in May 1917. Dalize is is also named in the elegiac 'La Colombe Poignardée et le Jet d'Eau' [The Bleeding-Heart Dove and the Fountain] (1918) alongside André Billy, Georges Braque, Max Jacob, André Derain and others (Fig. 2).

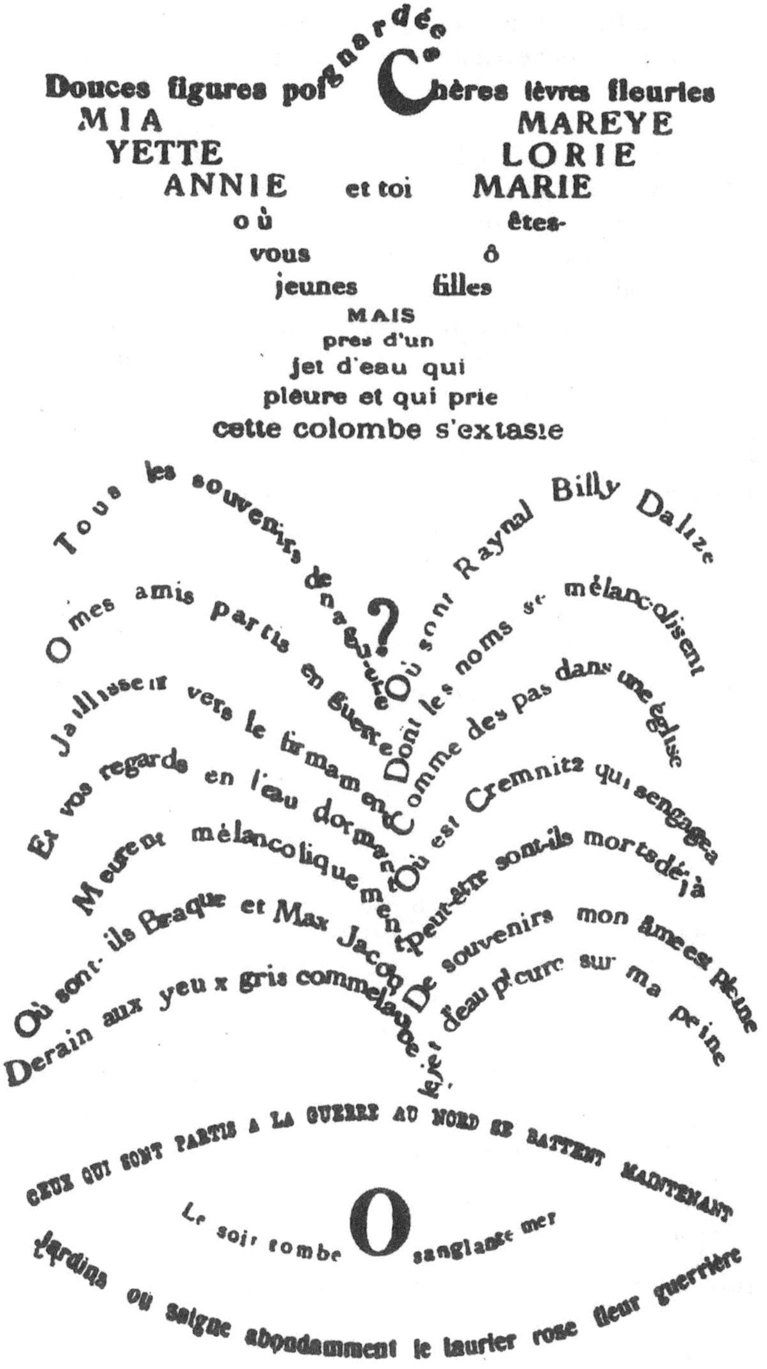

Douces figures poignardée Chères lèvres fleuries

MIA   MAREYE
YETTE   LORIE
ANNIE   et toi   MARIE
où   êtes-
vous   ô
jeunes   filles
MAIS
près d'un
jet d'eau qui
pleure et qui prie
cette colombe s'extasie

Tous les souvenirs de naguère
O mes amis partis en guerre
Où sont Raynal Billy Dalize
Dont les noms se mélancolisent
Comme des pas dans une église
?
Jaillissent vers le firmament
Et vos regards en l'eau dormant
Meurent mélancoliquement
Où sont-ils Braque et Max Jacob
Derain aux yeux gris comme l'aube
Où est Cremnitz qui s'engagea
Peut-être sont-ils morts déjà
De souvenirs mon âme est pleine
Le jet d'eau pleure sur ma peine

CEUX QUI SONT PARTIS A LA GUERRE AU NORD SE BATTENT MAINTENANT
Le soir tombe O sanglante mer
Jardins où saigne abondamment le laurier rose fleur guerrière

FIG. 4.2. *La Colombe Poignardée et le Jet d'Eau*

Apollinaire never found himself with a single group of writers and artists whom he could call his own. But he may have found something close to it in his comradeships developed in the army. But even if the war caused him to reflect on his apocalyptic beliefs and the consequences of a real-world cataclysm such as he was witnessing — the loss of life and breaking of bodies and minds, the destruction of the landscape — it did not suppress them entirely. World War I prompted Apollinaire to envision a new universe where the contradictions and binaries that structured the world were absorbed into one another. The poems of *Alcools* focus on how the apocalyptic moment resolves itself in the person and vision of the poet, whereas *Calligrammes* expands that vision, leaving the poet as a visionary in a world that cannot be fully contained within him as in the previous poems. From this point on, the skies will be resolved with the seas, the ideal with the material, the past with the future. But the recognition of this moment, where every undifferentiation is revealed, is, in the end, indescribable. Therefore, the loss suffered by those cultural innovators — who for Apollinaire certainly included the soldiers in the war — was all the more poignant precisely because neither the losses nor the gains could ever be fully articulated, but one could be hopeful that the latter was a revelation that compensated the former.

Notes to Chapter 4: The Late Arrivals

1. David G. Bromley, 'Constructing Apocalypticism', p. 35.
2. Ibid., p. 39.
3. Ibid.
4. Ibid., p. 35.
5. Marcel Raymond, *From Baudelaire to Surrealism* (London: Methuen, 1970), p. 175.
6. Ibid., p. 173.
7. Denis Boak, *Jules Romains* (New York: Twayne Publishers, 1974), p. 22. Boak lists a series of possible influences for Unanimism, including the social psychology of Gustave le Bon and Gabriel Tarde, the philosophy of Henri Bergson, and literary antecedents from Victor Hugo to Walt Whitman.
8. Ibid., p. 35.
9. Ibid., p. 23.
10. Martin, 'Futurism, Unanimism, and Apollinaire', p. 259.
11. Boak, *Jules Romains*, p. 23.
12. Quoted in Raymond, *From Baudelaire*, p. 178.
13. Boak, *Jules Romains*, p. 24.
14. Susan Harrow, '"Les Fiançailles": Cristallisation d'un amour', in *Guillaume Apollinaire 17*, ed. by Michel Décaudin (Paris: Les Lettres Modernes, 1987), pp. 119–34 (pp. 122–23).
15. *ŒPC*, I, 115.
16. Andreas Hoeck, 'The Johannine Paraclete: Herald of the Eschaton', *Journal of Biblical and Pneumatological Research*, 4 (Fall 2012), 23–37 (p. 30).
17. *ŒPC*, I, 115.
18. Ernst Haenchen, *John 2: A Commentary on the Gospel of John, Chapters 7–21*, trans. by Robert W. Funk (Philadelphia, PA: Fortress Press, 1984), p. 127.
19. Harrow, 'Les Fiançailles', p. 130.
20. Apollinaire, *Alcools*, ed. by Rees, p. 169.
21. Timothy Mathews, *Reading Apollinaire: Theories of Poetic Language* (Manchester: Manchester University Press, 1987), p. 54.
22. Didier Alexandre, '"J'ai fabriqué un dieu, un faux dieu, un vrai joli faux dieu": l'écriture

du sacré dans *Alcools*', in *Guillaume Apollinaire: Alcools*, ed. by Michel Murat (Paris: Éditions Klincksieck, 1996), 109–16 (p. 113).

23. L. C. Breunig, 'Apollinaire's "Les Fiançailles"', in *Essays in French Literature*, 3 (November 1966), 1–32 (p. 17).

24. Bromley, 'Constructing Apocalypticism', p. 39.

25. Bourdieu, *Les Règles de l'art*, p. 45.

26. This draft was originally published in *Guillaume Apollinaire: Textes inédits* (1952), but was later included in the complete works in the notes to 'Les Fiançailles' (see *ŒP*, 1059).

27. Apollinaire, *Alcools*, ed. by Greet, pp. 270–71.

28. Harrow, 'Les Fiançailles', pp. 123–24.

29. Ibid., p. 124; in a similar vein, Greet describes the stars in this line as 'elusive poems' (Apollinaire, *Alcools*, ed. by Greet, p. 270).

30. Breunig, 'Apollinaire's "Les Fiançailles"', p. 21.

31. *ŒP*, 136.

32. Ibid.

33. Apollinaire, *Alcools*, ed. by Rees, p. 177.

34. Apollinaire had conceived the idea, though quickly abandoned, of writing a series of poems based on the French Revolutionary calendar (Davies, *Apollinaire*, p. 176).

35. Boak, *Jules Romains*, p. 30.

36. Brian K. Blount, *Revelation: A Commentary* (Louisville, KY: Westminster John Knox Press, 2009), p. 279.

37. Weber, *Sociology or Religion*, p. 26.

38. Apollinaire, *Alcools*, ed. by Greet.

39. Jean Burgos, 'Une Poétique de la Rupture', in *Guillaume Apollinaire: Alcools*, ed. by Michel Murat (Paris: Éditions Klincksieck, 1996), pp. 63–80 (p. 69).

40. Bromley, 'Constructing Apocalypticism', pp. 38–39.

41. The first line of poem carries the date of 31 August, though the actual date of the overnight journey from Deauville to Paris was 31 July–1 August. The discrepancy is likely a result of Apollinaire misremembering the date.

42. Burgos, 'Une Poétique', pp. 76–77.

43. *ŒPC*, I, 160.

44. Malcolm Bull, *Seeing Things Hidden: Apocalypse, Vision and Totality* (London: Verso, 1999), pp. 119–20.

45. Weber, *Sociology of Religion*, p. 59.

46. David H. Gill, 'Through a Glass Darkly: A Note on 1 Corinthians 13,12', *Catholic Biblical Quarterly*, 25.4 (October 1963), 427–29 (p. 427).

47. Hans Conzelmann, *1 Corinthians: A Commentary on the First Epistle to the Corinthians*, trans. by James W. Leitch (Philadelphia, PA: Fortress Press, 1975), pp. 225–26.

48. J. G. Clark, 'La Poésie, la politique et la guerre: autour de "La Petite Auto", "Chant de l'honneur" et *Couleur du Temps*', in *Guillaume Apollinaire 13*, ed. by Michel Décaudin (Paris: Lettres Modernes, 1976), pp. 7–63 (pp. 17–18).

49. Bourdieu, 'Genèse et structure', p. 331.

50. Bull, *Seeing Things Hidden*, p. 79.

51. Bromley, 'Constructing Apocalypticism', p. 38.

52. Harrow, *The Material, the Real*, p. 73.

53. Ibid., p. 75.

❖

CHAPTER 5

Eschatological Panaesthetics

In 1911, Marinetti joined the Italo-Turkish War in Libya as a correspondent for the French newspaper *L'Intransigeant*, reporting on the activities of Italian forces. His partisan account of the war was published the following year as *La Bataille de Tripoli (26 octobre 1911): vécue et chantée* (1912). In between the periodic encomiums to Italian troops, the reporting is almost exclusively concerned with the sensations of war, as visual and aural analogies of weaponry and combat are made to painting, music, and dance. Marinetti describes a 'panaesthetic' experience within a hallucinatory space of physical extremities. For example, Marinetti speaks of cannon fire reciting 'toute sa poésie, par cœur' [all of its poetry, by heart].[1] But what is left out of the account is perhaps more telling still: there are no discussions of any kind of context for the war. The political decisions to go to war, national histories that might throw these nations into the conflict, demographic or social tensions contributing to the battle — all of these are ignored in favour of the immediate sensory experience of the battle. The battle is, for Marinetti, a moment outside of time, which, similar to the work of art, obeys rules and rationales completely in defiance of the heavy weight of history. With Marinetti, warfare becomes a model for artistic autonomy achieved outside of the auspices of art as such.

The characterization of warfare as a *theatrical* event was popularized by Carl von Clausewitz (1780–1831) in *On War* (*Vom Kriege*, 1832) where he envisioned a 'theatre of war' (*Kriegstheater* or *Kriegsraum*) in which the military battles take place. Clausewitz emphasized the theatre's general separation from other points in the overall area of warfare, not to say that everything outside of the theatre of war existed entirely free from the effects of the war, but to describe how areas where military operations took place could be effectively distinguished from arenas of strategizing, material supply, and political or civilian interests, which are nevertheless part of the total war effort. The theatre of war is

> strictly speaking, a sector of the total war area which has protected boundaries and so *a certain degree of independence*. [...] A sector of this kind is not just a part of the whole, but a subordinate entity in itself — depending on the extent to which changes occurring elsewhere in the war area affect it not directly but only indirectly.[2]

'Theatre of war' describes the sense of the battle as a place set apart from everyday life, a space where roles are assumed and dramas are enacted, and which only feels the effects of everyday life in obscured and indirect ways. Like the theatre of entertainment, the theatre of war offered the possibility of a space constructed in spite of, or in opposition to, the prevailing culture, where possibilities are played out between multiple antagonists. In their art and literature, the Futurists pushed for just such a space, but in *Monoplan*, Marinetti, drawing on his own experience of war, asserts the battlefield of modern warfare as the very place where the destruction and new creation of the universe could take place not only once, but repeatedly, giving the viewer a genuine sensation of the divine velocity that Futurism sought.

Battles of Body-Madness

What this section will propose is that apocalyptic literature can be broadly conceived as the refiguration of a space, not unlike a theatre, where the interior of that space allows the visionary a way to develop an imaginary that reflects upon the world outside of that imaginary. In what is possibly the most surreal section of *Monoplan*, the Pilot, tempting fate, flies into the volcanic Mount Etna on the island of Sicily to demonstrate his fearlessness. As described in Chapter 2, the Pilot, wishing for an interlocutor who can match his own bravado, takes up a discourse with the volcano itself. The latter's speech asserts two recurrent themes of *Monoplan*: destruction as a catalyst for change, and the future national glory of Italy. As the volcano then goes on to present a series of spectacles with its gas, ash, rocks, and lava, Marinetti speaks to the parallels between theatre and war. This conceptual alignment of two otherwise distinctive experiences was also expressed frequently in the manifestoes. In 'Le Théâtre Futuriste Synthétique' (1915), Marinetti draws Futurist theatre into the space of warfare through the peculiar equation of *war = Futurism = (avant-garde) theatre*:

> War, which is intensified Futurism, demands that we march and not that we moulder in libraries and reading rooms. **Hence we think that the only way that Italy can be influenced today is through the theater.** [...] But what is needed is a **Futurist Theater**, one utterly opposed to the passéist theater that makes a monotonous and depressing procession across the sleepy stages of Italy.[3]

Futurist theatre wished to replicate the 'fierce, overwhelming, and synthesizing velocity of the war',[4] condensing whole dramas into a few moments, suspending logic, and reconfiguring place and time. The theatre was also a place of a new, mutual experience between audience, actor, and writer that was not yet entirely articulable because it was intuitively, not intellectually, understood. This resistance to theorization was an effect of *physicofolie* or 'body-madness', the way in which Marinetti hoped Futurist theatre would express the language of instinct and matter, having as its driving force a desire that preceded cognition and enunciation. In an earlier manifesto, entitled 'Le Music-Hall' (1913), he wrote:

> Tandis que le théâtre actuel exalte la vie intérieure, la méditation professorale, la bibliothèque, le musée, les luttes monotones de la conscience, les dissections stupides des sentiments, bref: cette chose et ce mot immondes: '*psychologie*', le Music-hall exalte l'action, l'héroïsme, la vie au grand air, l'adresse, l'autorité

de l'instinct et de l'intuition. A la psychologie il oppose ce que j'appelle la *physicofolie*.[5]

[While current theatre exalts interior life, professorial meditation, the library, the museum, the monotonous struggles of the conscience, stupid dissections of sentiment, in brief: this filthy thing and word: '*psychology*', the Music-hall exalts action, heroism, life in mid-air, artifice, the authority of instinct and intuition. To psychology it opposes what I call *physicofolie*.]

Like war, the Futurist theatre folded the individual into a transformative experience that calls forth a response both cerebral and intuitive, even corporeal, to a universe inverted by speed and power. 'Le Théâtre futuriste synthétique' states, in this sense, that:

Il faut porter sur la scène toutes les découvertes et toutes les recherches [...] que le génie artistique et la science font chaque jour dans les zones mystérieuses du subconscient, parmi les forces encore mal définies, dans l'abstraction pure, dans le cérébralisme pur, la fantaisie pure, le record et la folie physique du Music-hall et des cirques.[6]

[We must bring to the stage every discovery and research [...] that artistic genius and science do every day in the mysterious zones of the subconscious, among still poorly defined forces, in pure abstraction, pure cerebralism, pure fantasy, the record and the physical madness of the Music-hall and circuses.]

What Marinetti makes clear in these manifestoes is that Futurist theatre served a preparatory function, establishing war as a place of experiment, sensory disaggregation, and body-madness, as well as goading participants, both actors and audience, into the physical and mental audacity that modern war required.

In the manifesto 'La Volupté d'être sifflé' [The pleasure of being booed] (1911), one of Marinetti's prescriptions for the theatre belies some of the popular pretensions of Futurism in recommending that theatre 'soumettre les acteurs à l'autorité des écrivains, arracher les acteurs à la domination du public qui les pousse fatalement à la recherche de l'effet facile et les éloigne de toute recherche d'interprétation profonde' [submit actors to the authority of writers, wrest actors from the domination of the public who inevitably pushes them to search for easy effects and draws them away from every search for deep interpretation].[7] The struggle here, between domination and artistic freedom, seems to favour the writer as the source of creativity, but the point is that actors are already dominated in the bourgeois theatre by popular sentiment and its legitimation by higher revenues. To achieve artistic freedom, actors must be led by artists whose necessity for artistic freedom is equal to, or exceeds, their own. This paradoxical figure of dominator/ emancipator is taken up by Mount Etna, embodying Marinetti's own Futurist aggression, as the Pilot enters the volcano and describes the bizarre scene before him and immediately informs the reader that we are in the realm of the theatrical. In this particular section the metaphors are of the stage, the spectacle, the audience, and the actor, all presented by the volcanic impresario. The first use of the term 'théâtre' is shortly after the Pilot enters the volcano and visualizes it as a space for the re-enactment of a creation drama:

> Voilà que le rauque entonnoir de ta gorge
> m'apparaît comme un théâtre incendié
> d'une ampleur incalculable,
> où furent conviés tous les peuples de la terre. (*MP*, 33)

> [There is the hoarse crater of your throat
> appearing to me like a burning theatre
> of incalculable width,
> where all the people of the world are invited.]

Here, Marinetti engages with the physical properties of the volcano, describing them in terms of theatrical venues. The hollow, circular shape of the volcano's interior walls, for example, serves as an amphitheatre for the ensuing entertainment. Elsewhere Marinetti compares the interior base of the volcano, which is covered by a sea of fire, to the theatre's orchestra:

> Dans le parterre du théâtre qui doit bien mesurer
> plus de vingt kilomètres de diamètre,
> se déploie largement une invitante mer de feu (*MP*, 34–35)

> [In the theatre stalls that must measure
> well more than twenty kilometres in diameter,
> an inviting sea of fire sprawls immensely]

Alongside this theatre's physical space, the Pilot sees fire, rocks, fumes, and ashes transfigured into a host of 'players'. A section of chapter three entitled 'Les Théâtres volcaniques' opens with a cabaret of acrobats and performers:

> Vous ne me voyez pas, belles flammes écuyères,
> et vous, tisons, qui basculez
> sur de très hauts trapèzes soudain mangés
> par le tourbillon des acteurs survenants! (*MP*, 64)

> [You can't see me, beautiful equestrian flames,
> and you, firebrands, who topples
> over from high on the trapeze suddenly eaten
> by the whirlwind of actors appearing!]

The Pilot is the one who sees, as the theatre 'appears' to him and the equestrians fail to see him, and so the theatrical spectacle seems to be an objectification of his own experience, culminating in the actors as a chaotic and consuming whirlwind. The fact that the Pilot can see while the players in this scene remain blind suggests the actor as ideally subordinate to the 'seeing' Pilot in much the same way that the ascription of sight to a visionary in apocalyptic literature lends authority to the prophet, as vision is analogous to a knowledge of the presently inconceivable. For example, the visions in the book of Revelation begin with John's vision, presented to him by the divine:

> After this I looked, and there in heaven a door stood open! And the first voice, which I had heard speaking to me like a trumpet, said, 'Come up here, and I will show you what must take place after this.' (Revelation 4. 1)[8]

Here we see a dual-layer of authority: on the literal level, the reader is dependent on John as the author of the vision, which itself resolves into a utopian space where justice is ultimately triumphant; but the vision is itself also 'staged' or 'authored' by the divine voice like a trumpet (or Mount Etna in *Monoplan*) where both the reader and John — as the primary personage of Revelation — mutually strive for an 'interprétation profonde'.

★ ★ ★ ★ ★

As described in Chapter 2, Martin Puchner defines the 'theatrical' as an action or speech that exceeds its contextual authorization — that is, surpasses the ability of the situation or audience to verify the action's or speech's 'legitimacy' or 'authenticity'. This is a mode or 'pose' of action and speech characterized by outsized confidence in its claims, deliberate inaccessibility in its form, and even an *a priori* dismissal towards those who might balk at either its vulgarity or obscurity. This 'pose', in the avant-garde manifesto, had a natural affinity with the theatre, especially the variety theatre of the Futurist soirées: 'Many avant-garde manifestos, by contrast, with their over-the-top statements and shrill pronouncements, are at home in avant-garde cabarets and theaters, where they were indeed declaimed with frequency.'[9] Similarly, Marinetti's own understanding of theatricality was intended to break out of traditional theatre and so he championed technological innovations in film and music, dream logic, and the incorporation of the most contemporary social and political events into the autonomous space of the theatre. Marinetti writes in 'Le Théâtre futuriste synthétique' that Futurist theatre is meant to be 'autonome, ne ressemble qu'à elle-même, tout en tirant de la réalité les éléments qu'elle combine capricieusement' [autonomous, resembling only itself, drawing entirely from reality the elements that it capriciously combines].[10] The manifesto does not so much describe a Futurist theatre that could be considered somehow 'realist', but a theatre that sets itself the task of transforming reality, as its starting point, into something only coherent with its own logic and, by implication, entirely generative of new artistic forms and modes of thought. But from there, as Puchner argues, the Futurists moved on to 'promoting the theatricalisation of life, of which the theatricalisation of the arts would be one form.'[11] The 'theatricalisation of life' suggests that theatre and theatrical manifestoes were more than just literary genres, but a way of thinking prior to conceptualization, that is, modes of existence, ways of performing, embodying, acting and behaving that would lead to new ways of conceiving and thinking about life.

Apocalypticism, as a religious attitude toward life, likewise attempts to steer the life of the individual and the community to an ideal future existence through the practice of the liminal group. John J. Collins locates this attitude and behaviour (what he calls the 'interpenetration of future expectation and present experience') in apocalyptic communities in ancient Judaism from about 200 BCE. In his discussion of the Dead Sea Scroll community, he describes its 'conviction of present participation in angelic life, coupled with the expectation of further fulfilment in the future', adhering to an ideal life that 'was not entirely relegated to a future utopia. It was also something eternally present in the heavenly court. This belief inevitably opened the way for some form of mystic participation in the higher form of life'.[12] The bizarre and fantastic images that confront the apocalyptic visionary — angels, gigantic beasts, heavenly courts — translated the cultural and political experiences of Jewish and Christian minorities into the mythical drama of divine creation and human redemption. Frequently, these visions occur in another spatial arena that corresponds with the divine sphere, to which the apocalyptic community conforms its activity.[13] This alternative plane of existence is further described by Elisabeth Schüssler Fiorenza: the 'symbolic universe' constructed by the revelation 'is a sheltering canopy' (a strikingly similar metaphor for religion to that used by the sociologist Peter L. Berger) under which the 'empirical community is transported to a cosmic plane and made majestically independent of the vicissitudes of individual existence'.[14] And indeed, this desire to be 'majestically independent' is echoed by the Futurist painter Fillía (1904–1936) regarding art having 'a spiritual function, to be a means of rendering images of a mysterious superhuman world. Man has a need to detach himself from the earth, to dream'[15] — a dream which, like the Futurist theatre, refers, in the last analysis, only to itself, re-symbolizing the world *away from the world*.

The theatricality of *Monoplan*, and the Futurist movement in general, suggests another form of an idealized future life, insulated from everyday language and practice. Or, to put it another way, theatricality is entirely open to the everyday, but so cavalier in its representation of that world that the latter is hardly recognizable as such. Biblical apocalyptic literature is constructed around what David E. Aune refers to as hierarchies of communication, separating the source, medium, believers and unbelievers, in which the central message 'is the core of a literary structure which is a surrogate for the cultic barriers which separate the profane from the sacred, the hidden from the revealed.'[16] The plot and message of apocalyptic literature is therefore characterized by increasingly obscure communications between the general *dramatis personae*, between the divine source or the scriptural tradition and the protagonist visionary, and between the visionary and the contemporary interpreter or reader. The 'théâtres volcaniques' in Marinetti's work establish levels of communication in the way one might read a play-within-a-play, each component reflecting on each other, and whose full meaning can only be revealed across the components. While the *dramatis personae* of the volcano communicate in typically theatrical ways, the overriding voices of the scene are between the Pilot and volcano itself — the latter described, tellingly, as 'le Volcan mon père' [my father the Volcano] (*MP*, 79). Immediately after the volcano concludes its discourse, the Pilot proclaims: 'J'ai compris, j'ai compris ma mission!...' [I understand, I understand my mission!...] (*MP*, 55). Other levels of communication can be deduced between the Pilot and his aeroplane, where the latter speaks something of an inner, contrarian voice, and, of course, between the Pilot-as-narrator and the reader.

Apocalyptic 'hierarchies of communication' are designed, therefore, to privilege the worldview of the 'elect' while simultaneously obscuring it to others. Marinetti's audience is an example of what he called in the 1920 pamphlet 'Al di là del comunismo' [*Beyond Communism*], the 'proletariat of gifted men', who 'will create

the theater free to all and the great Futurist Aero-Theater',[17] establishing the
principle of liberty for all (ironic, given Futurism's later political alliances) found
in the work of certain forwarding-looking practitioners. The use of theatrical
metaphors only highlights how, like most apocalyptic literature (especially the
book of Revelation), *Monoplan* is a work of self-conscious *staging* or construction
of an event between an audience and visionary mediator. In the book of Enoch,
one of the apocalypses of the biblical apocrypha, the narrator's vision is specifically
presented to him by the angels who lead him on his journey:

> And they *took me (and) led (me) away* to a certain place in which those who were
> there were like a flaming fire; and whenever they wished, they appeared as
> human beings. And they *led me away* to a dark place and to a mountain whose
> summit reached heaven. And *I saw* the place of the luminaries and the treasures
> of the stars and of the thunders (17. 1–2).[18]

The awestruck tone is typical of the apocalyptic visionary being presented with
grand and strange sights, like Apollinaire's poet in *La Petite Auto*, who is confronted
with figures that are laden with *interpretability* without the poet necessarily feeling
the need to *interpret* them.

   While the theatre-goers represented in the volcano receive a visual spectacle, the
Pilot is privileged to its obscure meaning, such as when he says to his visions, 'Je
suis digne de vous!' [I am worthy of you!], suggesting his reception of the imagery.
Shortly thereafter, when his vision of a grove of trees transforms into bayonets,
he proclaims, 'Je saisis le symbole' [I have seized the symbol] as yet another call
to war against Austria (*MP*, 61). In this, as in other writings, Marinetti is eager to
distinguish between the bourgeois theatre-goer and the (Futurist) spectator who has
genuine insight. In 'La Volupté d'être sifflé', he remarks that 'nous enseignons aux
auteurs le mépris du public et en particulier du public des premières représentations,
dont voici la psychologie synthétisée: rivalités de chapeaux et de toilettes féminines,
vanité d'une place coûteuse se transformant en orgueil' [we teach authors contempt
of the public and particularly the public of first performances, which is synthesized
psychology: rivalries of hats and feminine hygiene, vanity of expensive places
transformed into pride].[19] Marinetti advises Futurist writers to avoid instant fame:
'Nous enseignons aussi l'horreur du succès immédiat qui couronne les œuvres
médiocres et banales' [We also teach the horror of instant success that crowns
mediocre and banal works].[20] Success itself is not condemned, but only that success
that too easily conforms to audience expectations. The relationship to the audience is
the first of eleven prescriptions for a Futurist theatre in this manifesto, highlighting
the importance of eliciting unconventional reactions from a conventional public —
a task Marinetti views as always partially failing. Audiences are described as more
inclined to regard theatre attendance as a tactic in bourgeois pursuits of distinction
and ostentatious intellectualism. They attend the theatre not to *see* the spectacle and
put themselves in the role of visionary, but to *be seen* at the spectacle, to, in effect,
be a spectacle themselves. The audience is unreflective and capricious, and therefore
lacks any real authority to judge a work:

> Le public varie d'humeur et d'intelligence suivant les différents théâtres d'une ville, et les quatre saisons de l'année. Il est soumis aux événements politiques et sociaux, aux caprices de la mode, aux averses printanières, aux excès de la chaleur ou du froid, au dernier article lu dans l'après-midi. Il n'a malheureusement d'autre désir que celui de digérer agréablement au théâtre. Il est donc absolument incapable d'approuver, désapprouver, ou corriger une œuvre d'art.[21]

> [The public varies in mood and intelligence according to different theatres in a city, and the four seasons of the year. It is subject to political and social events, to the whims of style, to spring showers, to excesses of heat or cold, to the last article read in the afternoon. Unfortunately, it has no other desire than that of agreeably digesting the theatre. So it is absolutely incapable of approving, disapproving, or correcting a work of art.]

The audience described above could not, presumably, comprehend anything but the most apparent message of a work such as *Monoplan* — anti-Austrian and anti-Catholic sentiment, misogyny, the conflict of art versus money — without truly seeing it as a manifesto for an entire Futurist ethic which, presumably, could only be revealed to them in much more fraught situations such as theatre or, *a fortiori*, war. The Pilot's unusual vision of a theatre audience in the volcano watching the ensuing spectacle is an ample demonstration of this lack of direction:

> On y voit s'y presser tout en gesticulant
> plus d'un milliard de flammes
> spectatrices enthousiastes
> qui applaudissent et crient différemment
> un milliard de jouissances. (*MP*, 33–34)

> [We see it hurrying there while gesturing
> more than a billon flames
> enthusiastic spectators
> who applaud and cry out a billion
> different enjoyments]

While this audience is certainly engaged in the proceedings, such activity — wild gesticulations, various points of applause and shouting — is mainly incoherent and reactive, lacking an obvious sense of discrimination or interpretation. In Futurist soirées, provocation was meant 'to exploit [the audience's] power in order to create a new more spontaneous and participatory style of performance'. But, Walter Adamson continues, such provocation stages 'the separateness, absence, and difference of the Futurists at every turn',[22] which certainly can raise the charge of élitism, but a more complicated élitism given their engagement with popular forms and forums. The confrontation challenges the audience on the assumption that the majority will react with offence in the manner of a philistine public, such as in one of the only moments in *Monoplan* when the bourgeoisie are called out by name, precisely in connection with the theatre: 'et l'on écoute le pied lent du bourgeois qui revient | du théâtre et ralentit sa patiente sottise...' [and we hear the slow step of the bourgeois who returns | from the theatre and draws out his patient absurdity...] (*MP*, 230). There are two kinds of spectators: one that participates in the spectacle because they understand the Futurist project, and one that participates (often in similar ways) because they are the spectacle.

Marinetti, in his theoretical writings, is rarely so obscure about who is who. In many cases, like Apollinaire, he designates his Futurist allies by name with collectively authored manifestoes, and he condemns whole nations, even certain Italian cities such as Venice, with the appellation 'passéist' to goad sympathetic comrades in those places. The nature of apocalyptic literature, the manifesto form, and Marinetti's understanding of theatre all draw their legitimacy from an unrealized or unrealizable future. The artwork's legitimacy is deferred into the future, where it might be accepted by the broad public. Until then, 'tout ce qui est immédiatement applaudi ne surpasse pas la moyenne des intelligences; c'est partant du médiocre, du banal, du revomi ou du trop bien digéré' [everything that is immediately applauded won't surpass middling intelligence; it begins from the mediocre, the banal, the regurgitated or the too well digested].[23] The avant-garde group then becomes a kind of gnostic élite, privileged with the understanding of the future's art today, which is what allows them to engage a broader definition of art from popular culture to machinery, but is condemned to suffer the scorn of a supposedly unenlightened public.

The Murdered Moonlight

At the opposite pole of Marinetti's disdain for popular judgement is his suspicion of the obscurantism of nineteenth-century aestheticism, which Marinetti frequently grouped under the generalised term of Romanticism. One of the episodes inside Mount Etna is entitled 'Les Réservoirs du romantisme' [The Reservoirs of Romanticism], where the Pilot challenges a group of unnamed Romantic poets:

> Poètes romantiques, revenez donc en foule
> retrouver sur les bords de ce fleuve
> les plus fantastiques lanternes vénitiennes
> que vous avez rêvées!
> Elles sont enguirlandées de rose et maculées de sang...
> Vous trouverez sur les bords de ce grand fleuve de fard
> tout le fastueux bric-à-brac de votre rêve théâtral!... (*MP*, 73)

> [So come back together Romantic poets
> rediscover on the shores of this river
> the most fantastic Venetian lanterns
> that you dreamed of!
> They are garlanded with pink and stained with blood...
> You will find on these shores this great river of blush
> every sumptuous bauble of your theatrical dreams!...]

These lines recall the opening of the first Futurist manifesto that described an orientalist décor with overtones of hermeticism and mysticism: 'Nous avions veillé toute la nuit, mes amis et moi, sous des lampes de mosquée...' [We have been awake all night, my friends and I, under mosque lamps...].[24] The Futurists exist, in this moment, in the somnambulist state of a waking dream from which they will soon burst out into the light of day to bring forth the new movement. These dreaming figures also recall the opening of *Monoplan* insofar as the latter begins in the bedroom of the Pilot, as if he were asleep but also not definitively awake, as if he seeks to grasp the imaginative possibilities of dreaming without having to suffer sleep. The similarity in atmosphere of the manifesto's opening scene and that of the riverbank in the volcano suggests that the former can be understood as beginning within the space of Romanticism, with the intention of breaking out of this space. Indeed, this river scene has intriguing similarities to Coleridge's poem of high Romanticism, 'Kubla Khan' (written in 1797, but published in 1816). In the first instance, Coleridge's poem takes place 'Where Alph, the sacred river, ran | Through caverns measureless to man'.[25] It is at the river in the cavern of Mount Etna that the Romantic poets dream and, indeed, Coleridge's poem is subtitled as 'A Vision in a Dream'.[26] And like the Pilot, Kubla Khan hears 'Ancestral voices prophesying war!'[27] However, whereas Kubla Khan hears 'Ancestral voices', based on tradition or conventions across generations, the volcano's voice is primordial and self-generative. This is coherent with the entire scene's evocation of chthonic forces *against* the pressures of a tradition that confirm one's place in a continuity, but also conditions their existence. Recalling biblical typology, rivers are also associated with paradise, as the first river in Genesis flows out of the Garden of Eden (2. 10), and the river that flows from the throne of God in Revelation 22. 1 may signify a restoration of Eden. The Eden-like aspect of Xanadu, Kubla Khan's mythical palace in the poem, is readily apparent, as it is 'A sunny pleasure-dome with caves of ice',[28] and the scene in *Monoplan* conversely takes place in a cave of fire. Romanticism is then associated with a form of nostalgic reverie, powerful in sensuality, but always at a remove from real *action*, and ultimately a kind of *stasis*.

The struggle is between the interior and exterior existence: Romanticism's theatricalized interior life that has provided the poet with a rich, exciting, sensual imagination, but at the same time has insulated that poet from the external world of modernity. This scene, with its ornate Venetian lanterns and lavish odds-and-ends, is a 'rêve théâtral', meant to suggest that anything theatrical is overwrought and outmoded — indeed, Marinetti's views on Futurist theatre are intended to be anything but outmoded. The Futurist attempt to 'theatricalize' everyday life had to end in a bursting out into the daylight, 'Il faudra ébranler les portes de la vie pour en essayer les gonds et les verrous' [We will need to shake the doors of life to test their hinges and bolts].[29] Both sets of poets are also associated with the river, but in entirely different ways. The Romantic poets stand on a riverbank, only to find (four lines later) that it is a river of 'fard' [make-up]. In contrast, the sound of a tram in the manifesto is compared to the river Po in northern Italy: the tram passes 'sursautants, bariolés de lumières, tels les hameaux en fête que le Pô débordé ébranle tout à coup et déracine, pour les entraîner, sur les cascades et les remous d'un déluge, jusqu'à la mer' [jumping, many-coloured lights, such as the celebrating hamlets that the overflowing Po shake all of a sudden and uproot, to drag them, over the cascades and whirlpools of a flood, into the sea].[30] The distinction is between the 'embellishment' of the Romantic river, emphasized by the words 'enguirlandées' [garlanded], 'fard' [make-up], and 'maculées' [stained], and the violence of the tram, which is compared to the sound of the rushing waters of the river Po, sweeping the hamlets out to the chaos of the sea. Although the Pilot requests the entertainment and imagination of the Romantic poets, it is as a prelude to his escape from the volcano, bringing that energy into the world. As the Pilot states in this section: 'Car ce volcan est la synthèse | et la genèse de toute poésie' [For this volcano is the synthesis | and the genesis of all poetry] (*MP*, 73).

Given Marinetti's early, close relationship with Symbolism, the dramatic terms of his rupture with the movement that mentored him is notable. Symbolism was, for him, Romanticism's 'swan-song' — not a fruitless effort, but one that had to be rejected in order to move forward. In *Le Futurisme* (1911), Marinetti wrote in a chapter entitled 'Nous renions nos maîtres les symbolistes, derniers amants de la lune' [We renounce our Symbolist masters, last lovers of the moon] in which he expresses a deep, yet conflicted, love for 'les grands génies symbolistes: Edgar Poe, Baudelaire, Mallarmé et Verlaine' [the great Symbolist geniuses: Edgar Poe, Baudelaire, Mallarmé and Verlaine].[31] Marinetti accused them of searching into the 'beyond' for guidance, with a suspicion of technology and, most gravely, of seeking immortality:

> Nos pères symbolistes avaient une passion que nous jugeons ridicule: la passion des choses éternelles, le désir du chef d'œuvre immortel et impérissable. Nous considérons au contraire que rien n'est aussi bas et mesquin que de penser à l'immortalité en créant une œuvre d'art, plus mesquin et plus bas que la conception calculée et usurière du Paradis chrétien, qui devrait récompenser au million pour cent nos vertus terrestres.[32]

> [Our Symbolist fathers had a passion that we judge to be ridiculous: the passion for eternal things, the desire for the immortal and imperishable masterpiece. On the contrary, we consider nothing as base and petty as thinking of immortality when creating a work of art, more petty and base than the calculated and usurious conception of the Christian Paradise, which should reward at a million per cent our earthly virtues.]

For Marinetti, this struggle is simply another form of commerce — 'calculée et usurière' — that he condemns in the chapters on politics and finance, peddling art for 'symbolic' rewards rather than material. The pretence to immortality of which Marinetti accuses the Symbolists is simply another way of trading in the currency of nostalgia and tradition. Romantic and Symbolist practice is fundamentally oriented to a form of immortality analogous to a 'Paradis chrétien'.

In representing the Romantic or Symbolist traditions and their promises, Marinetti does not reject those traditions outright, but acknowledges their allure, perhaps even their necessity as starting points for bringing the act of dreaming into the world. In the early manifestoes, Marinetti is never shy about stating the importance of poets like Mallarmé and Verlaine, who were his 'pères' and 'grands génies'. The iconic image of the Symbolists' 'crime' is the moonlight, the image and object of their affections. In Marinetti's pre-Futurist works, the moon is an intensely ambiguous image of the confluence of life, death, and love, seductive and dangerous, powerful and empty, and Marinetti's struggle with Romanticism reflects this ambiguity.[33] While Marinetti understood and to some extent sympathized with the central dilemma of Romanticism as a desire for the 'Ideal' confronting the limitations of everyday life, he sought to transcend it. Cescutti writes:

> Ce drame qui s'exprime en de multiples formes duelles discordantes (matière et esprit, Dieu et l'homme, fini et infini, contenu et forme, passé et futur) caractérise toute la poésie depuis le romantisme. Il hantera Baudelaire, puis Rimbaud, Mallarmé, de même que la génération symboliste, *malades* d'un 'Idéal' également nommé 'Infini', 'Absolu', ou encore 'Inconnu'. Marinetti exacerbe le dilemme baudelairien jusqu'à provoquer la rupture.[34]

> [This drama which expresses itself in multiple dual, discordant forms (matter and spirit, God and man, finite and infinite, content and form, past and future) has characterized all poetry since Romanticism. It haunts Baudelaire, then Rimbaud, Mallarmé, as well as the Symbolist generation, sick with an 'Ideal' equally called 'Infinite', 'Absolute', or even 'Unknown'. Marinetti exacerbates the Baudelairian dilemma up to the point of provoking a rupture.]

As with Apollinaire, who also had a strained relationship to Symbolism, there is an effort to identify and aggravate contradictions, pushing 'la réflexion romantique à son paroxysme' [the Romantic reflection to its paroxysm][35] by forcing the presence, proudly unjustified, of idealized visions *within* the material world. Marinetti sought to move dialectically in and through the 'Ideal', antagonizing it to the breaking point, in order to modernize it as Futurist velocity or technology. Chapter 8, entitled 'Côte à côte avec la lune' [Side by side with the moon], deploys this image of the moon most frequently in a love scene — an uncharacteristically peaceful moment. The Pilot takes a brief respite from his war-mongering for a sexual interlude with a lover during a moonlit evening. Marinetti was keenly aware of the image of the moon in Symbolist poetry as 'la thématique romantique' [the Romantic theme] that 'diffusait autour de sa forme, à sa première apparition, une luminosité atténuée et diaphane, renvoyant aux tentations de la mélancolie et de la dissolution de l'être' [diffused around his form, in its first appearance, a diaphanous and thin luminosity, reflecting the temptations of melancholy and the dissolution of being].[36] In 'Tuons le Clair de Lune!!', the Romantic moon is a seductive force, causing the soldiers who are attacking the city of Gout to momentarily lose their fighting spirit:

> Mais lentement le sourire brillant et chaud de la Lune déborda hors des nuages craqués... Et comme elle apparaissait enfin toute ruisselante du lait grisant des acacias, les fous sentirent leur cœur se détacher de la poitrine et monter vers la surface de la nuit liquide...[37]

> [But slowly the shining and hot smile of the Moon burst out of cracked clouds... And as it appeared at last streaming with intoxicating milk from acacias, the madmen felt their hearts detach from their chests and float towards the surface of the liquid night...]

In Chapter 2, we saw how the image of the heart outside of the chest was one of Marinetti's metaphors for the Futurist overcoming the limitations of his body; but here, the heart passively drifts upward as if floating on water while the Futurists are lulled into a sense of ease. The latter image (written several years before *Monoplan*) inverts the former image: if the motor-heart of the Pilot actively drives him to his destiny, it is human heart of the pre-Futurist poet, still connected to Symbolist or Romantic idealism, which passively drifts. The Romantic Ideal of the moon casts an erotic or maternal spell, inducing calm and sexual pleasure, and the spell is broken when the refrain of the manifesto — 'Tuons le clair de lune!' — is shouted; from there, the soldiers erect massive electrical lamps to block out the moonlight: 'C'est ainsi que trois cents lunes électriques bifferent de leurs rayons de craie éblouissante l'antique reine verte des amours' [In this way, three hundred electric moons black out the old green queen of love with their dazzling rays of chalk].[38] *Monoplan* stresses this ambiguity by characterizing the moon as duplicitous: Mount Etna, figured as the moon's terrestrial counterpart, earlier states that 'J'ai pour complice la lune mensongère' [My accomplice is the lying moon] (*MP*, 46). Like the sea in *La Conquête des Étoiles*, the earthly forces are positioned as an antagonistic pairing to the celestial powers, and it is the role of the earth to assume the role that the sky occupied in a former era. In this chapter, the Pilot fully confronts the moon's allure:

> Avec un art infatigable, elle s'efforce
> d'embellir sans fin
> l'arche du ciel (*MP*, 203)

> [With a tireless art, it strives
> to embellish without end
> the bend of the sky]

The term 'embellir' again suggests the moon as something of a deceiver, even carrying misogynist undertones. The Pilot invokes the sense of the 'rêve théâtral' of Romanticism or the dreamlike space at the opening of the first Futurist manifesto: ornate and artistic, but confined to its own dream. The preceding lines might even make this allusion more explicit:

> Mon monoplan heureux partage mon plaisir,
> tandis que je contemple à loisir
> les soins minutieux
> que met la lune à déployer,
> jusqu'aux plus hautes frises du Zénith,
> ses gazes de turquoise
> poudrées d'argent. (*MP*, 203)

> [My gleeful aeroplane shares my pleasure,
> as I leisurely contemplate
> the careful minutiae
> that the Moon puts on display
> up to highest mouldings of the Zenith,
> its turquoise gauze
> powdered with silver.]

Like the ceiling of the Sistine chapel, the upper levels are elaborately and delicately painted. And in that sense, the art of the moon is not unwelcome and the Pilot is even pleased to see it, even though it is all so much meticulous embroidery, an art that is lovely, but nonetheless nostalgic and sentimental.

What Marinetti (to say nothing of Apollinaire and Pound) is cognizant of, in the writing of love in this manner, is how the revelatory and utopian dimension of art and literature elides the objective *object* and the receptive *subject*, how, as Bourdieu states, 'L'amour de l'art, comme l'amour, même et surtout le plus fou, se sent fondé dans son objet' [The love of art, especially like the most mad love, feels itself based in its object].[39] A similar and relevant observation by Karl Marx examines the means by which art inclines or interpellates the viewer to a desire for the paradisal vision:

> The need felt for the object is induced by the perception of the object. An *objet d'art* creates a public that has artistic taste and is able to enjoy beauty [...]. Production accordingly produces not only an object for the subject, but also a subject for the object.[40]

It is significant here that Marx resorts to the example of the *objet d'art*: a cultural product that elicits a particular perception, where 'production' is not simply material manufacture but interpretive work, that creates its own discourse in society, its own conceptual relationship to the world, its own *public* who intuitively understand its need for interpretation. The discovery of the subject (artist or public) in the object (artistic work) works to silence that interpretive labour, as well as the conditions for understanding the need for such labour, thus *naturalizing* in the manner of 'true love' that relationship.

Setting one's life to the pace and logic of another plane of existence or thought is foundational to apocalyptic literature, calling the believer to conform to the realm of the divine as a way to transcend death. Thus, the act of finding oneself in the work of art or religious belief, the seamless and all-too-natural alignment of belief to the 'beyond', manifests as a kind of death to the exterior world, only to have that death transcended in the next world. The tradition is located and fulfilled by the initial surrender of the Pilot, who allows himself to experience the appeal of the relationship between the artist and the artistic ideal. But the Pilot, at the height of the experience of love, enraptured by the lover's 'jardinet mignon' [sweet little garden] (*MP*, 208), sees an image of a bird 'aussie géant que moi' [as giant as myself] (*MP*, 208) that destroys the garden and 'ravage[] ce paradis' [ravage[s] this paradise] (*MP*, 209). This vision brings him back to the task at hand:

> Non, non, petite amie, je ne puis guère
> te faire une visite sérieuse cette nuit...
> Pardonne donc l'impolitesse involontaire.
> Adieu, petite amie...
> Je dois porter ailleurs ce gros pape enchaîné!... (*MP*, 209)

> [No, no, lover, I can hardly
> visit you seriously tonight...
> So pardon the sudden impoliteness.
> Goodbye, lover...
> I must carry this fat, shackled Pope elsewhere!...]

This is a crucial moment for the poet in particular, and for Futurism in general, in terms of stating its definitive 'No' to tradition and *passéisme*: after finding oneself in the Romantic ideal, a relationship characterized as love, the Futurist rejects it in favour of the razing of paradise.

John J. Collins' analysis of apocalyptic literature identifies a similar grounding of the subject within the object insofar as the longing of the believer is manifested, or more properly allegorized, in the world as it is imagined during and after the apocalypse, giving the believer a sense of having 'found' what they were looking for in the first place. Collins' argument indicates not a mere ideal, but an aspiration to an entire life practice that might extend beyond death, stating that 'If the hope of the apocalypticist was to be elevated to a heavenly life, then any information about *the heavenly regions where such life is most fully lived* is relevant to that hope.'[41] Apocalyptic sects mirrored their lives on the idea of heaven that was presented to them in accordance to the demands of a rigorously moralized life. Apocalypticism, distinguishing itself from prophecy, often understands such a life as the transcendence of death, of the moral life lived in full because it is, at last, stripped of the constraints of the fallen, material world. The hope, states Collins, 'is not primarily concerned with the end of anything. Rather it is concerned with the transcendence of death by the attainment of a higher, angelic form of life.'[42] If the Symbolists traded in a 'Paradis chrétien' in the form of 'les choses éternelles', Futurism tried to re-ground this form of revelation, in 'vertues terrestres'. The Pilot finds himself in the 'angelic' atmosphere of the love scene:

> Maison de mon amie, maison de Nazareth,
> dans vos traîneaux flottants de nuages diaprés
> qu'emporte l'attelage mélodieux des Anges!...
> Tout est blanc, tout est blanc, loin du rut et du sang!
> Plumage de tendresse... Cadences de velours...
> Mon monoplan se mêle au chœur des Séraphins... (*MP*, 210–11)

> [House of my dear, house of Nazareth,
> in your floating sleigh of many-colored clouds
> that the melodious team of Angels transports!...
> It's all white, all white, far from lust and blood!
> Plumage of tenderness... Cadences of velvet...
> My aeroplane is mixed with the choir of Seraphim...]

Noting that the house is a 'maison de Nazareth' suggests that the lover is modelled on the Virgin Mary. The gospel of Luke describes how Mary's pregnancy occurred by way of an angel's announcement while she resided in Nazareth (Luke 1. 26–27). This scene, then, recalls Mary's 'purity' and willingness to give herself, in both an erotic and spiritual sense, to God, and is itself the annunciation of the eschatological promise of Jesus. The eroticism of these lines in *Monoplan* implicates the Pilot in a similar divine communion, a relationship of affection and conception where the Pilot takes on both masculine and feminine positions, with the mystical and religious ideal that was always necessary for Futurism's positing of velocity as a figure of the apocalypse.

Death is constantly transcended in *Monoplan* through heroism or technology rather than by a dedication to the divine or the aesthetic, but it is transcended, nonetheless. For example, another instance in which Marinetti repeats the phrase 'côte à côte' is during the battle with Austria. The Pilot says to his Italian comrades: 'A bientôt le plaisir de mourir côte à côte, | ô rouges volontaires!' [Soon the pleasure of dying side by side, | O red volunteers!] (*MP*, 286). Death in an act of heroism or sacrifice is the closest one might get to transcending it, but as a perverse denial of death's finality. In the love scene of 'Côte à côte avec la lune', the imagery accepts death as an *afterlife*, rather than a form of continued existence in the Futurist camaraderie that Marinetti envisions, and this finality finds its counterpart in the sentimentalized hope of Romantic idealism. In one of the few references to Jesus in *Monoplan*, the Pilot refers to the death of Christ, but seems to reject any notion of martyrdom. Speaking to his 'amie', he states:

> Pour la seconde fois, je forme en volant
> une couronne d'épines épouvantable
> sur ton beau front qui saigne!...
> Allons donc! Il ne s'agit pas
> de Christ et de Calvaire! (*MP*, 201–02)

> [For the second time, I shape in mid-air
> A horrifying crown of thorns
> on your beautiful, bleeding forehead!...
> So let's go! It's not a matter
> of Christ and Cavalry!...]

'Calvaire' is the site of Christ's crucifixion, but also bears the connotation of an ordeal or suffering through which one is redeemed. The image of the 'couronne d'épines' is ambivalent: it is an image of martyrdom, but the description of it as 'épouvantable' undercuts any dignity for the martyr — it is merely appalling. The reference to Christ, then, is not simply a rejection of Christian agony or martyrdom, but a rejection of the resurrection as conceived in Christian theology, that is, as the promise of a heavenly afterlife, of a comfortable and eternal rest in paradise. Rather, the entire atmosphere of this chapter, from the lethargic meadows to the drunken odour of the hay, has a saccharine quality bordering on decay:

> Mais quand je plonge, ton haleine m'embaume,
> tes prairies indolentes
> me lancent par bouffées
> l'odeur ivre des foins et le parfum
> de ta gorge inquiète, et la volupté
> profonde de la terre... (*MP*, 202)

> [But when I dive, your breath embalms me,
> your lazy meadows
> hurl puffs at me
> the drunken odour of hay and the perfume
> of your worried throat, and the deep
> sensuousness of the earth...]

The sensual delights of the 'amie' ('ton haleine', 'ta gorge') are drunkenness and lassitude, and the sexualized 'foin' and the 'volupté | profonde de la terre', is sumptuous to the point of decomposition. From this perspective the Christian embrace of death with that promise of a future resurrection ultimately reduces the stakes of religious belief; this is opposed to the 'Religion-morale de la vitesse' of

Futurism, which promises a transcendence of death but, crucially, not in the terms of the resurrection of the individual ego promised by Christianity.

Marinetti's ambivalence towards Christianity and Romanticism is rooted in his understanding (and to some extent sympathy with) the longing for finding oneself in the other world of the artistic object; but he cannot concede what he sees as the highly interiorized loss of one's engagement in the world. Moving beyond the loss of oneself in 'l'absolu' or 'l'idéal', Futurism envisions resurrection as the subsumption of the ego into matter, a state that can be experienced through speed, war, and theatre. Peter Dayan has argued that the Symbolist concept (particularly of Mallarmé) of the 'Death of the Poet' constitutes a kind of death for the poet — not in the sense of oblivion, but more in the sense of one's social, everyday self: 'This death is not the death of the whole man, but merely of the individual, the "un tel" [one such as] — leaving the "soi" [self] intact. The poet abandons his everyday "élocutoire" [elocutionary] manner of thought in favour of "le rêve" [dream].'[43] In Marinetti's 'Manifeste technique de la littérature futuriste', he writes, 'Détruire le "Je" dans la littérature' [Destroy the 'I' in literature] only to replace him 'par matière, dont il faut atteindre l'essence à coups d'intuition' [by matter, whose essence must be achieved by jolts of intuition].[44] The literary 'I' was intellectualized and psychologized, and must die in order to realize itself as pure matter: 'Remplacer la psychologie de l'homme, désormais épuisée, par *l'obsession lyrique de la matière*' [Replace human psychology, sadly exhausted, by the *lyrical obsession with matter*].[45] The poet has to be *of* the world, but cannot quite be *in* the world in the sense that he or she maintains the self as a relational aspect of society or as a *kind* of individual whose psychology is defined and conditioned by that relation. What the Futurist must do, however, is maintain the sense of the dream without drifting off to sleep; the point was to assert the dream in a waking state because the apocalyptic vision is precisely one of heightened awareness, of the knowledge that it is a vision, but a vision of a deeper and more meaningful truth. The character of Gazourmah in *Mafarka le futuriste* (1909), who is described as dreaming but not sleeping, is representative of this goal: 'Aussitôt, des rêves bariolés la peupleront, mais le sommeil ne pourra s'asseoir sur ton front, haut plateau de ta vie' [Soon, variegated dreams will populate that high plateau of your life, but sleep will not be able to rest on your forehead].[46]

Polyphonic Warfare

Marinetti's reporting of the Italo-Turkish war is paradigmatic of what later came to be seen as the avant-garde and fascist aestheticization of war. Marinetti envisioned 'un vaste projet esthétique' [a vast aesthetic project] of Futurist writing and particularly performance that 'aspirait à un genre englobant qui, selon Hugo, devait être le "drame"' [aspired to an inclusive genre that, according to Hugo, had to be 'drama'],[47] and war is, in many instances of Marinetti's work, a terrifying shadow-play of death and heroism. Marinetti first sought to align this new 'genre' to the pace and diversity of the modern city in works such as *Destruction* (1904) and *La Ville charnelle* (1908), and later described *Mafarka le futuriste*, in the preface, as 'à la fois un chant lyrique, une épopée, un roman d'aventures et un drame' [at once a lyrical song, an epic, an adventure novel and a drama].[48] But the descriptions of modern warfare in *Monoplan*'s final chapter and *La Bataille de Tripoli* suggest that the aesthetic model that would redefine and break down the formal distinctions in the arts would be found on the battlefield.

Marinetti's own account of a battle against Turkish troops and local resistance in October 1911 in *La Bataille de Tripoli* pushes itself forward through a total engagement of the senses. Much of the commentary is a series of descriptions of the actual sounds that he hears at the front:

> Quand je levais la tête instinctivement, c'étaient bien des balles que j'entendais, mais des balles amoureuses dont le gazouillement idyllique se mêlait aux pépiements des moineaux dans les branches. Jamais mon oreille ne fut aussi heureuse et attentive qu'à distinguer les oiseaux vrais des illusoires.[49]

> [When I instinctively lifted my head, it was definitely bullets that I heard, but loving bullets whose idyllic tweeting mixed with the chirping of sparrows in the branches. My ears were never as happy and attentive as distinguishing the true birds from the illusory.]

The sounds are confused but joyful, and Marinetti finds an insouciant pleasure in distinguishing the chirpings of birds from the whistling of bullets. The sounds of battle are described as a 'vaste symphonie' [vast symphony][50] and Marinetti refers to the trenches as an 'orchestre' [orchestra].[51] In other sections the physical movements of war are seen in the light of dance and gymnastics. A confusing melee quickly becomes, in Marinetti's vision, the 'airs drôlatiques de derviches tourneurs' [amusing tunes of whirling dervishes], and the flights of bombs are described as 'volants trapèzes de flammes gymnastes' [flying trapezes of gymnast flames].[52] Marinetti begins to figure war as an aesthetic ur-form in which all other aesthetic conventions are contained. The references to music are particularly relevant, as Cescutti argues that music recalls an influence extending as far back as Wagner, in which the orchestration of multiple voices influenced such poets as Baudelaire, Mallarmé, and Verlaine who felt that it could 'libérer la poésie de la linéarité du langage' [liberate poetry from the linearity of language],[53] in an indication of the disintegration of time that is crucial to any eschatological viewpoint. Wagner's famous catchword was *Gesamtkunstwerk* [Total work of art], and in *Mafarka* Marinetti deploys similar phrasing at the very end that denotes totalizing and non-linear aesthetics: 'C'est ainsi que le grand espoir du monde, le grand rêve de la musique totale, se réalisait enfin dans le vol de Gazourmah... [...] Sublime espoir de la Poésie! Désir de fluidité!' [So the great hope of the world, the great dream of total music, was at last realized in the flight of Gazourmah... [...] Sublime hope of Poetry! Desire for fluidity!].[54]

In both *Monoplan* and *La Bataille de Tripoli*, Marinetti also attempts to engage less obvious senses, such as taste and smell. In *Monoplan*, the smells are said to mix and synthesize in a revolution of the Pilot's blood:

> Je hume avec ivresse l'odeur volumineuse
> et chargée de piment que répand la bataille.
> Odeur de laine chaude et de marrons brûlés.

Odeur de graisses et d'huile, d'urine et d'excréments
recuits par le soleil. Il s'y mêle de l'ail.
[...]
Puis tout se mêle, et la synthèse
désordonnée des puanteurs naïves
et des parfums mordants
s'acharne dans ma tête et révolutionne
mon sang!... (*MP*, 305–06)

[I inhale with intoxication the voluminous odour
filled with pepper that spreads across the battle.
Smell of hot wool and roast chestnuts.
Smell of fat and oil, urine and excrement
reheated by the sun. It's mixed with the garlic.
[...]
Then everything is mixed, and the untidy
synthesis of naïve stenches
and cutting perfumes
goads my head and revolutionizes
my blood!...]

The heady synaesthesia of munitions constitutes a radical re-orientation of the senses, if not, and particularly not, of the intellect ('révolutionne | mon sang!'). As above, Marinetti describes the war preparations as a form of cooking. Here he imagines the preparations of military trains as in a busy kitchen:

Sous nos pieds cette gare est bien la plus étrange
des cuisines surchauffées et fumantes,
avec ces bleus frétillements de rails-anguilles
entre les fours et les casseroles
des locomotives rangées...
Les clochettes électriques ont des bouillonnements
intenses
et des murmures de friture
dans leurs pots de faïence... (*MP*, 244)

[Under our feet this is the strangest station
of overheated and smoking kitchens,
with these blue wrigglings of eel-rails
between the ovens and saucepans
of orderly trains...
The electric bells bubble
intensely
and murmur with frying
in their earthenware pots...]

Similarly, *La Bataille de Tripoli* describes at one point the trenches as 'charcuteries'.[55] Rather than being a gratuitous diversion into the imagery of food, these sensations express a sense of power over the environment. For example, in the well-known Futurist manifestoes on cuisine, Marinetti suggested the replacement of the traditional restaurant with an aeroplane cockpit; as the diner was taking in the view, he would 'eat villages, farms and fields speeding by'.[56] Aerial distances were also conceived in the image of eating in a section entitled 'Aeropoetic Futurist Dinner': 'In front of the diners, [...] the round altimeter announces: 3000 metres eaten. Near it the tachometer, its dinner companion, announces: 20,000 revolutions devoured. On the other side of the altimeter the speedometer announces: 200 kilometres digested.'[57] This experience of war as a multiplicity of sensations, as dependent on the eschatological hybridizing of forms, constituted a change in the world and the self and, more significantly, the loss of separation of the self and history. Apocalypses are defined by the sense that all history is essentially contained in the eschatological moment itself and the compression of time and space into the single moment reveals not only the drama of history leading up to it, but the disintegration of forms that signal a new era.

Taking this hybridization of experience, self, and history further, Marinetti uses the language of theatre ('gradin en gradin') to evoke apocalyptic thought, by merging distinct spaces such as the air and the sea. In *Monoplan* the Pilot witnesses the space of the sea and the sky collapse into a single, unified space as the Pilot gets higher and higher:

> Je monte encore plus haut, de gradin en gradin,
> comme on gravit les marches d'un escalier géant.
> Je ne vois plus la ligne ténue de l'horizon...
> La mer bleue s'est haussée pour s'unir au ciel bleu (*MP*, 322)

> [I rise higher still, from tier to tier,
> as one climbs the steps of a giant ladder.
> I can't see the fine line of the horizon anymore...
> The blue sea has raised itself up to unite with the blue sky]

This image recalls the separation of ocean and sky found in the creation myth of Genesis: 'So God made the dome and separated the waters that were under the dome from the waters that were above the dome' (Genesis 1. 7). And yet, Marinetti essentially reverses the myth, re-establishing the pre-creation of chaos where absolute possibility is the sovereign principle. Marinetti lays out the history of Futurism and the machine as leading to the moment where creation itself can be conquered, and he reveals an entirely new vision that disregards the categories of perception that structure life. For instance, apocalyptic literature is often recognized by its bizarre, hybrid creatures that defy the boundaries that separate the 'normal' or 'accepted' from the 'perverse' or 'impure', notifying the viewer that the entirely new and unparalleled is at work. Daniel's four hybrid beasts ascend out of the sea only to be slain by the chosen one (Daniel 7. 1–8). The angel in Revelation 9 sounds a trumpet that releases from the pit 'locusts' whose 'faces were like human faces; their hair like women's hair, and their teeth like lion's teeth; [...] and they had tails like scorpions' (Revelation 9. 7–10). Another angel, in chapter 10, is clothed in cloud and has a face of light, and his legs are pillars of fire (Revelation 10. 1–2). The contradictory form of these figures, then, represents a kind of improbable collapsing together of the different states of creation. Similarly, Gazourmah is described, in *Mafarka le futuriste*, as a winged-man made of wood[58] and metal.[59] If the form of apocalyptic literature and art is to intimate a future so radically different that it is un-representable, then incongruity and open-ended-ness are paradoxically the most applicable representations, as they disrupt prior frameworks of perception with the intention of preparing those frameworks for the new era.

Addressing this portrayal of contradiction, Bull argues that the form of apocalypse can be understood as 'a revelation of the contradiction and indeterminacy excluded at the foundation of the world'.[60] Apocalyptic thought structures itself on the de-structuring of the distinctions and oppositions that ordered the world thus far, envisaging that de-structuring to re-create the world over again. Collins also notes the hybrid *formal* character of apocalyptic works:

> The question is complicated by the fact that some of these works are composite in character and have affinities with more than one genre. The book of Daniel, which juxtaposes tales in chaps. 1–6 and visions in chaps. 7–12, is an obvious example. [...] It would seem that Jewish apocalyptic writings that lack a common title and are often combined with other forms had not yet attained [...] generic self-consciousness.[61]

Monoplan, using the same indeterminacy of the 'composite character' of biblical apocalyptic literature, is an epic poem that is described in the subtitle as a 'roman'. Despite the lyric intensity of the work, which allows for direct communication of the singular experience of the poet, the *narrative* dominates, inscribing that experience into existing social possibilities, be they religious, artistic, technological, or erotic, and allowing those possibilities to be compared to and refracted through one another. The nature of those social possibilities is also contained in the subtitle, 'Roman politique', and *Monoplan* is as much national and nationalist as it is aesthetic and 'spiritual'. The polemics against the Catholic Church in *Monoplan* are not only an attack on religious idealism, but also on the political power of the church itself, whose monopoly on 'salvation' would be replaced, in theory, by Futurist machinery or materiality. On the other hand, the parliamentary scenes in *Monoplan* show a great variety of marginalized groups — from students, to homosexuals, to the poor — expressing themselves, and the organization of martial force would require that such an array must be shaped into a single unit or 'voice'. The use of multiple voices in this scene tends towards an appreciation of polyphony, but of course they are not properly *orchestrated* in the sense that Marinetti envisages in the final chapter of *Monoplan* or in *La Bataille de Tripoli*. Nonetheless, the polyphonic element, ultimately united under the banner of Italian nationalism, is a significant step towards the politics of Futurism. For example, Christine Poggi describes Carlo Carrà's (1881–1966) 1914 piece 'Manifestazione interventista (Festa patriottica-dipinto parolibero)' [Interventionist Demonstration (Patriotic Festival Painting Words-In-Freedom)] (Fig. 5.1), a wildly discordant picture of words and colours radiating out from the central words 'Italia' [Italy] and 'Aviatore' [Aviator], as an expression of the variety of modern life anchored to the national and technological element: 'With the term *Italia* firmly anchored at its centre, the nation appears as a centrifugally expanding force. The volatility and cacophony of modern life [...] are affirmed within this all-embracing, dynamic, but hierarchical structure.'[62]

The orchestration of polyphony culminated in Marinetti's *parole in libertà* [words-

FIG. 5.1. *Mattioli Collection, Italy*

in-freedom] as the lyrical form that would supersede *vers libre*.[63] Quoting Marinetti, Cescutti argues that, 'Sur le vers poétique, le "style orchestral, à la fois polychrome, polyphonique et polymorphe, *pouvant* embrasser la vie de la matière" actualise une dramatisation du langage qui sera à la base des "mots en liberté futuristes"' [On the poetic verse, the 'orchestral style, at once polychromatic, polyphonic and polymorphic, that *can* embrace the life of matter' actualizes a dramatization of language that will be the foundation of 'Futurist words-in-freedom'].[64] Once again, theatre imagery is used to assert a blending of genres and aesthetics in the battle scene:

> dans cet amphithéâtre de montagnes.
> Il nous faut traverser le parterre et monter
> sous les feux convergents des loges foudroyantes
> sur la scène invisible au rideau de fumée!... (*MP*, 300)

> [in this amphitheatre of mountains.
> We must cross the stalls and climb
> under the converging fires of lightning boxes
> on the invisible stage at the curtain of smoke!...]

> escalader la scène de ce théâtre de montagnes! (*MP*, 311)

> [climb the stage of this theatre of mountains!]

Cescutti argues, regarding his 1905 play *Roi Bombance*, that Marinetti's attention to the form of drama allows a multiple, open work in which various voices mutually influence each other, describing it as a 'véritable tentative de dramaturgie polyphonique, dressant une sorte de fresque multiple de la vie dynamique' [real attempt at polyphonic dramaturgy, erecting a sort of multiple fresco of dynamic life].[65] But as discussed above, music was just as important as a means to demonstrate the merging of forms:

> La campagne rayée de longs rangs militaires,
> comme une lyre immense aux cordes polychromes,
> vibre aux pizzicati de mille automobiles!... (*MP*, 289)

> [The countryside striped by long military ranks,
> like an immense lyre with polychromatic strings,
> pizzicato vibration of a thousand cars!...]

> Sur les falaises, les violons enragés du vent
> électrisent les boyaux miauleurs de la forêt,
> en chantant plus haut que l'orchestre
> formidable de la mer...
> Le ronflement de mon moteur se plaît à moudre
> cette arrachante polyphonie (*MP*, 339)

> [Over the cliffs, the enraged violins of the wind
> electrifying the mewling entrails of the forest,
> singing higher than the formidable
> orchestra of the sea...
> The snoring of my motor likes to grind
> this ripping polyphony]

The question of polyphony, then, becomes a political one, where the erasure of the distinctions between genres is presented alongside the interweaving of voices into a polyphonic unity where it's crucial to distinguish *unity* from *equality*, the former being a state in which individuals are located in a relationship to power based on the on the spiritual-aesthetic values of Futurism, and the latter being — in Marinetti's view, at least — largely as false a pretence as the Parliamentary respectability attacked in *Monoplan*.

In the concluding battle, the reader gets the first sense of how the aesthetic of the hybrid, polyphonic voice provides the foundation for what could be tentatively described as a fascist aesthetic. Indeed, in this chapter of *Monoplan*, Marinetti uses the word 'faisceau(x)' to speak of the 'bundles' of soldiers, a word that could refer to flexible reeds or sticks that were lashed to together to become stronger and more rigid. These bundles which were carried by Roman soldiers as a symbol of their authority, and would later become a symbol of fascism under Mussolini.[66] The Pilot sees the collection of munitions, for example, as 'faisceaux':

> chaque wagon ayant deux cents mètres de long,
> et portant en faisceaux
> des fusils, des tenailles
> et des morceaux de fer plus grands que des maisons. (*MP*, 326)

> [each car being two hundred metres long,
> and carrying bundles
> of rifles, pliers
> and pieces of iron larger than houses.]

But another usage of the term uses it in the sense of military units or groupings of combatants:

> Je suis sur vous, inébranlable comme un phare,
> dont la lentille souveraine
> groupe les moindres feux épars de la détresse
> et les mue en faisceaux de courage. (*MP*, 319)

> [I am above you, steadfast like a lighthouse,
> whose sovereign lens
> gathers the smallest, scattered fires from distress
> and changes them into bundles of courage.]

In these lines, the Pilot sees a melee of soldiers as a scattered and disparate collection. Like the light of 'un phare',[67] the Pilot's sight illuminates and concentrates, providing focus for the 'faisceaux' of soldiers who were 'lost'. 'Faisceaux' is used, then, to discuss the machinery of war and the soldiers that the Pilot guides as part of that machinery. Marinetti has embraced the polyphony of individuals only to transfigure them, within the machine-aesthetic that Futurism preached, in a death and rebirth radically distinct from the Romanticism or Christianity that Marinetti militated against. This was a death to the individual life that the soldier might have led before, and rebirth to the idea of Futurism or *Italia*.

★ ★ ★ ★ ★

However, the cycle of death and rebirth posed a problem for Futurism, being a 'natural', sometimes even 'maternal' force that challenged the masculine Futurist's ability to create *sui generis*. Poggi states that, therefore, this cycle 'must be opposed and displaced by both the machine and its symbolic ally, matter (physical substance/energy understood as inherently dynamic)'.[68] In this sense, the cycle of nature was closely connected to the Romantic Ideal: a longing for immortality that is experienced passively at the 'will' of a transcendent force. Marinetti clearly sees military order and mechanical aggression as a trait of Futurism; but, as argued above, he also sees war, armies, and machines as having aesthetic properties that speed up and expand understandings of time and space, emphasize multiplicity, and dissolve distinctions. Speaking of a group of soldiers in *Monoplan*, the Pilot states: 'Mon vol plané m'entraîne dans le vallon inassouvi | qui vient de dévorer notre avant-garde rouge' [My level flight leads me into the unsatisfied valley | that has just devoured our red vanguard] (*MP*, 315). Marinetti's use of 'avant-garde' draws upon the term's military origins, aligning its martial connotations with its association to the most experimental or radical ends of artistic Modernism. It is also significant that they have been devoured by the valley in these lines. Like the Pilot, who took his own 'Orphic' journey into the heart of the earth in the episode of his flight into Mount Etna, the soldiers undergo a similar experience, presumably allowing them to emerge as the same kind of 'avant-garde' as the Futurist Pilot. The association with being 'swallowed' by the earth prepares these soldiers for a rebirth similar to that of the Pilot's. To achieve this rebirth, the soldiers are martyred, but not simply in the physical sense; as part of an aesthetic experience, an artistic work in the guise of war, they will lose their psychological 'I'. The point is to goad the new avant-gardist into giving his life because he is nothing more nor less than matter; rather than humanize or anthropomorphize matter, the Futurist poet seeks to think with 'la sensibilité et les instincts des métaux, des pierres et du bois' [the sensibility and instincts of metal, rocks and wood].[69] Here is the complete inversion of the Romantic tradition as Marinetti sees it — the death of the 'I' not in the abstract, and therefore inert, Ideal, but in active matter. At the crucial point in the battle, the Pilot's body transforms into a living weapon and he announces the arrival of 'l'obus de mon corps!...' [the bombshell of my body!...] (*MP*, 346).

Mount Etna is, once again, Marinetti's touchstone as the paradigmatic figure of the re-absorption of the ego into matter, or the dissemination of the human consciousness into materiality, being a geological locus for the cycle of destruction and re-creation. What the Pilot sees in 'le spectacle des spectacles' (*MP*, 34) is no less than the repeated dissolution and creation of the world itself. He witnesses splitting crevasses and forming continents in the midst of a 'mer de feu' [sea of fire] as a spectator in a theatrical event:

> Des fleuves, des rivières
> et des ruisseaux resplendissants
> gorgés de lingots d'or, accourent à l'envi
> pour la nourrir en ruisselant
> hors des crevasses éloquentes
> qui s'ouvrent de distance en distance

> tout le long des gradins,
> parmi l'ondoyante moisson
> des flammes et des gaz spectateurs. (*MP*, 35)

> [Rivers, waterways,
> and radiant streams
> stuffed with ingots of gold, rushing in enviously
> to nourish it while cascading
> from eloquent cracks
> that open up from place to place
> along the length of the stalls,
> among waving harvest
> of flames and gaseous spectators.]

The theatre stalls split open among the rivers and streams that cut down the spectators of gas and flame as they feed the sea of fire. But just as this space is being divided and broken down, it immediately begins to reform:

> Et cette mer de feu se fige et s'empierre.
> Par groupes de caillots et d'îlots cousus, fondus,
> par rapides alluvions de rubis et d'agates,
> un continent se forme, vermeil, éblouissant... (*MP*, 36)

> [And this sea of fire congeals and fossilizes.
> By groups of pebbles and islets fastening together, melted,
> by quick alluvial deposits of rubies and agates,
> a continent forms itself, vermillion, dazzling...]

This is the apocalyptic dismantling of the world as theatrical entertainment — and not just for Marinetti but for writers and artists all over Europe at this time. For example, in 1919 the poet Blaise Cendrars (1887–1961) wrote 'La Fin du Monde filmée par l'Ange N-D' [The end of the world filmed by the Angel N D], a peculiar piece of poetry-for-the-screen written for the filmmaker Fernand Léger (1881–1955), who ultimately failed to produce it. In this piece, an angel at the top of Notre Dame Cathedral takes a camera and records the apocalypse and subsequent reformation of the world. Between the shock of World War I and the development of technologies such as photography and film, the apocalypse became something to watch or witness, preferably from the elevated position of the Pilot or angel. While not necessarily seeing the apocalypse as something specifically *of the theatre*, avant-gardists had become highly sensitive to its *theatricality* based often on a self-understanding of being 'above' or 'detached' from the end of the world because, in a sense, they had already embraced the end through the distancing of their own radical cultural practice.

However, Marinetti was not satisfied with a cycle of destruction and creation as a passive experience: Futurism was dedicated to asserting a form of control or orchestration over that cycle. In the first instance, this control was asserted by embracing the rejection of nostalgia and tradition. When the volcano finally speaks, it expounds upon its own nature as in destroying and rebuilding: 'Je n'ai jamais dormi. Je travaille sans fin | pour enrichir l'espace de chefs-d'œuvres éphémères!' [I have never slept. I work without end | to enrich the space of ephemeral masterpieces!] (*MP*, 44). It allies itself with eternity and warns against nostalgia, and ultimately its only exhortation seems to be a warning to those who might be attached to tradition:

> Malheur à ceux qui veulent enraciner
> leurs cœurs, leurs pieds et leurs maisons
> avec un ladre espoir d'éternité! (*MP*, 47)

> [Curse those who want to root
> their hearts, their feet and their houses
> with the miserly hope of eternity!]

> Gare à ceux qui s'endorment
> en adorant la trace des ancêtres
> sous les calmes feuillages de la Paix! (*MP*, 50)

> [Beware of those who fall asleep
> worshipping the tracks of ancestors
> under the calm leaves of Peace!]

While this does not really answer the Pilot's query about the 'devoirs' of his race (*MP*, 31), it expresses 'l'horreur de durer' [the horror of lasting] (*MP*, 45) implicated in the Futurist idolatry of speed and cult of youth. But when, after the volcano's discourse, the Pilot shouts, 'J'ai compris, j'ai compris ma mission!...' [I've understood, I've understood my mission!...] (*MP*, 55), he is aspiring to the same 'masculinized' power over matter (recall that the volcano is called 'père'), that creates and destroys through the aesthetic or technological manipulation of matter described by Poggi: 'Caught in this cyclic temporality, nature can never propel Marinetti into the future', and so the velocity of the machine 'allows Marinetti to confound the organic and the mechanical, the procreative and industrial, and thereby to seize for himself the illusory power of male autogenesis.'[70] When the volcano states, 'Ma vie est la fusion perpétuelle de mes débris' [My life is the perpetual fusion of my remnants] (*MP*, 44), it is embodying that same longing for autogenesis — the ability to create and re-create oneself irrespective of the cycles of time or biology.

At the end of *Monoplan*, the Pilot shouts, in a single line set off in its own stanza, 'Détruire! Il faut détruire!... il faut sans fin détruire!...' [Destroy! We must destroy!... we must destroy without end!...] (*MP*, 346). This is not just an eschatological moment; it is that moment repeated over and over. Futurism sought to live within that moment between death and rebirth, or between destruction and new creation. That is to say, it is living in the apocalyptic moment in the manner of apocalyptic sects, that is as incipient (religious) communities who have ordered their lives according to an understanding of how the future will be, and so therefore live within the space between a dying world and a new world. But the theme of rebirth is prominent in Marinetti, for the poet, for art, for the Italian nation:

> La vaste mer enceinte
> s'ouvre péniblement sous le soleil nouveau-né
> qui fait force de la tête... (*MP*, 281–82)

> [The vast pregnant sea
> opens up with difficulty under the new-born sun
> that strengthens my head...]

> Tu fus rebaptisé par le sang des héros.
> Quant à moi, j'en ruisselle!... Mes ailes
> sont imbibées d'une aurore éternelle... (*MP*, 318)

> [You were rebaptized by the blood of heroes.
> As for myself, I am flowing!... My wings
> are dipped in an eternal dawn...]

The old traditions have died, only to be replaced by the new Futurist sun (a symbol that would have more than passing fascist connotations), as Marinetti wrote in the 1924 manifesto 'Le Futurisme mondial' [Worldwide Futurism]: 'A un siècle de distance, face au grand soleil romantique de 1830 (qui ne fut, somme toute, qu'un soleil pour Chants du Crépuscule) voici la montée au zénith de gloire [...] du grand soleil futuriste' [A century gone, facing the great Romantic sun of 1830 (which was only, after all, a sun for Songs of the Twilight) this is the rise to the zenith of glory [...] of the great Futurist sun]. The messianic pretensions assert that Futurism will be the new Christianity and Marinetti/the Pilot, the new Pope. The final act of destroying the past is consummated when the Pilot releases his cargo, dropping the Pope as a bomb into the sea:

> C'est bien ici pourtant
> au beau milieu de ce grand lac italien
> Adriatique,
> que fut prédisposé depuis toujours
> le grand tombeau mouvant du dernier de nos Papes!... (*MP*, 343)

> [It's even here however
> in the middle of this great Italian
> Adriatic lake,
> that was always ready to be
> the great moving tomb of the last of our Popes!...]

> Je suis léger libre et puissant!...
> Je suis un italien délivré tout à coup
> de son lest chrétien
> et de ses lourdes entraves catholiques!... (*MP*, 344)

> [I am light free and powerful!...
> I am an Italian suddenly delivered
> from his Christian ballast
> and his heavy Catholic millstone!...]

By presenting the Futurist 'problem' as a religious or spiritual one, Marinetti raises the stakes for those involved. Futurism was not to be regarded as merely a political movement or artistic avant-garde (although it was both of those things); it was an occupation of the space of the higher spiritual Ideal that it claimed to overthrow in Romanticism or Catholicism with velocity and the machine.

Notes to Chapter 5

1. F. T. Marinetti, *La Bataille de Tripoli (26 Octobre 1911): vécue et chantée* (Milan: Edizioni Futuriste di 'Poesia', 1912), p. 23.

2. Carl von Clausewitz, *On War*, trans. by Michael Howard and Peter Paret (Princeton, NJ: Princeton University Press), 1976), p. 280; emphasis added.

3. F. T. Marinetti, Emilio Settimelli, and Bruno Corra, 'The Futurist Synthetic Theatre', in *Futurism: An Anthology*, ed. by Lawrence Rainey, Christine Poggi, Laura Wittman (New Haven, CT: Yale University Press, 2009), pp. 204–09 (p. 204); see also F. T. Marinetti, Emilio Settimelli, and Bruno Corra, 'Le Théâtre Futuriste Synthétique', in *Futurisme: Manifestes — Proclamations — Documents*, ed. by Giovanni Lista (Lausanne: L'Age d'Homme, 1973), pp. 256–60. This manifesto was first published in French in 1915. The Italian version, published shortly thereafter, contained several additions that were specifically directed towards Italian readers. Passages examined in this chapter that were not originally published in French will be quoted in English translation.

4. Marinetti, et al., 'Futurist Synthetic Theatre', p. 204.

5. F. T. Marinetti, 'Le Music-Hall', in *Futurisme: Manifestes — Proclamations — Documents*, ed. by Giovanni Lista (Lausanne: L'Age d'Homme, 1973), pp. 249–54 (p. 252).

6. Marinetti, et al., 'Théâtre Futuriste', p. 260.

7. Marinetti, *Le Futurisme*, p. 109.

8. David E. Aune enumerates the number of times that John refers to his vision of events with some variant of the phrase 'I saw': a total of forty-two times in the book (with twenty-six additional phrases referring to hearing), having 'the function of encouraging unconditional acceptance of the vision report at face value' (David E. Aune, 'The Social Matrix of the Apocalypse of John', *Biblical Research*, 26 (1981), 16–32 (p. 18)).

9. Puchner, *Poetry of the Revolution*, p. 5.

10. Marinetti, et al., 'Théâtre Futuriste', p. 259.

11. Martin Puchner, 'Screeching Voices: Avant-Garde Manifestos in the Cabaret', in *European Avant-Garde: New Perspectives*, ed. by Dietrich Scheunemann (Amsterdam: Rodopi, 2000), pp. 113–36 (p. 126).

12. John J. Collins, 'Apocalyptic Eschatology as the Transcendence of Death', in *Visionaries and Their Apocalypses*, ed. by Paul D. Hanson (Philadelphia, PA: Fortress Press, 1983), pp. 61–84 (pp. 71–72).

13. For example, Revelation is addressed to specific locales, but as Aune points out, 'John intentionally ignored local church officials since his role as a mediator of divine revelation transcended local community concerns' (Aune, 'Social Matrix', p. 25).

14. Elisabeth Schüssler Fiorenza, 'The Followers of the Lamb: Visionary Rhetoric and Social-Political Situation', *Semeia*, 36 (1986), pp. 123–46 (pp. 139–40).

15. Quoted in Poggi, *Inventing Futurism*, p. 265. While Futurism's later developments are beyond the bounds of this study, Poggi describes how the movement's post-war alignment with fascism brought out mystical or spiritual attitudes, which this quotation from 1931 expresses.

16. Dave E. Aune, 'The Apocalypse of John and the Problem of Genre', *Semeia*, 36 (1986), 65–96 (p. 91).

17. F. T. Marinetti, 'Beyond Communism', in *Futurism: An Anthology*, ed. by Lawrence Rainey, Christine Poggi, Laura Wittman (New Haven, CT: Yale University Press, 2009), p. 262; originally published in Italian.

18. Quoted from George W. E. Nickelsburg and James C. VanderKam, trans., *1 Enoch* (Minneapolis, MN: Fortress Press, 2004), p. 38; emphases added.

19. Marinetti, *Le Futurisme*, pp. 103–04.

20. Ibid.

21. Ibid., pp. 104–05.

22. Walter L. Adamson, *Embattled Avant-Gardes: Modernism's Resistance to Commodity Culture in Europe* (Berkeley: University of California Press, 2007), pp. 90–91.

23. Ibid., pp. 109–10.

24. Marinetti, 'Fondation et Manifeste du Futurisme', p. 83.

25. Samuel Taylor Coleridge, *Selected Poetry and Prose*, ed. by Elisabeth Schneider, 2nd edn (San Francisco, CA: Rinehart Press, 1971), pp. 120–21.

26. Ibid., p. 119.

27. Ibid., p. 121.

28. Ibid.

29. Marinetti, 'Fondation et Manifestes', p. 85.

30. Ibid.

31. Marinetti, *Le Futurisme*, p. 82.

32. Ibid., pp. 83–84.

33. Cescutti, *Origines mythiques*, pp. 352–53.

34. Ibid., p. 158.

35. Ibid., p. 246.

36. Ibid., p. 357.

37. F. T. Marinetti, 'Tuons le Clair de Lune', in *Futurisme: Manifestes — Proclamations — Documents*, ed. by Giovanni Lista (Lausanne: L'Age d'Homme, 1973), p. 109.

38. Ibid.

39. Bourdieu, *Les Règles de l'art*, p. 14.

40. Karl Marx, *On Literature and Art* (Moscow: Progress Publishers, 1976), p. 129.

41. Collins, 'Apocalyptic Eschatology', p. 74; emphasis added.

42. Ibid.

43. Peter Dayan, *Mallarmé's 'Divine Transposition': Real and Apparent Sources of Literary Value* (Oxford: Clarendon Press, 1986), p. 37.

44. Marinetti, 'Manifeste Technique', p. 135.

45. Ibid.

46. F. T. Marinetti, *Mafarka le futuriste: roman africain* (Paris: E. Sansot & Cie, 1909), p. 281.

47. Cescutti, *Origines mythiques*, p. 244.

48. Marinetti, *Mafarka*, p. vii.

49. Marinetti, *Bataille*, p. 33.

50. Ibid.

51. Ibid., p. 6.

52. Ibid., p. 41.

53. Cescutti, *Origines mythiques*, p. 254, n. 24.

54. Marinetti, *Mafarka*, pp. 305–06.

55. Marinetti, *Bataille*, p. 48.

56. F. T. Marinetti, *The Futurist Cookbook*, ed. by Lesley Chamberlain, trans. by Suzanne Brill (London: Trefoil Publications, 1989), p. 122.

57. Ibid., p. 124.

58. Marinetti, *Mafarka*, p. 293.

59. Ibid., p. 282.

60. Bull, *Seeing Things Hidden*, p. 83.

61. John J. Collins, *The Apocalyptic Imagination: An Introduction of the Jewish Matrix of Christianity* (New York: Crossroad, 1984), p. 3.

62. Poggi, *Inventing Futurism*, p. 52.

63. In a version of the manifesto 'Imagination sans fils et les mots en liberté' [Wireless Imagination and words-in-freedom] (1913), Marinetti condemns *vers libre* in terms suggesting that it is irreparably confined to the self of the poet, stating that it is 'imprisoned' in the psychological framework of Romantic and post-Romantic poetry that Futurism intended to transgress and transcend (in Rainey, et al., *Futurism: An Anthology*, p. 146).

64. Cescutti, *Origines mythiques*, p. 260.

65. Ibid.

66. 'Faisceau' is the French counterpart to the Italian 'fascio', which would be adopted by Mussolini as the symbol and name of the *Fasci Italiani di Combattimento*, the precursor to the Italian fascist party.

67. The image of the lighthouse, as a moral, spiritual, or aesthetic guide, is prominently used by one of Marinetti's 'grands génies symbolistes', Baudelaire, in his poem 'Les Phares' (1857), which lists famous painters and their influence on later generations.

68. Poggi, *Inventing Futurism*, p. 156.

69. Marinetti, 'Manifeste Technique', p. 135.

70. Poggi, *Inventing Futurism*, p. 156.

CHAPTER 6

❖

Failure and the *Phantastikon*

Pound preached a new aesthetic practice, which could potentially renew the tradition of beauty, at a time when the evidence of historical and political events suggested a decline; and he only felt confident enough to declare that the new era had arrived after Mussolini's 'March on Rome' in 1922, which he marked as Year Zero, often dating subsequent letters and publications accordingly. Therefore, Pound's advocacy seemed to occur in the period of its most untenable justifications. The failure of the prophet, however, may be a perverse legitimacy for his prophecy when measured against collapsing social, political, or cultural institutions in his contemporary world, leading from a prophetic eschatology to an apocalyptic eschatology. Paul Hanson provides an explanation for this transition in terms of Israelite prophecy, when the destruction of the temple in Jerusalem and the end of the Davidic monarchy precluded any probable avenue for God's salvation. Ezekiel, as an example of a more 'pragmatic' prophetic eschatology, predicts the rebuilding of the Temple upon the return of the Israelites to Jerusalem, whereas visionary groups, in periods where such a prospect seemed absolutely *otherworldly*, were led to proclaim that Israel must look to the improbable for salvation. From this point on, Hanson argues,

> The prophets no longer have the events of a nation's history into which they can translate the terms of Yahweh's cosmic will. Hence the successors of the prophets, the visionaries, continue to have visions, but they increasingly abdicate the other dimension of the prophetic office, the translation into historical events. At that point we enter the period of the transition from prophetic to apocalyptic eschatology.[1]

An eschatological belief looks outside of history to the cosmos or a sacred history — what must be typically represented by the poetic means of symbol or metaphor — to find confirmation of one's position. The break that is the eschatological moment is the construction of a negativity that implicitly declares all the known possibilities to be inadequate and, writes Gerhard von Rad,

> goes so deep that the new state beyond it cannot be understood as the continuation of what went before. It is as if Israel and all her religious assets are thrown back to a point of vacuum, a vacuum which the prophets must first create by preaching judgment and sweeping away all false security, and then fill with their message of the new thing.[2]

But this definition of eschatology lies at the extreme end of the continuum laid out by Hanson, where the prophet has first failed to locate God's ultimate salvation within worldly institutions and must seek after more visionary possibilities.

In 'Provincialism the Enemy', a series of articles he wrote in 1917 for *The New Age* (a magazine title that does not lack in apocalyptic pretention), Pound stated that, 'the lords of the temporal world never will take an artist with any seriousness'.[3] The emphasis on the 'temporal world' can be taken to mean that the appeal to any individuals or institutions of the 'here-and-now' is fruitless. Pound's position expressed an abandonment of the hope in the birthplace for the new era *within this world*, an abandonment that took the form of deeply anti-political attitudes expressed in much of his poetry as well as his letters and critical writings. Nevertheless, Pound needed to maintain a sense of a possible future, which was not to be found in Christian messianism. The second section of this chapter will accordingly examine how Pound felt, as expressed by Octavio Paz, that in Christianity,

> the future was mortal: the Last Judgment was to be the day of its abolition and the advent of an eternal present. The critical process of the modern age inverted the terms: the only eternity known to man was that of the future.[4]

Pound sought to recover the forces of spiritual renewal represented in the dead pagan gods of Pan, Dionysus, or even in a masculinized version of Christ. But Pound's major problem in conceiving a new millennium was not how to get out of history, but how to present history in a way that ran counter to its apparently inexorable degeneration. Pound's solution, the subject of the final section, was to chart a middle course between the visionary artist and the objective world to construct a point where beauty and history meet — a term he occasionally called the *phantastikon*.

The Old Lie

In a letter, dated 10 November 1917, that Pound had written to William Carlos Williams (1883–1963), Pound laments, using distinctly apocalyptic language, that the problem for the American artist was precisely America's politics:

> I thought the ————millennium that we all idiotically look for and work for was to be when an American artist could stay at home without being dragged into civic campaigns, dilutations of controversy, etc., when he could stay in America without growing propagandist.[5]

The apocalyptic moment that the modern artist aims for is one of complete divorce from the public sphere, which otherwise draws them away from their art and, more significantly, draws the art away from itself into political squabbles. The rejection of the public sphere as the site of the cultural renaissance that Pound sought is expressed as the denial of politics as a progressively self-perfecting and rational enterprise. In 'Provincialism the Enemy', Pound states: 'Fundamentally, I do not care "politically", I care for civilisation, and I do not care who collects the taxes, or who polices the thoroughfares.'[6] This dismissive attitude towards a particular structure of power is not the attitude one finds in prophets such as Amos, Hosea,

Micah, Jeremiah, or Isaiah. When Amos, for example, proclaims doom on those who 'afflict the righteous, who take a bribe, | and push aside the needy in the gate' (5. 12), he is making a judgment about the political relationships prevalent in Israel. Amos goes on to state that there is a solution, a possibility for God to relent in his anger if the relationship of the powerful to the powerless, in that same place of public intercourse, is reversed:

> establish justice in the gate;
> it may be that the Lord, the God of hosts,
> will be gracious. (5. 15)

This particular attitude is not typically considered an eschatological expression because there is no great, final moment of salvation in which justice will finally reign eternal. Rather, Amos explains an on-going dialectic between divine punishment and reprieve that finds its counterpart in everyday practices and relationships. Von Rad argues that, in this view, history was the measure of Israel's relationship to the eternal covenant with God, and contingent upon the way Israel behaved from generation to generation: 'No generation was exempted from that task; each one in succession was obliged to achieve this self-understanding in faith.'[7]

What concerned Pound was how to conceive of a culture divorced from questions of power and reform, that is, a continual series of struggles and compromises between individuals and groups seeking to maximize their own interests, as opposed to unencumbered ideals of poetic beauty. If that beauty is to be constantly subject to the mediation of politics and social interests, then 'the ideal of representative government to some extent conflicts with Pound's conviction that the arts are not democratic.'[8] Wyndham Lewis similarly eschewed democratic politics in favour of individual artistic production, and declared in the first issue of *Blast* that 'the vortex', that is the unique cultural moment distilled to its vital core, has 'nothing to do with "the People"'.[9] He went on to make an appeal to English Suffragettes that they take care not to mix art and politics because, 'political struggles of emancipation are questions of "votes" and not of "art", and *Blast* here signals a desire to keep art and politics [...] separate.'[10] Anti-political elements are at the root of apocalyptic literature because it projects salvation into the realm of the divine, where struggles over power only have meaning in highly mythical ways. As Hanson writes, prophecy, as opposed to apocalyptic literature,

> insisted upon translating the vision received from Yahweh into the categories of politics and plain history, and thus resisted the temptation of escape from the real world to the cosmic realm offered by myth and ecstasy. But [...] developments in the political realm made such translation increasingly difficult, as little within plain history could be identified with divine action and the political realm took on the appearance of unmitigated evil. A sudden resurgence of myth began to offer the possibility of escape rejected by early prophecy, and the result of this development was the death of prophecy and the birth of apocalyptic eschatology.[11]

'The wise' (משכלים, *maśkᵉlîm*) in Daniel 11 and 12, likely identified with the figure of Daniel himself (see Daniel 1. 3), are a signature instance of the anti-politics of the apocalyptic writer, since, as Collins writes, they are 'portrayed as activists, but they are not said to fight' against the persecution of Antiochus IV Epiphanes (215–163 BCE).

> Their activism lies in making the masses understand. The understanding they convey is presumably the revelation contained in the book of Daniel. The thesis of the visions is that the true meaning of events is not publicly evident but is known to the wise, through revelations. The real struggle is being fought out between the angelic princes.[12]

The 'angelic princes' are supernatural representatives of the nations at war, such as the archangel Michael, 'one of the chief princes' (10. 13), who battles on behalf of Israel against the 'princes' of Persia and Greece (10. 13, 20). This understanding of history, 'that whatever happens on earth is a reflection of a celestial archetype',[13] was very common in the mythologies of the ancient Near East and provided apocalyptic writers with the means to characterize political and military struggles as mere representations of grander, cosmic battles that were often already pre-determined. A rise or decline in fortunes was conceived as a change in a god's relationship to its national host. From the perspective of 'the wise' in Daniel, the key to the struggle was not to participate politically or militarily, but to understand its cosmic importance and impart that understanding to others. The reward for understanding was the election of 'the wise' to a divine or quasi-divine status, 'refined, purified, and cleansed, until the time of the end' (11. 35).

The day-to-day workings of the public sphere, in Pound, are designed to frustrate the interests of the artist, who must live and work in that public sphere but also struggle to avoid engaging it on its terms. *Mauberley* begins with a reminder of how incompatible 'E P' is with the society of Edwardian London. Politics in particular are viewed with a jaundiced eye. In section VI of *Mauberley*, Pound begins with the line, 'Gladstone was still respected' (*P*, 189) as an insult against the liberal Prime Minister W. E. Gladstone (1809–1898) and, probably more broadly, a representation of bourgeois, middle-brow morality that stifled good art.[14] An even more devastating critique is the line 'home to old lies and new infamy', an allusion to David Lloyd George's statement as Prime Minister during World War I that the soldiers would return to 'homes fit for heroes'.[15] The poet's priorities are radically different from the cynicism informing the activity of, not just the wider public, but the literary class in particular:

> For three years, out of key with his time,
> He strove to resuscitate the dead art
> Of poetry; to maintain 'the sublime'
> In the old sense. Wrong from the start — (*P*, 185)

Using the musical imagery of pitch and harmony ('out of key with his time'), E P is 'singing a different tune' in much the same way that Pound's partial adherence to various personae is designed as a jarring juxtaposition to the world around him. The reference to 'three years' would be roughly the time when Pound attempted and failed to develop an aesthetic through Imagism and Vorticism that could instigate a new renaissance, an effort that marks him off from the struggles of power within society, seemingly unconcerned with the strivings of political parties or social cliques, because he is attending to the efforts and art of the dead, resurrecting them by resurrecting their struggles.

The effort 'to maintain "the sublime" | In the old sense' is an anachronistic endeavour, but the idea of resurrecting or resuscitating the dead has clear apocalyptic connotations. Daniel 12. 2 is an example where, at the moment when Israel is rescued by the archangel Michael, 'Many of those who sleep in the dust of the earth shall awake'. But what is important about Daniel in this section is the characterization of the time just prior to the resurrection of the dead. It is a period of intense hardship, where Israel's suffering is at its greatest point: 'There shall be a time of anguish, such as has never occurred since nations first came into existence.' It is at this point, where it has reached the cusp of its apparent doom, that the nation is saved, transfigured at the moment where time seems irreversible and terminal. The stanza ends with Pound's judgement that E P was 'Wrong from the start — '; but are not all apocalyptic sentiments 'wrong from the start'? As both Pound and the author of Daniel felt, the beginning could only be truly understood by reference to the end. If anything, *apparent* beginnings or origins were an illusion or a deception. So the following stanza of *Mauberley* immediately mitigates the harsh judgment that Pound places on his own work. After stating that he was 'Wrong from the start — ', he reconsiders: 'No, hardly, but seeing he had been born | In a half-savage country, out of date' (P, 185). The fact of E P's beginning, his birth 'In a half-savage country' identifies (like Pound's frequent touchstone, the *Odyssey*) a hero starting from the point of furthest remove from his goal or home. He begins in a place filled with pettiness and cynicism, politics and propaganda, meant to emphasize the seeming impossibility of his ever reaching his 'millennium'.

Pound speaks from the standpoint of a different origin from most poets, allowing him to argue that his 'out of date' agenda was not 'Wrong', but in fact enabled him to see what his contemporaries were inured to by the 'deception' of politics. The poet is as distant from the millennium as anyone else, but his mentality is specifically drawn from that defeated hope: always lamenting modernity's lost potential that was, ironically, stifled by its own emphasis on the transient and the superficial, by greed and by 'usury age-old and age-thick' (P, 188). The line, 'His true Penelope was Flaubert' (P, 185) suggests that his goal, after a writer whom Pound regarded as 'the painter of the *essential* reality of his time',[16] is to expose the fundamentally practical terms of his reality. But the image that 'The age demanded' was neither beauty nor tradition but

> a mould in plaster,
> Made with no loss of time,
> A prose kinema, not, not assuredly, alabaster
> Or the 'sculpture' of rhyme. (P, 186)

This final image, the hastily put together as opposed to the carefully crafted, summarizes Pound's complaint: 'the cut stone is associated with clarity of ideas, the modelled with muddle.'[17] Because the 'age demanded' arts 'Made with no loss of time', those arts lack the proper perspective of the beginning and ending and will lose the sense that art is *regaining* something that was missing. Without that perspective, the arts will fail to understand the depths of deception that it is their responsibility to cut through.

★ ★ ★ ★ ★

Truth, in biblical apocalyptic literature, reveals not only the cosmic foundation of historical events, but in doing so reveals the illusion that is this world. As in Marinetti's formulation of the dream discussed in the previous chapter, the vision is false, but speaks to a deeper reality that, by contrast, makes the external world seem transient and deceptive. The concern for truth, particularly during a crisis such as World War I, is evidence of Pound's desire for a newer, better, and more real world beneath the deceptions that constitute the 'reality' of this world. The dualism of apocalyptic literature, which regards the history of the temporal world as a reflection of events in the divine sphere, emphasizes the question of deceit or illusion and the role of proper understanding and wisdom to see the 'truth', not simply as verifiable statements and facts, but as a unique and authentic perception that is not structured by external interests and that orders the world in a comprehensible way. However, Pound echoes Isaiah 59. 14, 'for truth stumbles in the public square', in suggesting that public discourse is not rigorous enough to withstand influence of deceit and lies:

> Died some, pro patria,
> non 'dulce' non 'et decor'...
> walked eye-deep in hell
> believing in old men's lies, then unbelieving
> came home, home to a lie,
> home to many deceits,
> home to old lies and new infamy;
> usury age-old and age-thick
> and liars in public places. (P, 188)

As opposed to the private vision of the poet, the public sphere is the place of 'civic campaigns' and 'dilutations of controversy', in short, the propaganda where truth is most suppressed. The apocalyptic sections of Daniel again provide parallels to the role of propaganda and duplicity by the powerful, describing the arch-enemy of 'the wise' largely through his practice of deception and efforts to 'obtain the kingdom through intrigue' (11. 21). He then conspires with foreign kings, though not necessarily in good faith: 'and after an alliance is made with him, he shall act deceitfully' (11. 23); 'The two kings, their minds bent on evil, shall sit at one table and exchange lies' (11. 27). When the arch-enemy finally gains power through deception, he invades several nations in an imperialist war before 'he shall come to his end' (11. 45) under unstated circumstances.

Pound himself is more moralistic on questions of truth and falsehood than we've seen with Apollinaire and Marinetti, who revel in the possibilities for obscurity in art and literature. Pound wrote that 'If Armageddon has taught us anything it should have taught us to abominate the half-truth, and the tellers of the half-truth, in literature.'[18] Pound tells the story of war, and the deceptions that led to war, from the perspective of the dead who suffered most from such lies. Echoing Wilfred Owen's characterization of 'The old Lie; Dulce et Decorum est | Pro patria mori', Pound sends his soldiers 'eye-deep in hell' for the sake of 'the old lie'.[19] They were the ones who, believing them to be true, died for the sake of deception but they return 'unbelieving'. The theme of descending into hell ('walked eye-deep in hell') — which Pound elaborated on at great length in Cantos XIV and XV, the so-called 'Hell Cantos', which also dwells at length on various kinds of deception — and returning with clarity of vision or supernatural power is widely attested in the myths of Orpheus and Odysseus, or Dante's journey into the heart of the Inferno before ascending to Paradise. The so-called 'harrowing of hell', the Christian tradition of Christ's descent into hell prior to his resurrection, where he scourges the damned and leads the sinless into heaven, is a particularly eschatological myth that indicates a new era where truth reigns. After the soldiers make their own 'descent', they return to a country that is still steeped in lies and deceptions, though they are now apparently more perceptive about distinguishing between lies and truth. Like the avant-garde, or 'the wise', these members of the dead are (or at least are envisioned as) a minority or an elect, so the question then is when exactly something resembling 'truth' can show itself to the world in general rather than to just these select few. The soldiers, having braved the war and paid for the lies that initiated it, having gone through 'hell and back', have reached the furthest point from truth and so have nothing to lose by asserting their intolerance of half-truths. Pound portrays them as lifting back the deceptions in a great revelation of truth:

> fortitude as never before
>
> frankness as never before
> disillusions as never told in the old days,
> hysterias, trench confessions,
> laughter out of dead bellies. (*P*, 188)

The experience of the war has a cleansing effect (Marinetti might even say 'hygienic') in terms of wiping away all of the falseness that led to it in the first place. Something new has indeed happened in these lines, signalled by the repeated phrase 'as never before'. There are no more illusions — only *dis*illusions, and ones so great that they were 'never told in the old days'. The 'unbelieving' soldiers make confessions in the trenches and corpses laugh, again alluding to the motif of the return of the dead. Pound also makes the point that this sort of revelation takes an uncommon level of courage, such as might be found in soldiers or indeed uncompromising artists, relating the word 'fortitude' to the plainspoken 'frankness', rather than to a more refined 'honesty' or 'authenticity'. In Pound's view, not only has Armageddon 'taught us to abominate the half-truth', but Armageddon is indeed required in order to reveal truth, suggesting again that truth can only be reached in the midst of the lie, that Paradise can only be reached via Hell in an inversion of the desire for a better, perhaps even utopian, world.

These lines in *Mauberley* demonstrate a 'doubling-down' that is itself the mark of apocalyptic. James Crenshaw states, similarly, that when Israelite prophecy was 'Confronted with the apparent injustice of God' it 'confessed God's healing presence *in the face of everything*'.[20] The Imagist and Vorticist aesthetics expressed Pound's faith that England was on the cusp of a new renaissance, but by the end of the war, that faith — in the institutions of politics, law, education, and even art — had been disconfirmed by history. In this sense, the laughter of the dead suggests an ambivalent form of mockery: on the one hand they may be mocking the belief that Pound ever thought that the history of the West could be anything other than decline and death; on the other hand, perhaps they are mocking death itself, looking beyond death, as if it were an open door, into the future. Rather than try to compete with the deception on its own terms, the poet simply asserts his higher 'truth' in the form of an unaccountable revelation, which, as we've seen with avant-garde strategies, operates at an unspoken level for the poet's potential audience — that is, it is not explicable, but it is accessible to intuition. This revelation defies conventional forms of legitimation, and, as Crenshaw writes, 'Once prophecy was shown to be incapable of bearing the burden of history, unable to validate itself in the present, and unwilling to deal with the problem of evil save in apodictic fashion, a void appeared in Israel's soul. Neither apocalyptic nor wisdom[21] [literature] suffered from the above weaknesses, and both rushed in to fill the vacancy.'[22] Collins offers a brief discussion of this connection to be found between apocalyptic and wisdom literature, both of which contend with mankind's inability to truly know God's plan. Collins writes,

> apocalypses do indeed present a kind of wisdom insofar as they, first, offer an understanding of the structure of the universe and of history, and, second, see right understanding as the precondition of right action. This wisdom, however, is not the inductive kind that we find in Proverbs or Sirach, but is acquired through revelation. [...] There is also an analogy between the wisdom literature and some apocalypses on the level of the underlying questions, insofar as both are often concerned with theodicy or the problem of divine justice.[23]

Furthermore, Collins states that while, for both wisdom literature and apocalyptic literature, wisdom is found 'in the order of the universe, [...] for the apocalyptist this wisdom is hidden and is obscured by iniquity on earth'.[24] 'The wise', in this sense, are those elite few who have already received the 'gift' of revelation, adhering to a common theme among esoteric traditions, as Leon Surette explains of the occult, 'history is seen as a story of conflict between superior individuals of small number [...] and an oppressive inferior mass'.[25] Whether that 'inferior mass' may end up as enlightened or damned may come down to the view of the apocalyptic visionary.

Referring to Ecclesiastes' famous list of 'times' (3. 1–8), von Rad argues that a basic precept of wisdom in ancient Israel was that time was not abstract, but determined by events, and that 'the utmost degree of wisdom was necessary not to miss the times appointed for things and their discharge, and to recognize their mysterious *kairos*.'[26] But what were the times that Pound and many of his contemporaries felt were upon them? There was a widespread belief that World War I was the 'War that will end war', to use H. G. Wells's famous phrase, precisely because it would destroy 'existing sociopolitical structures [...] forcing the creation of a new, greater structure to prevent any recurrence of war.'[27] But Pound went further with Imagism and Vorticism, often proclaiming it as a new thing in much broader terms: religious, psychic, and cultural. As Comens notes, Christianity in particular was a point of attack for Pound: '[T]he wartime imagery of hell, of Armageddon, and of an eventual perpetual peace was powerful enough to exert considerable influence'.[28] But rather than disavowing Christianity altogether, as the next section will demonstrate, there is a tension with a 'truer' and more vital version of the religion that Pound had in mind. While his 'remarkable veneration of scientific method and intense dislike of Christianity no doubt combine to blind him to these elements of a mythic narrative that, as we will see, clearly draws on the Christian apocalyptic',[29] it was really the Christianity of his own day — perceived as effete, bourgeois, narrow-minded — that he sought to contrast with an energetic, masculine, even chauvinistic, version of Jesus that, to his mind, had nothing to do with the contemporary church, and everything to do with the apocalyptic tradition of death and rebirth that he associated with his own art. Just as Marinetti sought to ground Futurism in the 'primordial' with *Monoplan's* discourse with Mount Etna, Pound will also seek a form of legitimacy in the notion of 'primitive Christianity'.

The Christian *Virtù*

An advertisement for the first issue of *Blast* that appeared on 1 April 1914 in *The Egoist* proclaimed the birth of Vorticism as 'The end of the Christian era'. Pound and Lewis were assuming a belief that was not uncommon at the time — Yeats also believed that the 'Christian era was coming to the end of its two-thousand year cycle'.[30] While Pound was at times sympathetic to the ecstatic aspects he perceived in early Christianity, he held the view that the church had degenerated into hoary, self-serving dogmatics. In *The Spirit of Romance* (1910; revd 1932), Pound regarded early Christianity — that is, Christianity at the time of Jesus and immediately after — as an 'ecstatic religion' that was not 'dogma or propaganda of something called the *one truth* or the *universal truth*'.[31] A few years later, in a letter to Harriet Monroe, he described Christianity as 'a bastard faith devised for the purpose of making good Roman citizens, or slaves, and which is *thoroughly different from that originally preached in Palestine. In this sense Christ is thoroughly dead.*'[32] In 'Provincialism the Enemy', he writes:

> Religious dogma is a set of arbitrary, unprovable statements about the unknown.
> A clergy, any clergy, is an organized set of men using these arbitrary statements
> to further their own designs. There is no room for such among people of any
> enlightenment.[33]

Is Pound implicitly contrasting the Christian clergy to his Imagist and Vorticist comrades as an established rival to a new spirituality? It's difficult to know, but in a reference to the 'holy Roman Church' as an institution that straitjackets civilization into provincial obedience, it's clear that he felt his role as a modern poet was to contend with the religious field, as well as the literary. But despite his negative assessment of the Church, Pound saw in early or 'primitive' Christianity a religion whose 'general object appear[ed] to be to stimulate a sort of confidence in the life-force'.[34] The 'end of the Christian era', picking up a certain revolutionary fervour, meant that 'the life-force' could be recovered once again and deployed to build a new man or new nation.

Satires on contemporary bourgeois morality and life, such as 'L'Homme Moyen Sensuel' (1917) or 'Mœurs Contemporaines' (1918), are some of Pound's most concerted efforts to skewer Christianity. The latter's relevant lines describe the enervating influence of religion on 'Mr. Hecatomb Styrax' and the people around him:

> His ineptitudes
> Have driven his wife from one religious excess to another.
> She has abandoned the vicar
> For he was lacking in vehemence;
> She is now the high-priestess
> Of a modern and ethical cult,
> And even now Mr. Styrax
> Does not believe in aesthetics. (*P*, 176)

The men in these lines are shown as sexually impotent or inexperienced (earlier in the poem, Styrax is described as a virgin until the age of 28) and parallels are drawn between religious ecstasy and aesthetic practice, drawing together these two fields in their ability to compensate for, or mediate, sexual desire. Styrax is a cuckold, but his wife's attempt to couple with the vicar is no more successful. The 'religious excess' of Styrax's wife is superficially comparable to sex, but more significantly, it's a failed quest for a spiritual-aesthetic meaning. There is a Dionysian fervour to her behaviour, concluding with her becoming, ironically and disappointingly, 'the high-priestess | Of a modern and ethical cult'. However, Styrax's wife can be commended as the only active element in these lines, genuinely seeking some kind of purpose, a journey that concludes with her defining her own purpose as the leader of a cult. At the same time, Styrax remains quite passive, a trait that is connected with his unwillingness or inability to 'believe in aesthetics'. Pound, therefore, draws out a comparison of aesthetic exploration to religious ecstasy, and to the fertility or vitality that is lost in contemporary Christian society. For example, in section III of *Mauberley*, Pound writes:

> Christ follows Dionysus,
> Phallic and ambrosial
> Made way for macerations (*P*, 186)

Christ, in these lines, is an instance of the fertile vitality of Dionysus but is then pushed aside for the degeneracy, the 'macerations' or softening, of modern life. The speaker is nostalgic for the excessive, ecstatic energies that (he believes) characterized primitive Christianity and embraced the cycle of death and rebirth, 'a religion of ecstasy, *virtù*, and the life force'.[35] In a very brief piece entitled 'Statues of Gods' (1939), Pound laments that 'The only Christian festivals having any vitality are welded to sun festivals, the spring solstice, the Corpus and St. John's eve, registering the turn of the sun'.[36] These elements are worthwhile because they still retain a residue of paganism, but moreover, they register a sense of cyclical time for an eternal energy or creative dynamism that goes through phases and might always regenerate and renew the world at the moment of death, as opposed to the terminal time of contemporary Christianity, which promises a definitive end to anxiety and suffering.

In 'L'Homme moyen sensuel', a poem that knowingly deploys cheap rhymes and no regular metre, the 'hero', Radway, has no clear purpose in life, and so adopts a highly bourgeois version of Christian socializing:

> Also, he'd read of christian virtues in
> That canting rag called *Everybody's Magazine*,
> And heard a clergy that tries on more wheezes
> Than e'er were heard of by Our Lord Ch . . . . J . . . .
> So he 'faced life' with rather mixed intentions,
> He had attended country Christian Endeavour Conventions (P, 259)

If 'christian virtues' (and perhaps Pound's first, un-capitalized 'christian' hints at the impotent, middle-brow nature of those virtues on offer) are designed for an undifferentiated 'Everybody', then they could only be the most bland and mediocre platitudes. The quotation marks around the phrase 'faced life' ironizes the idea that life can be based on the cant of magazines or the 'more wheezes | Than e'er were heard of by Our Lord Ch . . . . J . . . .'. The final insistence that even Christ would have found this version of Christianity peculiar and foreign recalls Pound's description of Jesus in 'Provincialism the Enemy': 'Christ's cross was not so much on Calvary as in His lamentable lack of foresight. Had He possessed this faculty we might imagine His having dictated to His disciples some such text as "Thou shalt not 'save' thy neighbour's soul by any patent panacea or kultur." '[37] The result is a life of 'mixed intentions', where the individual lacks a clear goal and passively floats through the world in a wash of prescribed cultural panaceas.

The figure of Jesus Christ in 'Ballad of the Goodly Fere' (1909) is, unlike Styrax or Radway, a more overtly masculine individual. As Witemeyer explains, Pound wrote the poem as an angry denunciation of 'a "cheap" conception of Jesus', and as the representation of a more 'vitalistic' protagonist.[38] The poem is written from the perspective of the obscure apostle, Simon the Zealot, who begins his account with the question of whether Jesus is now to be replaced by the Church and death: 'Ha' we lost the goodliest fere o' all | For the priest and the gallows tree?' (P, 31) The priest is a figure similar to the 'vicar [...] lacking in vehemence' of 'Mœurs Contemporaines', and who is contrasted to the saviour who 'cow[s] a thousand men | on the hills of Galilee' (P, 32), a 'mate of the wind and sea' (P, 33) who shows 'how a brave man dies on the tree' (P, 32). The vigorousness of his life is part and parcel with his willingness to embrace death, unlike Styrax and Radway, who, in avoiding danger and excitement, barely live to begin with. This Christ laughs at death in the same way the dead in *Mauberley* laugh from the trenches:

> Aye he sent us out through the crossed high spears
> And the scorn of his laugh rang free,
> 'Why took ye not me when I walked about
> Alone in the town?' says he. (P, 31)

Against the image of the gentle and forgiving saviour of the gospels, this Christ provokes and mocks the soldiers who arrest him. For example, in Matthew 26. 38, after going to Gethsemane with his disciples, Jesus expresses fear and sadness at his impending death: 'I am deeply grieved, even to death; remain here, and stay awake with me.' In the following verse he asks God to 'let this cup pass from me'.[39] Pound's Christ, on the other hand, embraces death: ' "I'll go to the feast," quo' our Goodly Fere, | "Though I go to the gallows tree." ' (P, 32). Witemeyer observes that this poem, being told from the perspective of Christ's apostle, is Pound's attempt to establish a greater level of authority than scripture through direct witness in order 'to create the illusion of a reliable and historically irrefutable first-hand witness'.[40] Like Apollinaire's article 'Des Faux' (discussed in Chapter 1), Pound has little regard for the historiography of the gospels. Simon Zelotes contradicts the Gospel version by asserting that his understanding of the figure of Christ comes from his own experience, the seemingly disinterested spontaneity of his account being superior to the redactable written accounts of the church. His denial of scripture — the lynchpin of Christian orthodoxy — is summed up in the following stanza:

> They'll no' get him a' in a book I think
> Though they write it cunningly;
> No mouse of the scrolls was the Goodly Fere
> But aye loved the open sea. (P, 32)

We see here how even though the Christ of this poem is a 'man of action', the church that eventually takes over his legacy is already attempting to limit the potential of that legacy in the unchallengeable prison of the text. This is contrary to the spirit of Christ: there is no ponderous intellectualism to him, or peevish moralizing — only an idealized, masculine courage that 'venerated the life force and the men who most embody it'.[41]

★ ★ ★ ★ ★

However, Christian apocalypticism, in its more common forms, needed to be repurposed as a more explicit act of creation. As noted above, Paz states that the trouble with contemporary Christian eschatology, from the avant-garde perspective, is that its vision of the apocalyptic moment maintains a definitive historical terminus. History ends in a utopian non-time, where suffering has been eradicated as has the creativity and development that finds its source in struggle and alienation:

> Christian eternity was the solution to all contradictions and anguish, the end of history and of time; our [Modernist] future, though the repository of perfection, is neither resting-place nor end; on the contrary, it is a continuous beginning, a permanent movement forward.[42]

Pound, like most avant-gardists, can't accept this 'utopic stagnation'; to the extent that modern society offers a well-served and well-ordered life, Pound balks: 'The denuded or mechanised life lacks attraction. No intelligent man goes toward it with his eyes open — whether it means a mechanical simplification, or a mechanical complication.'[43] What Pound wished to maintain was the apocalyptic sense of revealing an entirely, radically new epoch, without revelation itself becoming redundant. Pound's attraction to his version of primitive Christianity, in which he saw both the advent of a new epoch and the continuation of a tradition of revelation, as modes of perception specific to the poet or visionary, was driven by a desire to maintain the most vital aspects of tradition but, as he famously dictated, to 'Make it New'.

Yet, this effort is engaged in a struggle to conceptualize a new era when the symbols and materials of the present era are the only ones at hand. Unlike biblical myth, which offers a constellation of signs derived largely from the repetitions of nature and empire as the metaphors for a hidden, cosmic history, modernity's symbols are necessarily more transient and seemingly more superficial. In Revelation 6. 13–14, the eschaton is signalled by the collapsing of the heavens at the close of the season: 'the stars of the sky fell to the earth as the fig tree drops its winter fruit when shaken by the gale. The sky vanished like a scroll rolling itself up'. Like the Pilot's vision in *Monoplan* of the sea and sky collapsing together, there is the suggestion of a reversal of creation. If the sky and stars are the language used by the apocalyptist to glean the meaning of history, then the heavens vanishing 'like a scroll rolling itself up' suggests that this language is no longer relevant or the 'scroll' has been read to the end. 'Pan is Dead', a poem that confronts this problem, was first published toward the end of 1912, in Pound's collection *The Ripostes of Ezra Pound*, and is one of several poems where Pound broaches the subject of the potential return to some form of neo-paganism as a reaction to the secularism — the frivolity, even — of modernity. The poem is written as a dialogue between the speaker and a group of women who lament the death of their nature-god. Pound viewed the end of the pagan era as a paradigm shift into the Christian era ('Christ follows Dionysus'); but, at the same time, due to his belief that the Christian era was coming to a close, Pound speculated on the possibility of resurrecting a pagan spirit — specifically, a spirit that honoured the inevitability of death and renewal. Noting Pound's occasional interest in the occult, Surette provides a relevant note on the relationship between Christianity and paganism: by claiming that their traditions pre-dated Christianity, some occultists 'attempt[ed] to *recover* older, pagan beliefs and practices from *within* Christianity'.[44] In this respect, Pound wishes to draw out the vital and formative energy of early Christianity. As the comparative mythologies of scholars like James Frazer (1854–1941) asserted, that energy can be understood as being transcendent of all religion because it is the very notion of renewal in paganism that early Christianity initially appropriated. The opening of the poem refers the death of Pan in Plutarch's *Moralia*, which later traditions held to herald the birth of Christianity:[45]

> "Pan is dead. Great Pan is dead.
> Ah! bow your heads, ye maidens all,
> And weave ye him his coronal." (P, 67)

This was a common theme for several poets, including Apollinaire, who wrote the poem 'Mort de Pan' when he was an adolescent.[46] As A. David Moody explains, 'Behind this stands Elizabeth Barrett Browning's 'The Dead Pan', which celebrates the tradition that 'at the hour of the Saviour's agony, a cry of "Great Pan is dead"' was heard, and the pagan mysteries were no more.'[47] This is the sort of paradigm-shift that eschatologies take as their starting point and logical endpoint. It creates, in the words of Frank Kermode, in reference to Yeats, the fiction of 'a time of transition, the last moment before a new annunciation, a new gyre.'[48] The death of the god does not create an absence of belief, but shifts the world from one system of belief to another. Responding to the speaker in 'Pan is Dead', the women insist that without Pan's existence, and consequently his connection with nature, they simply are at a loss for *how* they might go about honouring the now-deceased god:

> 'There is no summer in the leaves,
> And withered are the sedges;
> How shall we weave a coronal,
> Or gather floral pledges?' (P, 68)

The problem with honouring Pan, from this perspective, is that the very terms by which he might be honoured — the celebration of nature, floral decoration, even forms of sexual intercourse — have died along with him. As a god of nature, Pan's death, presumably at the onset of Autumn, kills the symbols and materials by which he is known. The question directly asks, given that Pan — or any god — is created through the homage he receives, how a former era might be commemorated when its time is well and truly past; but at the same time, it implicitly raises the problem of how to imagine the new epoch when we inevitably lack the language and discourse for that age, especially when the discourse of an age is embedded in the very 'nature' of the age. To suggest that Pan can be honoured or represented independently of the natural world is to suggest that nature and Pan are not *analogues of each other*, which the myth emphatically denies. Pan is both the objective representation of the natural world and the subjective experience of it; Pan is not *like* nature, but rather is nature by means of an association that is fundamentally creative and poetic, where any celebration of nature *is* Pan. Speaking in terms of the Imagist principles of 'Pan is Dead', Comens tellingly formulates the problem in terms of nature, stating that, 'Pound discovered that the structure of the sentence, by miming *relations* in nature, could present, or re-enact, the structure of nature, beyond discursive capabilities.'[49] Imagist poetry, in Pound's view, was capable of constructing that relationship of identity, if not explaining it; and indeed, explaining it was precluded in the sense that it was a relationship 'beyond discursive capabilities' whose inarticulability was a mark of its place in an entirely other world.

Even if this obscurity renders the message more esoteric, this is still the *most truthful* expression of the world as the poet finds it. Pound wrote in his biography of Henri Gaudier-Brzeska that 'The image is itself the speech. The image is the word beyond formulated language.'[50] In his discussions of Imagism and Vorticism, Pound explains the concept of the 'primary pigment' in the arts as each art-form's own exclusive way of expression: the image in poetry, the colour scheme in painting, the sentence in prose, and so on. In 'Pan is Dead', as well as his discussion of the 'primary pigment', Pound makes the argument that what is expressed cannot be separated from the means of expression. The suggestion that a return to the language of Pan, as a pre-discursive language of nature, not entirely unlike Apollinaire's return to bodily language or Marinetti's return to the 'language' of wood and stone, might be similarly replicated in the modern era is expressed when Pound reverts to a language of Christianity to express the lament. If the reference to 'our Lord' is to be understood as potentially alluding to Christ as much as to Pan, then Pound would be suggesting a return to *the animating principles* of early Christianity without suggesting a return to Christianity itself. These principles are more vigorous and dynamic than the dogmatics of the contemporary church, and are more consonant with pagan religion:

> "[...] How should he [death] show a reason,
> That he has taken our Lord away
> Upon such hollow season?" (*P*, 68)

Witemeyer points to the 'Frazerian motif' of a god dying at the approach of winter in reference to this poem, presumably to be reborn in the spring,[51] and it is worth recalling that this motif of the seasonal cycle in apocalyptic thought can be found in the image of the 'fig tree drop[ping] its winter fruit' in Revelation 6. 13. The ambiguity of the term 'Lord' is telling. By using the locution more common to Christianity, Pound is alluding to the imminent end of the religion while at the same time asserting that this death was natural and provided an avenue to reimagine a new epoch. After the lament of the women that the summer has gone from the leaves, we are reminded that the 'hollow season' is only a 'season', rather than an eternity, and despite the evidence the tradition can be recalled and lived again.

The 'Filmy Shell'

As much of this study has examined, the apocalyptic mode of discourse plays on the divisions between what can be seen and not seen, or how what is seen can be real or imagined. The term *phantastikon*, which Pound briefly uses in his early works to describe the objectification of an inner response, is examined in this section to demonstrate how Pound hoped to mediate artistic subjectivity with a wider public. Jane Goldman defines apocalypse (in the sense of Modernist art and literature) as 'a non–linear, *revelatory response to image*, where a kind of instantaneous, epiphanic reading occurs in an intense moment of lyric aestheticism or subjective introspection.' She goes on to state that 'such aesthetic moments constitute an escape from the real, material world'.[52] Goldman's emphasis on 'lyric aestheticism', where such aestheticism is perceived as a total and independent structure that is withdrawn from the world is similar to Collins' view that apocalyptic thought is founded in the 'mystic participation in the higher form of life'.[53] For Pound, aesthetics became their own 'higher form of life', although an 'escape from the real, material world' did not necessarily require ignorance or unconcern of the world, as might be thought of Decadent or Symbolist theories of art. It did mean that the poetic content, necessarily drawn from this world, was shot through with the vital tradition that the modern world was lacking, transforming that content into something entirely aesthetic, idealized, or new.

Pound's essay 'I Gather the Limbs of Osiris' (1911–12) describes an aspect of art and poetry that he felt was fundamental: that every artwork tends toward a kind of absolute independence from the world, that 'every masterpiece contains its law within itself, self-sufficing to itself'.[54] An excellent poem or painting is not simply its own 'take on the world', it is its own self-contained, conceptual system that is a development in the history of that system. It may draw elements from the world in the same way that the language of Pan draws from nature. Importantly, Pound felt that the element of the world from which the poet extracted his or her imagery attained a kind of truth within the artwork that was not mimetic. Again, using the concept of the primary pigment, he wrote that, 'The primary pigment of poetry is the IMAGE. The Vorticist will not allow the primary expression of any concept of emotion to drag itself out into mimicry.'[55] Rather, the image achieves its truth when it takes a step outside of the history or the temporal world from which it came and represents something original or 'primary'. The image, in this sense, becomes the starting point from which the poet can contemplate the revelation of something altogether new. Witemeyer takes this revelation of the image a step further and suggests that it is part of the poet's ability to create an 'imaginative "world"'.[56] Drawing from a quotation by Pound himself — 'The essential thing about a poet is that he build us his world' — Witemeyer states that the faculty Pound called the *phantastikon* was the ability to see 'patches of the macrocosmos' reflected in the poet's consciousness.[57] From these 'patches', the poet can build 'different worlds out of what they see, out of what is reflected by the "filmy shell" of the consciousness.'[58] Pound's metaphor of the translucent 'filmy shell' then describes a poet who has a view of the external world, but that consciousness itself provides a secondary reflection, where select aspects of the external world are obscured, highlighted, or overlaid with the poet's own self-image. However, the 'filmy shell' also implies the instability of the world, and so cannot be easily equated with the world-building exercise described by Berger, who insists that 'the world-building activity of man is always and inevitably a collective enterprise. While it may be possible [...] to analyze man's relationship to his world in purely individual terms, the empirical reality of human world-building is always a social one.'[59]

This poetic world-building is not entirely that of biblical apocalyptic literature, which typically understands revelation as the unveiling of an otherworldly conflict, and this world as a mere reflection of that conflict. The understanding of apocalyptic thought that came to prominence in Romanticism, particularly with such poets as William Blake, is much more oriented towards sensory re-alignment and a withdrawal from history. Comens states that it 'consists in a perceptual revolution that can occur at any moment: the ordinary world dissolves in favour of a new, visionary reality, the equivalent of the millennium. In this view, it is only our perceptual inability that condemns us to live in a "fallen" world, for the (visionary) *real* world exists now, ahistorically.'[60] Early in *Mauberley*, Pound highlights a predominant theme throughout the poem, the distinction between the truth of the world as the poet perceives it, and the daily deceptions the poet attempts to cut through. When he speaks of what the 'age demanded' he writes:

> Not, not certainly, the obscure reveries
> Of the inward gaze;
> Better mendacities
> Than the classics in paraphrase! (*P*, 186)

The tradition here is rejected by the public. Despite being a 'paraphrase', a form supposedly meant to cater to a broad audience, the 'age demanded', nevertheless, another kind of mendacity. The 'inward gaze', on the other hand, is a hint of Romantic aestheticism, the poet searching an interior world of subjective experience in order to find his truth, and these lines represent something of a criticism of that tradition of subjectively visualizing another world as a sufficient break with the external world. The 'inward gaze' recalls Goldman's 'intense moment of lyric aestheticism or subjective introspection': it is a sensation of a world that exists outside of time and therefore does not rely upon history or society for any sort of legitimation. However, the 'inward gaze' is 'obscure': while the strength of its imagination is evident, it fails to find truth '*in* things' — autonomy runs the risk of an inert solipsism. Pound wished to draw out the truth from within history through a more visionary approach to it, but not to abandon history entirely in the sense of the Romantic or 'inward gaze'. He hoped to assert an aesthetic that imposed the truth of history onto the world, expressed in the form of the image or 'primary pigment' of poetry. If the 'inward gaze' was, at least in isolation, an evasion of history, then Pound intended for Imagism and Vorticism to become a form of revelatory historiography of the 'patches of the macrocosmos' that are effective in their negativity or distance from history as such.

Pound's criticism of a *purely* visionary aesthetics is brought to bear later in the poem, where he documents the failure of the Pre-Raphaelites. He's certainly sympathetic to the visionaries and their *sight* as poets and painters. The title of section VI is 'Yeux Glauques', referring to the bright, watery eyes common to Pre-Raphaelite paintings ('The Burne-Jones cartons | Have preserved her eyes'[61] (*P*, 189)). There is an aqueous quality to this gaze, which sees something beyond or through the material existence of everyday life. But at the same time, this vision is represented as 'thin' and 'vacant', lacking substance to what is being seen:

> Thin, like brook-water,
> With a vacant gaze.
> [...]
> The thin, clear gaze, the same
> Still darts out faun-like from the half-ruin'd face (*P*, 189)

The visionary experience is certainly something that Pound feels sympathy for, but he does not seem to regard it as a 'perceptual revolution'. The reference to the faun is an allusion to Rimbaud's 'Tête de faune', a short and peculiar poem demonstrating the sudden, unexpected appearance of the truly magical in a scene of the otherwise mundane.[62] Rimbaud writes that from out of dense foliage, 'Un faune effaré montre ses deux yeux' [A frightened faun shows its two eyes] but then suddenly 'il a fui' [it fled].[63] The image indicates the desire of the Pre-Raphaelites to uncover, however briefly, the truly magical, the thing that cannot exist within the rationality of the real world. But the *truly magical* does not necessarily equate the *true*, either as the poetic *virtù* or the mundane truth of 'the world as it is', and the image of the 'faun-like' gaze lacks substance and connection to the history or social world that the Pre-Raphaelites find themselves in. It 'darts out from the half-ruin'd face' in that it exists in the baroque sensibilities of the Pre-Raphaelites, who do not draw their inspiration from 'history' as a unified tradition, but from the fragmented remnants of the past. To the extent that this kind of imagery reveals a 'truth', it's one that still resides in the purely imaginative without taking account of the concrete reality around it and without finding or constructing the tradition from within reality. While Pound felt that the visionary transformation of the world was inadequate in itself, it was a necessary precondition for the 'the historical or literal apocalyptic' that attempts to construct a historiography of God's relationship to Israel or, in the Modernist sense, a tradition of beauty that finds new expressions in new eras. Rather than excusing itself from history, Comens states the 'historical or literal apocalyptic'[64] in biblical apocalyptic literature accounts for the rise and fall of empires, or the persecution of God's people, as a fundamental part of a greater, cosmic reality between God and history. Because the 'apocalyptic basis common to the visionary and the ethical made the adoption of the historical apocalyptic a relatively easy, almost unobtrusive step',[65] Pound was able to maintain aspects of the visionary while shifting to the epic, which ultimately led him to the *Cantos*.

★ ★ ★ ★ ★

In 1917, Pound published 'III Cantos' in the magazine *Poetry* as a first attempt at the epic that would be become his primary project for the remainder of his life. The bulk of these three cantos were abandoned, save for a few sections that reappeared in *A Draft of XVI Cantos* (1924), but these first three, sometimes referred to as the 'Ur-Cantos', are often considered central for understanding the questions and concerns Pound dealt with in attempting a modern epic poem.[66] In the closing lines of Canto I, Pound uses the word *phantastikon*, in a section reflecting on the power of the poet's imagination, the ability of the poet to build 'my own phantastikon' (*P*, 234) for himself:

> And now it's but truth and memory,
> Dimmed only by the attritions of long time.
> 'But we forget not.'
> No, take it all for lies.
> I have but smelt this life, a whiff of it —
> The box of scented wood
> Recalls cathedrals. And shall I claim (*P*, 233–34)

The poet holds to a particular truth, a steadfast belief, but that truth is tied to memory, instances of a sensory experience of the external world, which is fading in the poet's own mind. A second voice interrupts asserting a platitude possibly in relation to honouring the war's dead: 'we forget not'. But the immediate response suggests that this is a lie, and recalls the recounting of lies in *Mauberley*. Pound proclaims that the only truth he can honestly hold to is that provided by his own senses, his own practice as a poet, and the tradition of poetry: 'I have smelt but *this life*'. Those finer details of 'this life' provide the starting point for a new *phantastikon* examined below. 'The box of scented wood' — perhaps an image of a funeral coffin — a solid example of the material world, bears no obvious relation to cathedrals, let alone the history of Christianity, but that may be precisely the point: it is the consciousness of the poet that selects the association and creates the relation between the box of wood and cathedrals. Just as in 'Pan is Dead', where the leaves and sedges are part of a discursive system of the nature god's, the box of wood is made to speak something that cannot be truly articulated because it exists in a 'future' state of which no proper discourse yet exists. But the poet declares the discourse regardless ('And shall I claim').

The image of the cathedral is significant in that it is a sacred site that alludes to that particular future state. It exists in this world for the purpose of compelling the worshipper to consider the supernatural world or the afterlife. The cathedral is, in this sense, the nexus between these two worlds, a place where we are asked to consider the 'beyond'; and so the scented wood is connected to this 'beyond' through that nexus of inner experience, tradition, and the material world. The cathedral is the anteroom of the apocalypse — not quite the new world that lies outside of history, but the space that suggests that new world as an objective, present fact, presenting a struggle between the artist and his or her creation:

> Confuse my own phantastikon,
> Or say the filmy shell that circumscribes me
> Contains the actual sun;
> confuse the thing I see
> With actual gods behind me?
> Are they gods behind me?
> How many worlds we have! [...] (P, 234)

Of these same lines, Peter Liebregts writes that, 'Pound openly wondered whether he now had to solve the question of the ontological status of immediate experience, that is, whether he had to state whether this vision did objectively appear to him from without, or whether it was a mere subjective projection from within.'[67] The dilemma that Pound raises is that the sensation of reality experienced by the *phantastikon* can draw the poet out of reality altogether, confusing the 'actual sun', for instance, with the memory and imagination of sunlight. Pound had to take the objective materials of the world and transform them into a subjective representation which was so powerfully wrought, that it tended toward objectivity in its own right. By posing these lines as questions, Pound seriously considers that he has a choice or, perhaps more accurately, that he should remain, as long as possible, in the productive tension between choices. Choosing the pure imagination would send him back to the outdated era of the Pre-Raphaelites, with a genuinely visionary capacity but unconnected with the world around him; but choosing objectivity would lead him back to the place of the failed prophet, predicting and moralizing, always threatened by the possibility of being disconfirmed and disproven. In this way, the *phantastikon* is Pound's attempt to find a way forward that did not entirely accede to either option, an attempt to 'steer a middle course between subjectivity and objectivity'.[68] The 'thing I see' can be, perhaps should be, confused with the 'actual gods behind me', giving the thing itself the power of creation.

In the next lines, Pound shifts emphasis on creation in the arts, exploring how artists shape themselves through artistic endeavours that render new worlds around them as a necessary by-product. Furthermore, the *phantastikon* is common across the arts, as these lines address painting as well as writing. This was one of Pound's goals in formulating Vorticism, which Pound hoped would become, 'a designation that would be equally applicable to a certain basis for all the arts':[69]

> Oh, we have worlds enough, and brave *décors,*
> And from these like we guess a soul for man
> And build him full of aery populations.
> Mantegna a sterner line, and the new world about us:
> Barred lights, great flares, new form, Picasso or Lewis. (*P*, 234)

With the phrase, 'Oh, we have worlds enough', Pound indicates his doubts about the ease of creation by mediocre artists and writers, shoddy worlds crowding out the space for the truly great *phantastikon*. The following image of 'brave *décors*' indeed does not suggest a deep respect for what seems like merely aesthetic accoutrements of the bourgeoisie. Nor does Pound express great confidence that such *décors* can demonstrate much of anything about the individual who possesses it. We are meant to merely 'guess' at the 'aery', and therefore insubstantial, 'populations' of the man's soul, rendered by imagination but perhaps lacking the solidity of an informed tradition. But surely Pound does not consider Picasso or Lewis as mediocre souls; his reference to the Italian painter Andrea Mantegna (1431–1506) contrasts the 'sterner line' with the 'aery populations', Mantegna representing something more solid and substantial than the *décors*. Mantegna's form is the basis for clearer *phantastikon* bearing solidity that weighs on the history of the form, if not history itself. Moreover, 'new form', suggested as attributes of Picasso and Lewis, would certainly be, coming from Pound, a genuine honour. Where Pound makes the key contrast is in the phrase, 'the new world about us'. From this perspective the 'new world', flowing from the 'sterner line' of Mantegna's art, is objective and now exists 'about us', rather than as 'aery populations' within the confines of the soul. As Liebregts states, it is the 'struggle between the subjective and objective [...], between the "creatio ex nihilo" [creation from nothing] and the "ex nihilo, nihil fit," [out of nothing, nothing comes] that Pound faced' in this canto.[70] Therefore, these lines propose the process by which the truly great artists impose subjective visionary experience onto the world as objective fact, compelling the world to conform to their vision rather than vice versa. In this sense, the question, 'Are they gods behind me?', is a legitimate one because Pound is never entirely certain which *phantastikons* are compelling enough to become 'creatio ex nihilo'.

The irony of Pound reflecting on the language of gods and cathedrals is that it highlights a religious tradition he often had very little regard for. In the Christian tradition, he felt that there was, at one time at least, the possibility of rebirth, renewal, and 'creatio ex nihilo', but apparently he now felt that it was left to poetry to take up the mantle of creation. Bourdieu describes how, in many cases, the poet carries into his poetry

> des concepts originellement élaborés dans la tradition *théologique*, notamment la conception de l'artiste comme 'créateur' doté de cette faculté quasi divine qu'est l'"imagination" et capable de produire une 'seconde nature', un 'second monde', un monde *sui generis* et autonome.[71]

> [concepts originally elaborated in the *theological* tradition, notably the conception of the artist as 'creator' equipped with this quasi-divine faculty of the 'imagination' and capable of producing a 'second nature', a 'second world', a world *sui generis* and autonomous.]

In light of this statement, Pound can be seen as the creator of the 'second monde', of the new world after the apocalypse. Isaiah 65. 17 predicts a new creation that lies outside of history, one that would be so great that even the memory of the old world would fade:

> For I am about to create new heavens
> and a new earth;
> the former things shall not be
> remembered
> or come to mind.

This new creation comes to pass in the final chapters of Revelation: 'Then I saw a new heaven and a new earth; for the first heaven and the first earth had passed away' (21. 1). Pound likely had such ability in mind, but he believed that the arts could do this better than religion, because the arts had more vital traditions on which to draw. Furthermore, the arts were more numerous, so that we could always proclaim, 'How many worlds we have!' Surette states that Pound lived in an era where 'to be pagan was to be antichristian, and to be antichristian was to be revolutionary.'[72] But this statement can be taken a step further, where to be revolutionary is to be grounded in the ability to imagine a separate world. This other world might speak *to* our world and *of* our world, but it never can be fully identified with our world. This practice of world-making is sometimes based on utopian thought or cosmic speculation, and it might have a variety of methods to get from here to the 'beyond', but it is always based on, as von Rad defines eschatology, a consummation of the historical process beyond the scope of the world's history.[73] And yet, Pound does not take this process to mean a total abandonment of history or the social world, but rather seeks to propose an entirely different entrance into history. In fact, this entrance was, he felt, proposed by the past itself. Pound (echoing Eliot's famous point in 'Tradition & the Individual Talent') saw the history of art as a 'complete order' that changes when something is added to it, but is 'eternally living and relevant because it exists in a timeless order.'[74] Apocalyptic writing is a way of casting back one's eyes over history in light of a timeless order; it points out relationships in the world that cannot be understood except in terms of a new era that has yet to manifest itself. Pound was searching for a 'more totalizing narrative, an Ur-narrative, [...] an apocalyptic narrative that could subsume all others.'[75] But the apocalyptic thinker is painfully and irreparably confined to this world, so his only hope is to convince, in spite of all the evidence, others of his vision. In this sense, a correspondent commented on Pound's work in the following way: 'I see, you wish to give people new eyes, not to make them see some new particular thing.'[76] The two poems that this correspondent was referring to — 'The Return' from *Ripostes* and 'Heather' from *Lustra* — were described by Pound as 'an objective reality' and 'a state of consciousness', a contradiction akin to his attempt to map a course between the Romantic, visionary apocalypse and the historical apocalypse.

Notes to Chapter 6

1. Hanson, *Dawn of Apocalyptic*, p. 16.
2. Gerhard von Rad, *Old Testament Theology*, trans. by D. G. M. Stalker, 2 vols (Edinburgh: Oliver and Boyd, 1965), II, 115.
3. Pound, *Selected Prose*, p. 160.
4. Octavio Paz, *Children of the Mire: Modern Poetry from Romanticism to the Avant-Garde*, trans. by Rachel Phillips (Cambridge, MA: Harvard University Press, 1974), p. 150.
5. A profoundly ironic statement for somebody who became an enthusiastic propagandist for Mussolini. Ezra Pound, *The Letters of Ezra Pound, 1907–1941*, ed. by D. D. Paige (London: Faber and Faber, 1951), pp. 180–81.
6. Pound, *Selected Prose*, p. 169.
7. Von Rad, *Old Testament Theology*, II, 303.
8. Bruce Comens, *Apocalypse and After: Modern Strategy and Postmodern Tactics in Pound, Williams, and Zukofsky* (Tuscaloosa: University of Alabama Press, 1995), p. 30.
9. Jane Goldman, *Modernism, 1910–1945: Image to Apocalypse* (Basingstoke: Palgrave Macmillan, 2004), p. 164.
10. Puchner, *Poetry of the Revolution*, p. 115.
11. Hanson, *Dawn of Apocalyptic*, p. 282.
12. Collins, *Apocalyptic Imagination*, p. 89.
13. Ibid., p. 88.
14. Ruthven, *Guide*, p. 134.
15. Ibid., p. 133.
16. Michael Alexander, *The Poetic Achievement of Ezra Pound* (London: Faber and Faber, 1979), p. 117; emphasis added.
17. Ruthven, *Guide*, p. 130.
18. Ezra Pound, *Pound/Joyce: The Letter of Ezra Pound to James Joyce, with Pound's Essays on Joyce*, ed. by Forrest Read (London: Faber and Faber, 1967), p. 139.
19. Pound may not have been alluding to Owen, as both poems were first published at nearly the same time, but to the Roman poet Horace, from whom Owen also borrowed the title of his poem. In any case, it's not clear that Pound had read Owen's poem when composing *Mauberley* (Ruthven, *A Guide*, pp. 132–33).
20. James L. Crenshaw, *Prophetic Conflict: Its Effect upon Israelite Religion* (Atlanta, GA: Society of Biblical Literature, 2007), p. 105; emphasis added.
21. Crenshaw refers to the so-called 'wisdom tradition' in biblical literature, exemplified in the Old Testament by Proverbs, Ecclesiastes, and Job. This tradition frequently attempts to ground moral and ethical decisions upon observation of the natural world, and struggles with doubt, disillusionment, and ignorance.
22. Crenshaw, *Prophetic Conflict*, p. 106.
23. Collins, *Apocalyptic Imagination*, p. 17.
24. Ibid., p. 144.
25. Leon Surette, *The Birth of Modernism: Ezra Pound, T. S. Eliot, W. B. Yeats, and the Occult* (Montreal, PQ, and Kingston, ON: McGill–Queen's University Press, 1993), p. 38.
26. Von Rad, *Old Testament Theology*, II, 101.

27. Comens, *Apocalypse and After*, p. 16.
28. Ibid., p. 28.
29. Ibid., p. 29.
30. Moody, *Ezra Pound: Poet*, p. 256.
31. Ezra Pound, *The Spirit of Romance* (London: Peter Owen, 1952), p. 95.
32. Pound, *Letters*, p. 68; emphasis added.
33. Pound, *Selected Prose*, p. 160.
34. Pound, *Spirit of Romance*, p. 95.
35. Hugh Witemeyer, *The Poetry of Ezra Pound: Forms and Renewal, 1908–1920* (Berkeley: University of California Press, 1969), p. 82.
36. Pound, *Selected Prose*, p. 71.
37. Ibid., p. 164. Pound's term 'kultur' was used polemically to describe provincial and even nationalistic cultures that enforce obedience and orthodoxy (see also Pound, *Selected Prose*, p. 160).
38. Witemeyer, *Poetry of Ezra Pound*, p. 81.
39. The Gospel of John relates the same event in the opposite manner, where Jesus says, 'And what should I say? — "Father, save me from this hour?" No, for this reason that I have come to this hour' (12. 27).
40. Witemeyer, *Poetry of Ezra Pound*, p. 82.
41. Ibid., p. 83.
42. Paz, *Children of the Mire*, p. 30.
43. Pound, *Selected Prose*, p. 166.
44. Surette, *Birth of Modernism*, p. 49.
45. Ruthven, *A Guide*, p. 190.
46. *ŒP*, 707.
47. Moody, *Ezra Pound: Poet*, p. 177.
48. Frank Kermode, *The Sense of an Ending: Studies in the Theory of Fiction* (Oxford: Oxford University Press, 2000), p. 98.
49. Comens, *Apocalypse and After*, p. 39; see also Dasenbrock, *Literary Vorticism*, p. 108: 'For Pound, in contrast [to Lewis], the essence of any situation is a relation: for example, the faces in the crowd are related to petals [...]. [T]hese relations aim at the same analytic representation that the Vorticist artists wish to attain [...]. Pound, too, is active and exploratory, not simply passively receiving an aesthetic from Lewis and the other Vorticists.'
50. Ezra Pound, *Gaudier-Brzeska: A Memoir* (London: Laidlaw & Laidlaw, 1939), p. 102.
51. Witemeyer, *Poetry of Ezra Pound*, p. 108.
52. Goldman, *Modernism*, p. 11; emphasis added.
53. Collins, 'Transcendence of Death', p. 72.
54. Pound, *Selected Prose*, p. 25.
55. Ezra Pound, 'Vortex. Pound.', in *Blast 1*, ed. by Wyndham Lewis (Santa Barbara, CA: Black Sparrow Press, 1981), 153–54 (p. 154).
56. Witemeyer, *Poetry of Ezra Pound*, p. 50.
57. Ibid.
58. Ibid., p. 51.
59. Berger, *Sacred Canopy*, p. 7.
60. Comens, *Apocalypse and After*, p. 35.
61. A reference to Edward Burne-Jones's 1884 painting 'Cophetua and the Beggar Maid'; Ruthven, *Guide*, p. 134.
62. Ibid.
63. Rimbaud, *Œuvres complètes*, p. 70.
64. Comens, *Apocalypse and After*, p. 42.
65. Ibid.
66. See Goldman, *Modernism*, p. 136; Peter Liebregts, '"Bricks thought into being ex nihil": Ezra Pound and Creation', in *Ezra Pound, Ends and Beginnings: Essays and Poems from the Ezra Pound International Conference, Venice 2007*, ed. by John Gery and William Pratt (New York: AMS Press, 2011), 81–96 (p. 86).

67. Liebregts, 'Bricks thought into being', p. 89.
68. Ibid.
69. Pound, *Gaudier-Brzeska*, p. 93.
70. Liebregts, 'Bricks thought into being', p. 86.
71. Bourdieu, *Les Règles de l'art*, p. 405.
72. Surette, *Birth of Modernism*, p. 78.
73. Von Rad, *Old Testament Theology*, II, 113–14.
74. Witemeyer, *Poetry of Ezra Pound*, p. 4.
75. Comens, *Apocalypse and After*, p. 32.
76. Pound, *Gaudier-Brzeska*, p. 98.

CONCLUSION

❖

The intention of this study has been to take a fresh look at the relationship between sociality amongst poets who were dedicated to establishing a basis for conceiving the future, and the literary legacy that these poets took up or entered into, as well as that which they left behind. The precise nature of 'society', evident in my use of sociological analyses of religion and art, is riven by the tension between the mundane, or even profane, reality as each poet found it, and an ideational vision of a modern society that could be expanded and contracted in the work of these poets, from a clique of artists and writers, to a social milieu in London or Paris, the nations of France or Italy, or even European culture itself. Nevertheless, it bears repeating that the poets who form the subject of this study were strongly influenced by the libertarian and anarchist philosophies that had made their mark by the end of the nineteenth century, and all had a profound investment in the power of individual conscience and action. That ideational vision is, moreover, structured by a sense of the past in its broadest and most fantastic conceptions, often indistinguishable from myth and constellated in unusual ways. Community, citizenry, nation, and civilization are most evidently viewed 'through a glass, darkly', as intimations of a utopian notion of society whose image is broken by the real experience of an encounter with the world and imperfectly reassembled by the poet's own notion of him- or herself as a social actor. This line of research raises a number of issues, such as: the relative worth of tradition versus a modernized future, especially a future characterized by war or other forms of cultural upheaval; the formal experiments of avant-gardism that might best represent or prefigure an ultimately unimaginable future; the possibility of establishing artistic values in the Modernist era that have a social function or status analogous to those established by religious thought and practice.

Early in this study, I addressed that aspect of the avant-garde that seeks to collapse the distinction between art and life — that is, strip art of its autonomy. However, I also claimed that this intention was followed by an effort to reconstruct that autonomy at another level, within a context of secular modernity. The Bible has played a significant role in this study for the way it plays on these questions of society and artistic autonomy through its canonical status as both literature and scripture, and in asserting itself (and being asserted) as transcendent of social or historical context, that is *always relevant as a source of wisdom*. The exegesis of its meaning, moreover, is not exclusively — perhaps not even primarily — through individual interpretation, but through doctrine and convention, liturgical tradition, and collective cultural history. On the other hand, the Bible's 'conservative' attributes, seen as the source of the sexual, political, and economic standards of the day, made it ripe for subversion by avant-gardists eager to shed bourgeois morality as they looked towards the future. But the Bible itself is also a collection of subversions and affronts to the hierarchies and mores that govern society, given a reading that, to borrow Bloch's terminology, can 'discern' them.[1] Readings of the Bible 'against the grain' of conventional or orthodox exegesis can draw out moments of rebellion and revolt against the Lordship model of the divine, in favour of a religiosity that demands attention to *human* potentials and capacities. Against what these poets saw as the rationalizations of modernity — the shallow functionalism and utilitarianism of culture, the obeisance to technology, the commodification of artistic value — the Bible provided a resource for exodus, for the constant journey into freedom. As such, the Bible's canonicity and broad familiarity could serve the avant-garde by instilling a *faith*, with its implications of joy racked with doubt, in the transition to modernity. Even more, they look forward to the change as a beautiful necessity, such as Apollinaire and Marinetti, who make the transition as a new, multiplied sense of the body and consciousness rather than as an individual, or Pound, who makes the transition as emissary for a variegated but continuous tradition.

Notions of social cohesion as organized by bourgeois morality or mandates by the state were largely rejected by these poets, who favoured an 'organic' sociality that seemed to culminate in the desperate situation of warfare, which shattered conventional notions of selfhood. In this latter context, early indications of Marinetti's and Pound's eventual adherence to Italian fascism manifest through a fascination with an aestheticized *order* that became a metaphor for a new social order. It's beyond this study to really account for that eventual and unfortunate change in their artistic and political priorities, which is partially why this study concludes where it does. Prior to these intimations of a militantly self-perfecting order, however, the early works addressed here emphasize an experimental sense of 'wandering', an openness that is not to be read as a lack of determination. A comment by Frye crystallizes the way in which biblical literature, in spite of its doctrinal legacy, establishes an intentional disorientation as a principle of faith:

> Metaphors of unity and integration take us only so far, because they are derived from the finiteness of the human mind. If we are to expand our vision into the genuinely infinite, that vision becomes decentralized. We follow a 'way' or direction until we reach the state of innocence symbolized by the sheep in the twenty-third Psalm, where we are back to wandering, but where wandering no longer means being lost. There are two senses in which the word 'imperfect' is used: in one sense it is that which falls short of perfection; in another it is that which is not finished but continuously active, as in the tense system of verbs in most languages. It is in the latter sense that 'the imperfect is our paradise,' as Wallace Stevens says, a world that may change as much as our own, but where change is no longer dominated by the single direction toward nothingness and death.[2]

What Frye is pointing to is how the Bible so often attempts to keep hold of the undecidable and transient; an attribute perhaps best summed up in the moment when Moses asks God to reveal his name, and the latter states, in one possible rendering, 'I will be what I will be' (Exodus 3. 14). However, is a longing for high-spirited wandering the only drive at work in these poets' use of biblical literature, or is something more structured at work? This study concludes by summarizing the tensions between sociality and individuality, wandering and destination, that these poets must inevitably negotiate.

The poets, then, must first contend with the concept of an audience *as identity*. A poem such as Apollinaire's 'Sur les prophéties' is attuned to the poet's or prophet's need for an audience by envisioning the lack of an audience in a positive sense, that is, when an audience becomes its own generator of creative, inspired language. In this poem, Apollinaire begins the piece by placing himself in the role of audience ('Tout ce qu'elle m'a dit du passé était vrai et tout ce qu'elle | M'a annoncé s'est vérifié dans le temps qu'elle indiquait' [Everything she told me about the past was true and everything she | Pronounced to me was confirmed in the time she indicated]) (ŒP, 185) but then he looks ahead to a time when the public, in its broadest configuration, is capable of prophecy in its own right, no longer dependent on the fortune-tellers, but self-sufficiently exploring the possibilities of the future. Looking again at the end of the poem, it seems that the role of the modern poet is to assist that audience to believe that they too can become speakers of and for the future:

> Mais il y a longtemps qu'on fait croire aux gens
> Qu'ils n'ont aucun avenir qu'ils sont ignorants à jamais
> Et idiots de naissance
>
> [But for a long time people were made to believe
> That they had no future that they were forever ignorant
> And idiots from birth] (ŒP, 186)

But where does that leave the poet or prophet who, until this apocalyptic endpoint where life and art finally collapse into onto another, relied on audiences, even small and elite ones, to establish their legitimacy as the one who called forth that audience to modernity? Has prophecy, which is distinguished by speech that sets itself askew to the world, not ceased to exist if the prophet and audience are eventually indistinguishable?

What 'Sur les prophéties' understands by imagining the end of prophecy through its own universalization is the way in which an audience builds a 'plausibility structure'. The plausibility structure, as described by Berger, and in which we can find analogues in the concepts of *ideology* and *habitus*, relies on the ongoing dialogue between the speaker, the social object, and the external world, and was a way in which ideas could cohere into powerful reality functions. As Pound says in *ABC of Reading*, 'Any general statement is like a cheque drawn on a bank. Its value depends on what is there to meet it.'[3] Every acknowledgment of some feeling of dissonance, from apprehension to appreciation, confusion to outrage, allows a subject to reflect upon and calibrate the kind of 'reality' they are presenting. The poets of this study certainly concentrate much of their work on discordant visions, but in a way that tests out reality functions, pushing ahead and pulling back as they and their presumed audience see fit. The use of the Bible is a paradigmatic example of this push and pull, being a well-known text, yet one that is always moving beyond itself in its reliance on prophecy.

In 'Sur les prophéties', the future is one where everyone either presents the same prophetic vision, or each individual presents an individually distinctive vision — which may amount to the same thing. More importantly, that future represents the final confirmation of the reality proposed by the modern poet, thereby rectifying a *belated* or *deferred* identity between (avant-garde) poet and (contemporary) public. That is why this poem is also about the power of an audience to legitimate the poetic view, particularly when that plausibility structure becomes an unspoken and unquestionable practice of everyday life, as Apollinaire envisions. As the audience is already partially attuned, in a crucially latent sense, to the message of salvation of the faithful, condemnation of the corrupt, and re-establishment of order in the world, the avant-gardists could effect a certain blindness to their own works. Even when a manifesto enumerates principles of technique and style, the actual intention of the manifesto cannot be articulated in so straightforward a fashion, given that such enumerations are often clearly aspirational and contingent. These silent assents between audience and poet build a circle of legitimacy in which the latter articulates the sensibilities and concerns in their (select) audience, and that audience bestow the status of revelation on the poet's work. However, because the message is always straddling the line between commitment and novelty, the desired audience is always somewhat deferred to the future. A *general public* for the avant-garde is necessarily more of a hope than a reality. Pound forcefully proposes the problem of an ever-incomplete audience, for the audience is the thing that should be changed by the poet. When Pound states of his poetry, 'I am by no means sure it would be true prophecy', he is expressing the contradiction that, on the one hand, prophecies must be confirmed by an external source to be deemed 'true' and, on the other hand, there is no adequate source in the contemporary world to which the prophet could legitimately appeal to make that confirmation.

'Sur les prophéties' can also be read as a form of premonition that is less obviously optimistic, inasmuch it demonstrates something more discontinuous and uncertain, given that prophecy and apocalypse are also the primary discursive modes of crisis. In periods with mild or manageable social tensions, Berger argues that plausibility structures are stable and can be shared by the broadest segments of the society. However, in periods of high social tension and crisis, plausibility structures are fragmented among the population and may easily change according to the pressures of events and developments that cannot be swiftly incorporated into them. Socialization, which, when successful, leads to the 'establishment of symmetry between the objective world of society and the subjective world of the individual', becomes increasingly precarious, leading to 'various degrees of asymmetry', and demonstrating a plausibility structure for the fiction that it is.[4] While the most evident drivers of change in this study seem to be technological and martial, the events that challenge the integrity of the plausibility structure need not be entirely material, but may be constituted as radical developments in psychology and the understanding of consciousness, or changes in the philosophy of ethics and morality. If the avant-garde poet-prophet is the symptom of the crises of the Modernist period, the silence of the plausibility structure makes him appear as the harbinger of crisis, and the prophetic poem foresees a period of intensifying fractures and discontinuity, perhaps even anticipating postmodernity's proliferation of worldviews as itself the standard of a secularized civilization.

The fracturing that confronted Apollinaire, Marinetti, and Pound struck at the *auratic* quality of art, that is, art's autonomy. As this study has examined, the works of these poets negotiated those fractures by straddling a series of lines between art and the social worlds outside of art: they could be politically engaged, but hold politics at a distance; they could speak of the materials and practices of everyday life, but in mystical ways; they might treat warfare as an aesthetic event; they could adopt popular styles and registers for much more traditional frameworks, and vice versa. In an analysis of Baudelaire's discussion of the poetic 'halo', Somigli draws out the relationship of the aura to the threat of commodified art in modernity, and identifies a paradox: if capitalism

> can strip the artist of the halo, that means that the halo itself is not an 'eternal' characteristic of the artist, as the idealist tradition might want to suggest. This raises the question of where the 'halo' comes from, a question that points to the historicity and the constructed nature of the halo itself.[5]

Pound was keenly aware of how the aura or halo was historically constituted, and therefore its 'eternality' had to be historically verified in age after age (a problem that would receive its most thorough response in the *Cantos*). When he famously referred to the poetic epic as 'a poem including history',[6] he is (as indicated by his subsequent insistence on how the comprehension of Greek drama depends on a knowledge of Homer) referring mainly to *literary* history, to the *historical* development of the closed circle of the tradition. It is this closed circle upon which the autonomy, aura, or halo is built. However, what this study has shown with regard to these poets is a breakdown of autonomy and permeation of other social fields into art. In periods of crisis, such as World War I, the halo cannot be constituted on the same basis as before, which Apollinaire, Marinetti, and Pound were all well aware of. Inasmuch as the halo denotes the dedication of the poet to a 'higher' purpose, it is derived from religion and it was to religion that many Modernists turned for its re-constitution. The religions of art that rose to prominence in the late nineteenth century tried to fulfil a similar function of spirituality; but the ability of religion itself to provide a stable plausibility structure was itself in crisis, which many Modernists were more than happy to assist in, as doing so could provide an opening for art to fill newly secularized spaces. What we have then seen in these poets is not a one-or-the-other effort to accelerate the dissolution of artistic autonomy or re-establish it as it once was. Rather, Apollinaire, Marinetti, and Pound attempt to reconstitute the artistic field in a number of ways, not least of which is on a *biblical* if not exactly *religious* basis, annexing scripture to questions of aesthetics and literature. Moreover, they allowed their own problems of poetry and modernity to be cast as issues with the gravity of those presented in the Bible. That is, the Bible carves out a space for a particular set of viewpoints, recasting contemporary questions as biblical questions, questions of prophecy and revelation.

Along with Greek and Roman literature, biblical literature provided a means to reconceptualize a major concern for Apollinaire, Marinetti, and Pound: the figure of the nation. The nation, be it France, Italy, or America, wanders in exodus not simply from one place to another, but into an entirely new relationship to the divine, it discovers its identity only in a state of exile, hoping to become the 'kingdom' where the highest achievements of human freedom and imagination are realized. While nationalism, which haunts each of these figures of the nation, is not the only basis for conceiving a future sociality, it is one that each of the poets had some sympathy with — sometimes, as with Marinetti, in its most chauvinistic forms, at other times, as in much of Apollinaire's work, in more welcoming and accessible ways. Nationalism appealed to these poets not only because of their particular views on the cultural divisions that intensified, leading up to and throughout World War I, but as a way to come to grips with changes in (mass) culture and (mass) politics within a spiritualized ideal that obscured or resolved social and political divisions under the *condition* of the nation. Adamson states that 'Nationalism's ideal [...] was that of a retotalized social world in which divisions between the divine and human, rational and emotional, public and private sides of life would be overcome';[7] this effort is not entirely distinct from the scepticism of 'bourgeois democracy' in prophetic discourse. At the very least, the all-or-nothing tenor of prophetic discourse finds it difficult to come to terms with the compromise and deliberation so often necessary for the functional political and social negotiation and cohesion in liberal democracies. However, while it's well-known that Marinetti and Pound moved towards fascist politics in the post-war era, it's not the intention of this study to argue that, at this early phase, the poetry examined was in sympathy with the authoritarianism that manifested itself as fascism developed across the 1920s and '30s. As poets, first and foremost, they took creativity and imagination seriously and much of their engagement with the nation insists on room for improvisation, experiment, and play. This is not to suggest that fascism doesn't engage imagination and fantasy — it certainly does — but that the tension between social and cultural order on one hand, and fiction or even revelation on the other, had not been resolved (or perhaps suppressed) the way it was under fascist regimes. The notion of order promoted by Pound and especially Apollinaire is not meant as *diktat*, but as a structure that hones the imagination, and is always itself open to change. The nation, in this particular context, is a 'condition' that allows for a deferred and un-determined result within a structured space that is by no means an 'empty signifier'. It allows the social subject, depending on their prior sympathies with the avant-garde, to step into the space of autonomy that is normally reserved for art.

Earlier in this study, I made reference to Carlo Carrà's piece 'Manifestazione interventista (festa patriottica-dipinto parolibero)' as an example of the Futurist vision of public life under the aegis of 'Italia': the word at the centre of the painting is one from which social life radiates like the rays of a sun. But two further points can be made regarding this painting. Let's not neglect the wildness of the piece, inspired (as indicated in the title) by Marinetti's Words-in-Freedom: the seemingly haphazard shifts of colour and fading that are combined in the red, white and green of the Italian flag, which is knowingly placed throughout the painting, the profusion of language and onomatopoeia, the lines that often run askew to the centrifugal flow of the image. Under the condition of the nation in this piece, it seems, there is ample room for deviation and parleying with difference. Secondly, there is no reason why a viewer must read the painting centrifugally. Rather, we might reverse the directionality, making 'Italia' the culmination of the unbridled (Futurist) activity in the work. Indeed, this more dialectical formula of nationalism is simply the objective view inverted into a subjective one, whose centrifugal structure, that seemingly lives the social field from the inside out, is the cornerstone of art and religion as well.

Recalling Adamson's quotation above, describing nationalism as the overcoming of 'divisions between the divine and human, rational and emotional, public and private', nationalism must always find new divisions in order to overcome them. Apocalyptic thought can therefore serve the ends of nationalism by always proposing a final, almost organic suturing of those divisions. For example, in 1917 Apollinaire wrote the poem 'Tristesse d'une Étoile', where he described the relationship of the soldier to France:

> Et je porte avec moi cette ardente souffrance
> Comme le ver luisant tient son corps enflammé
> Comme au cœur du soldat il palpite la France
> Et comme au cœur du lys le pollen parfumé
>
> [And I carry with me this ardent suffering
> As the glow-worm carries his flaming body
> As France beats in the soldier's heart
> And as in the lily's heart the scented pollen] (ŒP, 308)

The 'ardente souffrance' is in reference to both Apollinaire's head wound and his poetic vocation, which, earlier in the poem, he calls 'le secret malheur qui nourrit mon délire' [the secret misfortune that feeds my desire]. And it is this deep loss felt by the poet that is compared to the 'natural' relationship that the soldier feels to France. Apollinaire takes the image a step further by comparing France to the lily's pollen. France, in these lines, becomes an outward expansion, the creation of a new reality that never quite forecloses the possibility of further creation. In this way, there is certainly a nationalist undertone to 'Tristesse', where France is no longer simply established, but is constantly growing and finding new borders to cross and new soil to fertilize. The relationship between the soldier and France is organic and the expansion of France is a 'natural' extension of that relationship. What makes this kind of thought apocalyptic is how Apollinaire transforms, through the poetic image, loss into growth and how he transforms the individual into the embodiment of an ideal.

This 'lost', organically cohesive society is the recurring concern for the poets in this study, where the distinction between citizen and nation, prophet and public, has been replaced by a relationship less structured by the functionality of politics or the economy, but one that most resembles, aesthetically and socially, love — mutually supportive and self-sacrificing, and all the more powerful for existing, largely, in silence. In 'Les Fiançailles' we find it among the 'late-comers'; in *Monoplan*, there are intimations of it in Marinetti's characterization of the Sicilians or the students or, especially, the soldiers. However, in lieu of this future society, the poet offers up the self as allegory for a new sociality. Pound's use of the *personae* is a clear example: taken as discrete instances in the poems, the *personae* provide Pound with a fractured consciousness, re-historicized through the lens of the adopted figure by which he evaluates the modern world. But when read across his works, less individually, the *personae* form an occult lineage whose various figures Pound himself adopts and speaks. Marinetti, on the other hand, looks towards the religion of velocity, dispersing his 'I' into matter. He thus tends towards a total allegorizing of the body-as-cosmos, a quasi-mysticism that envisions the self as everywhere and nowhere at once. What we see here is that the self is sanctified in a way that the group is not; or, more specifically, the group is sanctified through the self whose secret or cosmic history is read as a salvation history, the hope of the society pre-ordained through the life of the poet.

The fracturing of the self concedes its centrality in the modern world, but does so in a way that undermines the bourgeois self in its privatizing acquisitiveness. With the commodification of art comes the commodification of the *effects of art*, such as pleasure, knowledge, and even sympathy. Unlike scripture, which can provide a model for communal exegesis, the commodification of art reduces the ability to imagine another collective, social life to the imagination of another life of *one's own*. This is certainly not an unimportant operation, as the *stahlhartes Gehäuse* [steel-hard shell], in Max Weber's famous formulation for capitalism,[8] protects one against the endlessly dynamic flow, and instability, that avant-gardists so often championed, as much as it encloses or traps one into individualized practices and beliefs. In theory, the imagination of hope can be as extensive and numerous as every individual who experiences themselves as a member of the elect. Against the state where election is a form of personal property, the poets in this study propose a joyful death of the 'lonely soul and its solid middle-class God'.[9]

The 'privatized', however, needs to be parsed from autonomy: the latter, which has been rendered in terms of the *field* or the *sphere*, may be experienced individually, but it is a particularly social phenomenon, as states of autonomy can never be confirmed without reference to other actors within a comparable context. The faith of the avant-garde troubles *private* faith, as it claims its own hopes from fields beyond the strictly aesthetic. Bloch summarizes how private faith has foreclosed many of the possibilities of the audience, of *having an audience*, that these poets are pushing against:

> this My-Own, with its sense of being spoken to in the Bible in what is claimed to be a purely individualistic manner, free from the impersonally social 'one...' and the worldly 'it is,' is the private straw this Christian remnant clings to. The bodily, the social, the cosmic: it can all, for them, be discarded from religion as worldly, as the world: the soul need not bother about it, need neither act nor even understand: Scripture speaks from existence to existence, and in no other way, least of all 'about' anything.[10]

In their polemics and suspicion of idealism, particularly of the Symbolist tradition, Apollinaire, Marinetti, and Pound reclaim the 'wordly' in the guise of the material and the social, but in doing so, they also reclaim the world outside of the social, namely death. As Marinetti once prophesied that the Futurists would be discarded, the audience invoked by the avant-garde is that of a *hearing* given to mortality itself, so clear in any realization that society is founded upon the work of the *trépassés*.

As described above, apocalyptic thought in particular always runs the risk of replacing social and cultural decline with a utopian eternity where neither decline nor progress is conceivable, and what we find in the work above is an effort to hold onto a ruptural aesthetic that also continually prepares the ground for yet another rupture. Bloch describes the language of the Bible as a 'calling to',[11] in that it announces itself as the language of the kingdom to every new generation. It seeks to become the reason and moment for its own reception. Its audience is always being called to welcome the modern, whether as a potential continuation of the past, given the audience's willingness to take up the tradition for a new era, or as the transcendence or destruction of tradition as preparation for a new creation. But more specifically, it calls on the audience to prepare itself for passing. In an exegesis of 'Autumn malade', a brief poem by Apollinaire in *Alcools*, Bourdieu states that 'The poet pronounces the *fatum*, but also proffers an exhortation to *amor fati*. From the future anterior of prophecy, he jumps suddenly [...] to the imperative. "Die", accept death, learn how to die.'[12] In Bourdieu's analysis, the poem concludes in the mode of the apocalyptic, where prophecy itself fails, but *something* persists in the radically unknown, and 'gives way to a continuous progress towards silence, to a gradual fading of the elusive threshold where the transition from totality to nothingness takes place, where existence passes into non-existence. Life is this continuous passage, right up until the ultimate discontinuity.'[13] It has been the goal of this study to demonstrate how Apollinaire, Marinetti, and Pound envision the *amor fati* of death as the re-integration of the self into a new kind of social life, of the material and temporal incompleteness of the self. The individual must always come to an end, thrown back into social life where its limitations disappear beyond every horizon. The individual is subject to an audience with its own self, which announces its death and, in the manner of scripture, its eternal life.

Notes to the Conclusion

1. Bloch, *Atheism in Christianity*, pp. 57–70.
2. Frye, *Great Code*, p. 168.
3. Ezra Pound, *ABC of Reading* (New York: New Directions, 2011), p. 25.
4. Berger, *Sacred Canopy*, p. 15.
5. Somigli, *Legitimizing the Artist*, p. 10.
6. Pound, *ABC of Reading*, p. 46.
7. Walter L. Adamson, 'Apollinaire's Politics: Modernism, Nationalism, and the Public Sphere in Avant-Garde Paris', *Modernism/Modernity*, 6.3 (September 1999), 33–56 (p. 52).
8. Weber, *Protestant Ethic*, p. 121.
9. Bloch, *Atheism and Christianity*, p. 29.
10. Ibid., p. 28.
11. Ibid., p. 10.

12. Pierre Bourdieu, 'Apollinaire, Autumn Ill', trans. by John Speller, *Paragraph*, 35.1 (March 2012),
    131–36 (p. 132).
13. Ibid., p. 135.

BIBLIOGRAPHY

❖

Primary Sources

Apollinaire

APOLLINAIRE, GUILLAUME, Œuvres Poétiques, ed. by Marcel Adéma and Michel Décaudin (Paris: Gallimard, 1956)
——Alcools, ed. and trans. by Anne Hyde Greet (Berkeley: University of California Press, 1956)
——Œuvres complètes de Guillaume Apollinaire, ed. by Michel Décaudin, 4 vols (Paris: André Balland et Jacques Lecat, 1966)
——Alcools, ed. and trans. by Garnet Rees (London: Athlone Press, 1975)
——Œuvres en prose complètes, ed. by Michel Décaudin, 3 vols (Paris: Gallimard, 1977–1993)
——Calligrammes: Poems of Peace and War (1913–1916), ed. and trans. by Anne Hyde Greet and S. I. Lockerbie (Berkeley: University of California Press, 2004)

Marinetti

LISTA, GIOVANNI (ed.), Futurisme: Manifestes — Proclamations — Documents (Lausanne: L'Age d'homme, 1973)
MARINETTI, F. T., La Conquête des étoiles: poème épique (Paris: E. Sansot & Cie, 1902)
——Mafarka le futuriste: roman africain (Paris: E. Sansot & Cie, 1909)
——Le Futurisme (Paris: E. Sansot & Cie, 1911)
——Le Monoplan du pape: roman politique en vers libre (Paris: E. Sansot & Cie, 1912)
——La Bataille de Tripoli (26 Octobre 1911): vécue et chantée (Milan: Edizioni Futuriste di 'Poesia', 1912)
——Marinetti: Selected Writings, ed. by R. W. Flint, trans. by R. W. Flint and Arthur A. Coppotelli (New York: Farrar, Straus and Giroux, 1972)
——Scritti Francesi, ed. by Pasquale A. Jannini (Milan: Mondadori, 1983)
——The Futurist Cookbook, ed. by Lesley Chamberlain, trans. by Suzanne Brill (London: Trefoil Publications, 1989).
RAINEY, LAWRENCE, CHRISTINE POGGI and LAURA WITTMAN (eds), Futurism: An Anthology (New Haven, CT: Yale University Press, 2009)

Pound

POUND, EZRA, Gaudier-Brzeska: A Memoir (London: Laidlaw & Laidlaw, 1939)
——The Letters of Ezra Pound, 1907–1941, ed. by D. D. Paige (London: Faber and Faber, 1951)
——The Spirit of Romance (London: Peter Owen, 1952)
——Pound/Joyce: The Letters of Ezra Pound to James Joyce, with Pound's Essays on Joyce, ed. by Forrest Read (London: Faber and Faber, 1967)
——Selected Prose, 1909–1965, ed. by William Cookson (London: Faber and Faber, 1973)
——Collected Early Poems of Ezra Pound, ed. by Michael John King (London: Faber and Faber, 1977)

——'Vortex. Pound.', in *Blast 1*, ed. by Wyndham Lewis (Santa Barbara, CA: Black Sparrow Press, 1981), pp. 153–54; original printing, *Blast*, ed. by Wyndham Lewis, 1 (1914)

——*Personæ: The Shorter Poems of Ezra Pound* (London: Faber and Faber, 2001)

——*ABC of Reading* (New York: New Directions Press, 2011)

Other Sources

ADAMSON, WALTER L., 'Fascism and Culture: Avant-Gardes and Secular Religion in the Italian Case', *Journal of Contemporary History*, 24.3 (July 1989), 411–35

——.'Apollinaire's Politics: Modernism, Nationalism, and the Public Sphere in Avant-Garde Paris', *Modernism/Modernity*, 6.3 (September 1999), 33–56

——.*Embattled Avant-Gardes: Modernism's Resistance to Commodity Culture in Europe* (Berkeley: University of California Press, 2007)

——.'How Avant-Gardes End — and Begin: Italian Futurism in Historical Perspective', *New Literary History*, 41 (2010), 855–74

ADÉMA, MARCEL, *Apollinaire: le mal-aimé* (Paris: Libraire Plon, 1952)

ALEXANDER, MICHAEL, *The Poetic Achievement of Ezra Pound* (London: Faber and Faber, 1979)

ALEXANDRE, DIDIER, ' "J'ai fabriqué un dieu, un faux dieu, un vrai joli faux dieu": l'écriture du sacré dans *Alcools*', in *Guillaume Apollinaire: Alcools*, ed. by Michel Murat (Paris: Éditions Klincksieck, 1996), pp. 109–16

ALLEN, LESLIE C., *Ezekiel 1–19* (Dallas, TX: Word Books, 1994)

ALTER, ROBERT, *Canon and Creativity: Modern Writing and the Authority of Scripture* (New Haven, CT: Yale University Press, 2000)

——.*The Art of Biblical Poetry* (New York: Basic Books, 2011)

AUNE, DAVID E., 'The Social Matrix of the Apocalypse of John', *Biblical Research*, 26 (1981), 16–32

——.'The Apocalypse of John and the Problem of Genre', *Semeia*, 36 (1986), 65–96

BATES, SCOTT, 'Les Collines, dernier testament d'Apollinaire', in *Guillaume Apollinaire 1*, ed. by Michel Décaudin (Paris: Lettres Modernes, 1962), pp. 23–39

BENJAMIN, WALTER, 'On Language as Such and On the Language of Man', in *Walter Benjamin: Selected Writings, Volume 1: 1913–1926*, ed. by Marcus Bullock and Michael W. Jennings, trans. by Edmund Jephcott (Cambridge, MA: Harvard University Press, 1997), pp. 62–74

BERGER, PETER L., *The Sacred Canopy: Elements of a Sociological Theory of Religion* (New York: Anchor Books, 1969)

BLENKINSOPP, JOSEPH, *A History of Prophecy in Israel* (Louisville, KY: Westminster John Knox Press, 1996)

BLOCH, ERNST. *Atheism in Christianity: The Religion of the Exodus and the Kingdom*, trans. by J. T. Swann (London: Verso, 2009)

BLOUNT, BRIAN K., *Revelation: A Commentary* (Louisville, KY: Westminster John Knox Press, 2009)

BLUM, CINZIA SARTINI, *The Other Modernism: F. T. Marinetti's Futurist Fiction of Power* (Berkeley: University of California Press, 1996)

BOAK, DENIS, *Jules Romains* (New York: Twayne Publishers, 1974)

BOER, ROLAND, 'The Privatization of Eschatology and Myth: Ernst Bloch vs. Rudolph Bultmann', in *The Privatization of Hope: Ernst Bloch and the Future of Utopia*, ed. by Peter Thompson and Slavoj Žižek (Durham, NC: Duke University Press, 2013), pp. 106–20

BOHN, WILLARD, *Apollinaire and the International Avant-Garde* (Albany: State University of New York Press, 1997)

——.'The Poetics of Flight: Futurist 'Aeropoesia'', *MLN*, 121.1 (Jan. 2006), 207–24

BOURDIEU, PIERRE, 'Éléments d'une théorie sociologique de la perception artistique', *Revue internationale des sciences sociales*, 22.4 (1968), 640–64

——.'Le Marché des biens symboliques', *L'Année Sociologique*, 22 (1971), 49–126

——.'Une Interprétation de la théorie de la religion selon Max Weber', *European Journal of Sociology*, 12.1 (May 1971), 3–21

——.'Genèse et structure du champ religieux', *Revue française de sociologie*, 12.3 (June–September 1971), 295–334

——.'La Production de la croyance: contribution à une économie des biens symboliques', *Actes de la recherche en sciences sociales*, 13 (February 1977), 3–43

——.*Les Règles de l'art: genèse et structure du champ littéraire* (Paris: Seuil, 1992)

——.*The Field of Cultural Production: Essays on Art and Literature*, ed. by Randal Johnson, trans. by Claud Du Verlie (New York: Columbia University Press, 1993)

——.'Autumn, Ill', trans. by John Speller, *Paragraph*, 35.1 (March 2012), pp. 131–36

BREUNIG, L. C., 'Apollinaire's "Les Fiançailles"', *Essays in French Literature*, 3 (November 1966), 1–32

——.ED., *The Cubist Poet's in Paris: An Anthology* (Lincoln: University of Nebraska Press, 1995)

BROMLEY, DAVID G., 'Constructing Apocalypticism: Social and Cultural Elements of Radical Organization', in *Millennium, Messiahs, and Mayhem: Contemporary Apocalyptic Movements*, ed. by Thomas Robbins and Susan J. Palmer (Routledge: New York, 1997), pp. 31–46

BULL, MALCOLM, *Seeing Things Hidden: Apocalypse, Vision and Totality* (London: Verso, 1999)

BÜRGER, PETER, *Theory of the Avant-Garde*, trans. by Michael Shaw (Minneapolis: University of Minnesota Press, 1984)

BURGOS, JEAN, 'Une Poétique de la Rupture', in *Guillaume Apollinaire: Alcools*, ed. by Michel Murat (Paris: Éditions Klincksieck, 1996), pp. 63–80

BURROW, J. W., *The Crisis of Reason: European Thought, 1848–1914* (New Haven, CT: Yale University Press, 2000)

CALINESCU, MATEI, *Five Faces of Modernity: Modernism, Avant-Garde, Decadence, Kitsch, Postmodernism* (Durham, NC: Duke University Press, 1987)

CARMODY, FRANCIS J., *The Evolution of Apollinaire's Poetics, 1901–1914* (Berkeley: University of California Press, 1963)

CARROLL, ROBERT P., 'Twilight of Prophecy or Dawn of Apocalyptic?', *Journal for the Study of the Old Testament*, 14 (1979), 3–35

——.*Jeremiah: A Commentary* (London: SCM Press, 1986)

CASILLO, ROBERT, 'Troubadour Love and Usury in Ezra Pound's Writings', *Texas Studies in Language and Literature*, 21.2 (Summer 1985), 125–53

CAWS, MARY ANN, 'The Poetics of the Manifesto: Nowness and Newness', in *Manifesto: A Century of Isms*, ed. by Mary Ann Caws (Lincoln: University of Nebraska Press, 2001), pp. xix–xxxii

CENDRARS, BLAISE, *Poésies Complètes*, ed. by Claude Leroy (Paris: Denoël, 2001)

CESCUTTI, TATIANA, *Les Origines mythiques du futurisme: Marinetti, poète symboliste (1902–1908)* (Paris: Presses de l'Université Paris–Sorbonne, 2008)

CHAMPIGNY, ROBERT, 'Le Temps chez Apollinaire', *PMLA*, 67.2 (1952), 3–14

CLARK, J. G., 'La Poésie, la politique et la guerre: autour de "La Petite Auto", "Chant de l'honneur" et *Couleur du Temps*', in *Guillaume Apollinaire 13*, ed. by Michel Décaudin (Paris: Lettres Modernes, 1976), pp. 7–63

CLAUSEWITZ, CARL VON, *On War*, trans. by Michael Howard and Peter Paret (Princeton, NJ: Princeton University Press, 1976)

COLERIDGE, SAMUEL TAYLOR, *Selected Poetry and Prose*, ed. by Elisabeth Schneider, 2nd edn (San Francisco, CA: Rinehart Press, 1971)

COLLINS, JOHN J., 'Introduction: Towards the Morphology of a Genre', *Semeia*, 14 (1979), 1–20

——.'Apocalyptic Eschatology as the Transcendence of Death', in *Visionaries and their Apocalypses*, ed. by Paul D. Hanson (Philadelphia, PA: Fortress Press, 1983), 61–84

——.*The Apocalyptic Imagination: An Introduction to the Jewish Matrix of Christianity* (New York: Crossroad, 1984)

——.*Daniel* (Minneapolis: Fortress Press, 1993)

COMENS, BRUCE, *Apocalypse and After: Modern Strategy and Postmodern Tactics in Pound, Williams, and Zukofsky* (Tuscaloosa: University of Alabama Press, 1995)

CONZELMANN, HANS, *1 Corinthians: A Commentary on the First Epistle to the Corinthians*, trans. by James W. Leitch (Philadelphia, PA: Fortress Press, 1975)

COUFFIGNAL, ROBERT, *L'Inspiration Biblique dans l'œuvre de Guillaume Apollinaire* (Paris: Lettres Modernes, 1966)

——.'Zone' d'Apollinaire: structure et confrontations* (Paris: Minard, 1970)

CRENSHAW, JAMES L., *Prophetic Conflict: Its Effect upon Israelite Religion* (Atlanta, GA: Society of Biblical Literature, 2007)

DASENBROCK, REED WAY, *The Literary Vorticism of Ezra Pound & Wyndham Lewis: Towards the Condition of Painting* (Baltimore, MD: Johns Hopkins University Press, 1985)

DAVIES, MARGARET, *Apollinaire* (Edinburgh: Oliver & Boyd, 1964)

DAYAN, PETER, *Mallarmé's 'Divine Transposition': Real and Apparent Sources of Literary Value* (Oxford: Clarendon Press, 1986)

DE PAULIS-DALEMBERT, MARIA PIA, 'F. T. Marinetti: La Réécriture de l'imaginaire symboliste et futuriste entre le français et l'italien', *Chroniques italiennes web*, 12 (December 2007), 1–30

EKSTEINS, MODRIS, *Rites of Spring: The Great War and the Birth of the Modern Age* (London: Black Swan, 1990)

ELIOT, T. S., *Collected Poems, 1909–1962* (London: Harcourt, Brace & Company, 1963)

ELLIOTT, ROBERT C., *The Power of Satire: Magic, Ritual, Art* (Princeton, NJ: Princeton University Press, 1960)

ESPEY, JOHN J, *Ezra Pound's* Mauberley: *A Study in Composition* (London: Faber and Faber, 1955)

EYSTEINSSON, ASTRADUR, '"What's the Difference?" Revisiting the Concepts of Modernism and Avant-Garde', in *Europa! Europa? The Avant-Garde, Modernism and the Fate of the Continent*, ed. by Sascha Bru et al. (Berlin: Walter de Gruyter, 2009), pp. 21–35

FIORENZA, ELISABETH SCHÜSSLER, 'The Followers of the Lamb: Visionary Rhetoric and Social-Political Situation', *Semeia*, 36 (1986), 123–46

FLINT, F. S., 'Imagisme', in *The Norton Anthology of English Literature*, ed. by Jahan Ramazani and Jon Stallworthy, 6 vols (New York: W. W. Norton, 2012)

FREEDMAN, DAVID NOEL, ed., *The Anchor Bible Dictionary*, 6 vols (New York: Doubleday, 1992)

FREEDMAN, DAVID NOEL, ALLEN C. MYERS, and ASTRID B. BECK, eds, *Eerdmans Dictionary of the Bible* (Grand Rapids, MI: William B. Eerdmans, 2000)

FRYE, NORTHROP, *The Great Code: The Bible and Literature* (London: Routledge & Kegan Paul, 1982)

——.*Words with Power: Being a Second Study of the Bible and Literature* (New York: Harcourt Brace Jovanovich, 1990)

GAZZOLA, GIUSEPPE, 'Prolegomena on a New Edition of Marinetti's *Versi e prose*', in *Futurismo: Impact and Legacy*, ed. by Giuseppe Gazzola (Stonybrook, NY: Forum Italicum, 2011), 76–85

GERTH, H. H., and C. WRIGHT MILLS, 'Introduction: The Man and His Work', in *From Max Weber: Essays in Sociology* (London: Routledge, 1948)

GILL, DAVID H., 'Through a Glass Darkly: A Note on 1 Corinthians 13,12', *Catholic Biblical Quarterly*, 25.4 (October 1963), 427–29

GOLDMAN, JANE, *Modernism, 1910–1945: Image to Apocalypse* (Basingstoke: Palgrave Macmillan, 2004)

GOTTWALD, NORMAN K., *The Hebrew Bible in Its Social World and in Ours* (Atlanta, GA: Scholars Press, 1993)

HAENCHEN, ERNST, *John 2: A Commentary on the Gospel of John Chapters 7–21*, trans. by Robert W. Funk (Philadelphia, PA: Fortress Press, 1984)

HANSON, PAUL D., *The Dawn of Apocalyptic: The Historical and Sociological Roots of Jewish Apocalyptic Eschatology* (Philadelphia, PA: Fortress Press, 1979)

HARROW, SUSAN, ' "Les Fiançailles": Cristallisation d'un amour', in *Guillaume Apollinaire 17*, ed. by Michel Décaudin (Paris: Lettres Modernes, 1987), pp. 119–34

——.*The Poetics of the Quest: A Study of Development and Continuity in the Poetry of Guillaume Apollinaire* (unpublished doctoral thesis, University of Edinburgh, 1988)

——.*The Material, the Real, and the Fractured Self: Subjectivity and Representation from Rimbaud to Réda* (Toronto: University of Toronto Press, 2004)

HOECK, ANDREAS, 'The Johannine Paraclete: Herald of the Eschaton', *Journal of Biblical and Pneumatological Research*, 4 (Fall 2012), 23–37

HOLBERT, JOHN C., ' "Deliverance Belongs to Yahweh!": Satire in the Book of Jonah', *Journal for the Study of the Old Testament*, 21 (1981), 59–81

JOYCE, PAUL M., *Ezekiel: A Commentary* (New York: T. & T. Clark, 2007)

KAISER, OTTO, *Isaiah 1–12: A Commentary*, trans. by John Bowden, 2nd edn (London: SCM Press, 1983)

KERMODE, FRANK, *The Sense of an Ending: Studies in the Theory of Fiction* (Oxford: Oxford University Press, 2000)

KING, RICHARD, 'Mysticism and Spirituality', in *The Routledge Companion to the Study of Religion*, ed. by John R. Hinnells (New York: Routledge, 2005) pp. 306–22

LIEBREGTS, PETER, ' "Bricks thought into being ex nihil": Ezra Pound and Creation', in *Ezra Pound, Ends and Beginnings: Essays and Poems from the Ezra Pound International Conference, Venice, 2007*, ed. by John Gery and William Pratt (New York: AMS Press, 2011), pp. 81–96

LOCKERBIE, S. I., 'Le Rôle de l'imagination dans *Calligrammes*, deuxième partie: les poèmes du monde intérieur', in *Guillaume Apollinaire 6*, ed. by Michel Décaudin (Paris: Lettres Modernes, 1967), pp. 85–105

MALLARMÉ, STÉPHANE, *Œuvres complètes*, ed. by Bertrand Marchal, 2 vols (Paris: Gallimard, 1998–2003)

MARCUS, DAVID, *From Balaam to Jonah: Anti-prophetic Satire in the Hebrew Bible* (Atlanta, GA: Scholars Press, 1995)

MARKS, HERBERT, 'On Prophetic Stammering', in *The Book and the Text: The Bible and Literary Theory*, ed. by Regina Schwartz (Oxford: Blackwell, 1990), pp. 60–80

MARTIN, MARIANNE, 'Futurism, Unanimism, and Apollinaire', *Art Journal*, 28.3 (Spring 1969), 258–68

MARTZ, LOUIS L., *Many Gods and Many Voices: The Role of the Prophet in English and American Modernism* (Columbia: University of Missouri Press, 1998)

MARX, KARL, *On Literature and Art* (Moscow: Progress Publishers, 1976)

MARX, WILLIAM, 'The 20th Century: Century of the Arrière-Gardes?', in *Europa! Europa? The Avant-Garde, Modernism and the Fate of the Continent*, ed. by Sascha Bru et al. (Berlin: Walter de Gruyter, 2009), pp. 59–71

MATHEWS, TIMOTHY, *Reading Apollinaire: Theories of Poetic Language* (Manchester: Manchester University Press, 1987)

MEEKS, WAYNE, ed., *The Harper Collins Study Bible: New Revised Standard Version with Apocryphal/Deuterocanonical Books* (San Francisco, CA: HarperCollins, 1993)

MOLONEY, FRANCIS J., *The Gospel of John* (Collegeville, MN: The Liturgical Press, 1998)

MOODY, A. DAVID, *Ezra Pound: Poet, A Portrait of the Man and his Work*, I: *The Young Genius, 1885–1920* (Oxford: Oxford University Press, 2007)

NICKELSBURG, GEORGE W. E., and JAMES C. VANDERKAM, eds, *1 Enoch: A New Translation* (Minneapolis, MN: Fortress Press, 2004)

OVERHOLT, THOMAS, *Channels of Prophecy: The Social Dynamics of Prophetic Activity* (Minneapolis, MN: Fortress Press, 1989)

——.'Prophet, Prophecy', in *Eerdmans Dictionary of the Bible*, ed. by David Noel Freedman, Allen C. Myers and Astrid B. Beck (Grand Rapids, MI: William B. Eerdmans Publishing Company, 2000)

PASCAL, BLAISE, *Pensées and Other Writings*, trans. by Honor Levi (Oxford: Oxford University Press, 1995)

PAZ, OCTAVIO, *Children of the Mire: Modern Poetry from Romanticism to the Avant-Garde*, trans. by Rachel Phillips (Cambridge, MA: Harvard University Press, 1974)

PERLOFF, MARJORIE, *The Futurist Moment: Avant-Garde, Avant-Guerre, and the Language of Rupture* (Chicago, IL: University of Chicago Press, 1986)

POGGI, CHRISTINE. *Inventing Futurism: The Art and Politics of Artificial Optimism* (Princeton, NJ: Princeton University Press, 2009)

POGGIOLI, RENATO, *The Theory of the Avant-Garde* (Cambridge, MA: Harvard University Press, 1968)

POLK, TIMOTHY, *The Prophetic Persona: Jeremiah and the Language of the Self* (Sheffield: JSOT Press, 1984)

PONDROM, CYRENA M, *The Road from Paris: French Influence on English Poetry, 1900–1920* (Cambridge: Cambridge University Press, 1974)

PRATT, WILLIAM, 'Ezra Pound and the Image', in *Ezra Pound: The London Years, 1908–1920*, ed. by Philip Grover (New York: AMS Press, 1978), pp. 15–30

PUCHNER, MARTIN, 'Screeching Voices: Avant-Garde Manifestos in the Cabaret', in *European Avant-Garde: New Perspectives*, ed. by Dietrich Scheunemann (Amsterdam: Rodopi, 2000), pp. 113–36

——.*Poetry of the Revolution: Marx, Manifestos, and the Avant-Gardes* (Princeton, NJ: Princeton University Press, 2006)

RAD, GERHARD VON, *Old Testament Theology*, trans. by D. M. G. Stalker, 2 vols (Edinburgh: Oliver and Boyd, 1965)

RAINEY, LAWRENCE, *Institutions of Modernism: Literary Elites and Public Culture* (New Haven, CT: Yale University Press, 1998)

RAYMOND, MARCEL, *From Baudelaire to Surrealism* (London: Methuen, 1970)

READ, PETER F., *Society and Religion in the Poetry of Guillaume Apollinaire* (unpublished doctoral thesis, University of Hull, 1981)

RIMBAUD, ARTHUR, *Œuvres complètes*, ed. by Antoine Adam (Paris: Gallimard, 1972)

RUTHVEN, K. K., *A Guide to Ezra Pound's 'Personae' (1926)* (Berkeley: University of California Press, 1969)

SCALISE, PAMELA J., 'Scrolling through Jeremiah: Written Documents as a Reader's Guide to the Book of Jeremiah', *Review and Expositor*, 101 (Spring 2004), 201–25

SHATTUCK, ROGER, *The Banquet Years: The Origins of the Avant-Garde in France, 1885–World War I* (New York: Vintage Books, 1968)

SINGSEN, DOUG, 'The Historical Avant-Garde from 1830 to 1939: l'art pour l'art, blague and Gesamtkunstwerk', *Modernism/Modernity*, 5.2 (2020) <https://doi.org/10.26597/mod.0154> [accessed 6 December 2020]

SOMIGLI, LUCA, *Legitimizing the Artist: Manifesto Writing and European Modernism, 1885–1915* (Toronto: University of Toronto Press, 2003)

STEEGMULLER, FRANCIS, *Apollinaire: Poet among the Painters* (London: Rupert Hart-Davis, 1963)

SURETTE, LEON, *The Birth of Modernism: Ezra Pound, T. S. Eliot, W. B. Yeats, and the Occult* (Montreal, PQ, and Kingston, ON: McGill–Queen's University Press, 1993)

SWARTZ, DAVID, *Culture and Power: The Sociology of Pierre Bourdieu* (Chicago, IL: University of Chicago Press, 1997)

VERLAINE, PAUL, *Œuvres Poétiques complètes*, ed. by Y.-G. Le Dantec and Jacques Borel (Paris: Gallimard, 1962)

WEBER, MAX, *The Theory of Social & Economic Organization*, ed. by Talcott Parsons, trans. by A. M. Henderson and Talcott Parsons (New York: The Free Press, 1947)

——.*From Max Weber: Essays in Sociology* (London: Routledge & Kegan Paul, 1977)

——.*The Sociology of Religion*, trans. by Ephraim Fischoff (Boston, MA: Beacon Press, 1991)

——.*The Protestant Ethic and the 'Spirit' of Capitalism and Other Writings*, ed. by Peter Baehr and Gordon C. Wells (London: Penguin Books, 2002)

WHITMAN, WALT, *Leaves of Grass* (New York: The Modern Library, 2001)

WILLARD, CHARLES B., 'Ezra Pound's Appraisal of Walt Whitman', *Modern Language Notes*, 72.1 (January 1957), 19–26

WILSON, ROBERT, *Prophecy and Society in Ancient Israel* (Philadelphia, PA: Fortress Press, 1973)

WITEMEYER, HUGH, *The Poetry of Ezra Pound: Forms and Renewal, 1908–1920* (Berkeley: University of California Press, 1969)

——.'Early Poetry, 1908–1920', in *The Cambridge Companion to Ezra Pound*, ed. by Ira B. Nadel (Cambridge: Cambridge University Press, 1999), pp. 43–58

ZIMMERLI, WALTHER, *Ezekiel 1: A Commentary on the Book of the Prophet Ezekiel, Chapters 1–24*, trans. by Ronald E. Clements (Philadelphia, PA: Fortress Press, 1979)

INDEX

❖

www.ingramcontent.com/pod-product-compliance
Lightning Source LLC
Chambersburg PA
CBHW080606090426
42735CB00017B/3351